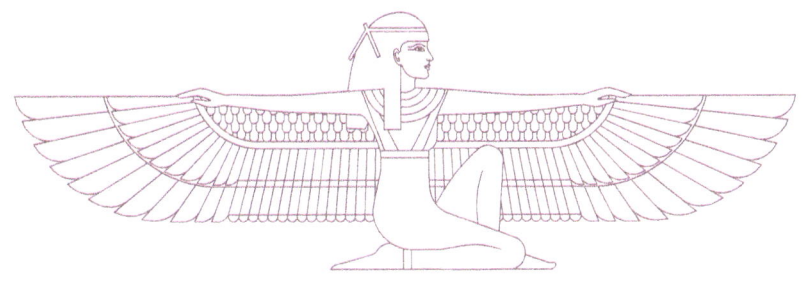

The Winged Isis

The goddess Isis was immensely popular from very ancient times. The sister and wife of Osiris, their only son was fathered after Osiris was killed and had ascended to heaven. This conception led to their son, Horus, being acclaimed as born of a perpetual virgin – and possibly became an inspiration for the conception story in the gospels of Matthew and Luke. Ancient references associate Horus with the Giza pyramids and with Baalbek Terrace - which are geometrically aligned to each other.

The 'Winged Isis' symbolizes her ability to fly, albeit with mechanical aids. Worship of Isis endured many millennia – growing to become the most popular deity across the Roman Empire at the time of Jesus visit.

This book is dedicated to those whose Soul longs to fly and discover the truth about our origins.

The Truth Will Set You Free
SECOND EDITION

Prequel

Younger Dryas meteor impacts, the Flood & Atlantis

Highlighting contributions from other disciplines not yet reflected in the conventional understanding of history

GLYN THOMAS

Quintology Publishing
www.quintologypublications.com

Copyright © 2024 by Glyn Thomas & Gregory Thomas

All rights reserved, including the right to reproduce this work in any form whatsoever, without permission in writing from the publisher except for brief passages in reviews or in citations and references.

Printed by Ingram Spark and affiliates – Lightning Source UK Ltd, Milton Keynes, United Kingdom (see inside back page)
Second Edition, published May 2024.

First edition entitled:- *The Flood and the Origin of the Pagan Gods*

Paperback ISBN: 978-1-7384439-0-1
Ebook ISBN: 978-1-7384439-1-8

Typeset, layout and cover design by Gregory Thomas
www.gregthomas.design

Contents

Series introduction
1 How the conventional understanding of human history emerged
2 Conventional views are highly resistant to change
3 Mars – sustaining life 4 billion years ago?
4 Earth – violent events enabled life but caused extinctions
5 Earth - major extinction level events in past 600 million years
6 Catastrophic events impacting hominids in past 1 million years
7 The Hiawatha impact 10765BC & the Younger Dryas Period
8 The human dimension of the Hiawatha impact
9 Atlantis, an ancient story now gaining evidence of a factual origin
Map Younger Dryas ended by twin meteor impact off Kefalonia c9620BC
10 Pre Younger Dryas culture at many sites in Turkey
11 Egyptian engineering points to an earlier advanced culture
12 Sumerians – legacy knowledge & links to Stonehenge
13 Cuzco & Tiahuanaco, Peru/Bolivia – ancient technology
14 Indonesian anomalies
15 Longyou Caves, Zhejiang Province – an anomaly
16 Antikythera Mechanism – an anomaly
17 Egyptian colonies in Central America?
18 Were survivors of destroyed cultures acclaimed as gods?
19 Conclusions
Appendix: Key family members of the ancient 'gods'
Index
Bibliography
Books in this series
Symbols used on covers in this series

Series Introduction
- why these booklets were written

From quite an early age, I have been fascinated by cosmology, geology, history and politics. In ancient cultures, politics was inseparable from religion – political power flowed through religious structures. The pharaoh or emperor was the high priest, the priests themselves constituted the civil service, the priests were the government scribes.

During my working life, the pressure of work combined with a heavy load of obligatory professional reading to crowd out reading for personal interest. So, following retirement in 2013, I was delighted to be able to delve into specialist material on the topics above. What I found both astonished and disappointed me. I am astonished by the extent that our knowledge in most fields has been radically transformed. When I was a boy, cosmologists were unsure whether our universe was continuing to expand or beginning to contract; climatologists believed we were heading towards another ice age; and some believed our Sun might be unique in having orbiting planets – possibly, our solar system was a special exception created by a benevolent God. Now I learn that the Vatican has a committee tasked with determining procedures and exchanges following First Contact with any intelligent aliens. My disappointments stem from the stubborn resistance of many conventional historical beliefs to accept hard evidence from more recent discoveries and the low level of lateral thinking which seems to stem from academics closeting themselves in narrow chimneys of specialist knowledge.

This last observation is one major spur behind the decision to author this series. I genuinely feel that significant new learning may be found by joining up the deep knowledge to be found in various isolated chimneys.

PREQUEL – YOUNGER DRYAS METEOR IMPACTS, THE FLOOD & ATLANTIS

Certainly, there is much that I have found both startling and persuasive – sufficiently so that it spurred me to want to share with you. Some read the title of this series and feel a phrase they personally revere may have been hijacked. The phrase "the Truth will set you free" being attributed to Jesus according to the Gospel of John 8:32. Knowledge of the real truth is indeed liberating. Those who may react to my adoption of the phrase for this series may feel I am setting myself up as a rival purveyor of the truth – I can assure those having such thoughts that their concern is misplaced.

Many believe the real truth is what they find in the bible. The journey thought this series will present fairly solid evidence that Jesus rejected most major tenets of Jewish faith as recorded in the books of the Old Testament – and much evidence for this is in the bible itself ! Not only that, but for most of the past 2,000 years, the official church played down the Old Testament as being unimportant. For most of the period that the Catholic Church reigned supreme, say AD325 to AD1500, very little attention was paid to the books of the Old Testament. This was partly due to a widespread hatred of the Jews and partly as many of the senior hierarchy (understanding Hebrew) knew that the Old Testament did not really support the idea that there was only one God. For this reason and the inconvenient fact that much Catholic dogma has no biblical foundation, Catholic adherents were prohibited from reading or owning a copy of any books of the bible. The penalty of breaching this ecclesiastic law was excommunication and commitment to everlasting hell. And when that was felt insufficient, the sentence would be imposed immediately by burning the individual at the stake. It is hard to believe, but Catholics were only permitted to read the bible by a papal edict issued in 1943.

It was access to the bible, and in the vernacular translated into many languages, that triggered the growth of Protestantism. Reading the bible revealed the "untruths" in Catholic dogma and ignited the religious enmity between the two camps. Given Christians had been banned from reading their most sacred book for over a millennium, its text was devoured with gusto. 'Sola Scriptura' (Scripture alone) became a watchword, devout Christians started towards believing the bible is the 'Word of God' and therefore its text is inerrant – everything it says is true.

A moments thought, without even questioning anything stated in the bible, suggests this to be a naive reaction. Having been under the sole control of the church for over a millennium, the learned leadership of the church was fully aware of the contradictions between biblical texts and Catholic dogma. It would be naive to assume no attempts were made to conform texts to dogma that had been evolved by the papacy. This series will identify plenty of evidence of this. One example we shall cover in detail, is the invention of the Trinity – which despite its centrality to conventional Christian dogma is only mentioned twice in the bible – in Matthew 28:19 and 1John 5:7. The text of Matthew 28:19 was changed during the third century and was hotly debated at the Council of Nicaea in AD325. No copy of 1John 5 with the Trinitarian formula has been found dated earlier than AD1215 – and there are thousands of extant copies of 1John dated prior to this showing the original pre-Trinitarian text.

The primacy of conforming biblical texts to dogma is enshrined in the written instructions issued to the English bishops tasked by James I with drawing up the official King James Version of the bible. The translations were to be based upon selected Greek and Hebrew texts judged most authentic - BUT where any translation contradicted dogma, the text was to be altered to conform with dogma!

As we shall discover, not only were elements of belief fabricated but some of Jesus teaching was distorted and twisted to support political objectives after the Roman Empire decided to stop fighting Christianity and to subvert it to achieve its political agenda. My conclusions in this series reveal what I have found may be the original teaching of Jesus – hence the use of the well-known title phrase.

This Prequel focuses on events prior to when conventional history teaches the first civilisations arose – in Sumer and Egypt. The evolution of life on planet Earth has been subject to numerous catastrophic disasters, many of which have been extinction level events. The meteor impact which wiped out the dinosaurs 65 million years ago is relatively well known but less well understood is that there have been dozens of such events over the last 540 million years. The development of life on this planet from the formation of Earth, 4543million years ago, up to the start of the Cambrian period 540 million years ago had only progressed to bacteria – but then, in the Cambrian period, the diversity of lifeforms exploded. Indeed, there may have been up to a dozen events in just the last 20,000 years which all but wiped out humanity on at least one continent. So much for the biblical story that after God wiped out humanity (saving only Noah and his family) with The Flood, he covenanted never to be so cruel again and sealed his promise by creating the rainbow in memoriam.

Despite the paragraphs above, this Prequel to the series barely touches on conventional religion but does set the scene for the reader to re-characterise their understanding of what are conventionally labelled "pagan"gods. This booklet will give the reader real insights and the latest research findings to look anew at the conventional account of "ancient history" covering the period from 4000BC to the rise of the Roman Empire.

Some of my conclusions may appear radical, none are intended to offend. If you know of evidence that contradicts or supports any observation or conclusion I have made, I would be delighted to hear from you at:

www.quintologypublications.com.

This site also contains much information concerning the other books in this series together with maps and various documents that may be downloaded.

1

How the conventional understanding of human history emerged

1.1 Conventional history for Western societies emerged out of the post Imperial Roman period of the Dark Ages (cAD500 to c1400) into a period of renewed learning and innovation – the Reformation, with its attendant focus on culture, the arts and education. Academics had knowledge of Latin and Greek but no understanding of the written records from any earlier civilization – whilst monuments, tablets and pottery were found displaying Egyptian hieroglyphs and Mesopotamian cuneiform – none could be translated. So, from the Reformation onwards through to the 19th Century, students saw the Bible as the only authoritative source of human history prior to Alexander the Great.

1.2 The first breakthrough came with Napoleon's troops unearthing what became known as the Rosetta stone dating from 196BC (with a text written in three scripts – ancient Egyptian hieroglyphs, Demotic Egyptian dating from c650BC and ancient Greek) in 1799 – which opened the door to understanding all Egyptian texts that had hitherto been totally indecipherable.

1.3 However, cuneiform writing remained a mystery for another 60 years. The cuneiform writing system had been in use for more than three millennia, through several stages of development, with examples now dated from the 34th century BC down to the second century AD. The original Sumerian script was adapted for the writing of the Akkadian language (the lingua franca of the Middle East from c.2000BC until gradually replaced by Aramaic over the course of the first millennium BC) as well as Elamite, Hittite, Hurrian and Ugaritic (Canaanite) languages. Cuneiform writing was gradually replaced by the Phoenician alphabet during the Neo-Assyrian Empire (911-612BC). By the second century AD, the cuneiform script had become extinct, and all knowledge of how to read it was lost until it began to be deciphered in the 19th century.

1.4   In 1835 Henry Rawlinson, a British East India Company army officer, visited the Behistun Inscriptions in Persia. Carved in the reign of King Darius of Persia (522-486BC), they consisted of identical texts in the three official languages of the empire: Old Persian, Babylonian (Akkadian), and Elamite. The Behistun inscription was to the decipherment of cuneiform what the Rosetta Stone was to the decipherment of Egyptian hieroglyphs. Rawlinson correctly deduced that the Old Persian was a phonetic script and he successfully deciphered it. In 1837 he finished his copy of the Behistun inscription, and sent a translation of its opening paragraphs to the Royal Asiatic Society. It took until 1847 to complete and publish the first part of the Rawlinson's Memoir, followed by the second part in 1849.

1.5   After translating the Persian text, Rawlinson and, working independently of him, the Irish Assyriologist Edward Hincks, began to decipher the older Akkadian text. They were greatly helped by the excavations of the Frenchman Paul Émile Botta and the Englishman Austen Henry Layard of the city of Nineveh from 1842. Among the treasures uncovered by Layard and his successor Hormuzd Rassam were, in 1849 and 1851, the remains of two libraries, now mixed up, usually called the Library of Ashurbanipal, a royal archive containing tens of thousands of baked clay tablets covered with cuneiform inscriptions. The extensive libraries were impeccably organised with detailed catalogue tablets in each section – these have helped prioritise translations but also reveal that only a minority of the tablets were recovered from the ruins.

1.6   By 1851, Hincks and Rawlinson could read 200 Babylonian signs. They were soon joined by two other decipherers: young German-born scholar Julius Oppert, and versatile British Orientalist William Henry Fox Talbot. In 1857, the four men met in London and took part in a famous experiment to test the accuracy of their decipherments. Edwin Norris, the secretary of the Royal Asiatic Society, gave each of them a copy of a recently discovered inscription from the reign of the Assyrian emperor Tiglath-Pileser I. A jury of experts was empanelled to examine the resulting translations and assess their accuracy. In all essential points, the translations produced by the four scholars were found to be in close agreement with one another.

1.7 A vast treasure trove of up to two million cuneiform tablets are estimated to have been excavated in modern times, of which it is estimated that between 30,000 – 100,000 have been read or published. What we have learned from those tablets translated so far is truly astonishing – revealing a very high level of civilization dating back to the very earliest tablets translated. We have elaborate records of history, star maps, stellar observations, tables of star rising predictions, legal codes, commercial contracts, shipping manifests, medicine, crop cultivation, cooking recipes, school text books, school exam papers, children's school reports, and records of many other topics. The British Museum holds the largest collection (c.130,000), followed by the Vorderasiatisches Museum Berlin, the Louvre, the Istanbul Archaeology Museums, the National Museum of Iraq, the Yale Babylonian Collection (c.40,000) and Penn Museum. Most of these have "lain in these collections for a century without being translated, studied or published", as there are only a few hundred qualified cuneiformists in the world.

1.8 Therefore, over the past 200 years we have recovered much ancient knowledge, either from original texts or from ancient copies which duly acknowledge even older, then pre-existing versions, which texts state have been faithfully copied. The use of baked clay tablets to record the cuneiform texts has enabled these to endure for periods in excess of 5,000 years. Such tablets, excavated from all over the Fertile Crescent of Mesopotamia, have enabled us to achieve a reasonable understanding of the languages of most civilisations predating the Greek. In addition, scientific advances in geology, climatology and archaeology have revealed many intriguing details. The newer specialism of astro-archaeology has yielded dating techniques employed by ancient builders when dedicating temples and monuments. The most likely meaning of many intriguing statements in the Torah have been identified, shedding light and explanations on historical accuracy of some sections of the Old Testament whilst revealing other parts to be well intentioned priestly imagination or "leaps of faith" arising from a lack of understanding of why events occurred.

1.9 So, for the privileged few, such as you the reader hereof, your accumulated knowledge of history and your interest to understand more is increasingly rewarded by the wealth of information readily available. However, the reality is that you are becoming an ever smaller minority. Educators used to regard history as an essential ingredient in the development of a well-informed citizen. Sadly, many education departments have downgraded history as a school subject and some governments control the syllabus of the subject as a way to justify their undemocratic hegemony over their country.

1.10 The much greater tragedy is the woefully poor level of education available today to a large portion of humanity. An article in The Economist dated 16 November 2018 reported on uneven progress achieved for the UN's Millennium Development Goal that by 2015 all the world's children would complete primary school. *"On paper this has largely been achieved: nine out of ten children are now enrolled. Alas, the figure is not as impressive as it sounds. Even though most of the world's children go to school, an awful lot of them learn pretty much nothing there. According to a recent World Bank study of seven sub-Saharan African countries, half of nine-year-olds cannot read a simple word and three-quarters cannot read a simple sentence. The reason is terrible teaching. The same study found that only 7% of teachers had the minimum knowledge needed to teach reading and writing effectively. When classrooms were inspected to see whether a teacher was present, half the time the answer was no."*

1.11 The internet is magnifying accessible information but facts are being diluted and distorted. It used to be that news media viewed themselves as paragons of accurate and responsible reporting, editorial standards sought to ensure all reports were fact-checked and reliable. The rise of alternative media and resulting channel fragmentation has resulted in 'speed to market' (24 hour news channels) often downgrading factual accuracy, whilst competition has led to 'free' news relying solely on advertising revenue. The result has been to slash costs by cutting journalistic staffing and investigative reporting to focus on attention grabbing headlines sourced from anywhere and anybody. (Sadly, this paragraph was written pre-Trump – so the depressing trend described above has subsequently deteriorated even further.)

1.12 The dependability of time, available from countless sources, is something we now take for granted – but it is actually a quite recent innovation. When we check the time and date showing on our smartphone, we cannot imagine the precise time showing on our device is any different to that of others anywhere in our timezone – New York and Miami or

Hong Kong and Beijing – but it wasn't always so. Even 150 years ago, time was a local concept – only the spread of railways triggered and supported the synchronization of time across nations. Railways developed first in the UK and as they spread across the country it was important to operate to a timetable and that required time in each city to be exactly the same. Even this fairly obvious need was slow to be met. The Great Western Railway adopted a common system wide time in 1843 but it was not until 1883 that all UK railways adopted Greenwich Mean Time (GMT). Other countries followed, with occasional quirks – until 1911 the clocks on the exterior walls of all French railway stations showed standard Paris Mean Time (itself 9 minutes out of sync with GMT) but clocks inside stations and the trains ran five minutes later – to allow passengers more time to catch their trains! Until the new fangled railways forced standardisation, time was measured in each locality by measuring from the sunrise, usually at a solstice for which precise astronomical measurements were published. But time could and did vary by up to 20 minutes between different localities – which had no method (or interest) in checking whether the next city had exactly the same time. Rural life was driven by the sun itself.

1.13   Similarly, until the 20th Century, no community was affected by light pollution. Everyone enjoyed spectacular views of our galaxy and of more remote galaxies – on every clear night. Clouds permitting, fully half the time, the human population could wonder at the heavens. Naturally, knowledge of the constellations was commonplace – the names of the 12 signs of the zodiac were very familiar. Intriguingly, these same zodiac designations have been traced back to the earliest known human civilization – the Sumerian, centred around modern day Basra, which collapsed around 1960 BC, contemporary with the departure of the provincial governor and his children (one of whom became the Jewish patriarch, Abraham). There is evidence which suggests the identification and naming of the constellations dates back far earlier than even the Sumerian empire.

2

Conventional views are highly resistant to change

2.1 One feature of conventional history, brought home to me during my research since 2013, is the surprising resistance to change. The 'establishment', particularly academics with tenure, appear extremely reluctant to accept changes to any historical assumptions that have been the foundation of their discipline, their own work and that imply their teaching could have been wrong. I set out five examples below, in chronological sequence, where massive evidence proves, at least to my satisfaction, that conventional history desperately needs updating.

A meteor impact triggered the Younger Dryas period

2.2 When Bretz published his theory in 1923 that the Channelled Scablands of eastern Washington State had been so formed by a single massive flooding of glacial meltwater caused by an as yet unknown event he was ridiculed by the scientific community who insisted that explanations dependent upon catastrophic events were tantamount to basing science upon an 'act of God' and dismissed his arguments. Conventional geology insisted that the erosion had been caused by numerous repeated floodings gradually creating the Grand Coulee and the downstream erratics fields. It was only research by Graham Hancock working with Randall Carlson, a self styled 'catastrophist geologist', published in 2015 that showed clearly that the geological features could only have arisen from a monumental flooding event. Their work identified evidence of a meteor impact event without locating the impact site. This was prior to the discovery of the Hiawatha glacier crater. This discovery is covered in detail in chapter 7.

The age of the pyramids and the sphinx

2.3 Conventional history states that the Great Pyramid of Giza was constructed by Pharaoh Khufu (aka Cheops) between 2585BC and 2566BC, and the second very slightly smaller pyramid and the Sphinx were constructed by his successor, Khafre, who also reigned for around 20 years. However, there are many problems with this attribution. Firstly, the only association between the main Giza pyramid and Khufu is a single inscription "Khufu woz 'ere" scrawled on a tunnel wall inside the pyramid, which is now generally interpreted as engraved by workers denoting their activity. It is definitely not an official pharaonic imprimatur and carries no indication of a surrounding cartouche – indeed some have suggested that an early Egyptologist desperate to 'discover' the identity of the builder scratched the marking himself. It is true that there are a few simple temple buildings near the Giza pyramid which have also been attributed to Khufu – but the contrast between the stupendous monumental Giza pyramid and small, simple nearby temples should also alert us to the improbability of Khufu being the origin of both. Once you appreciate just how tenuous the link to Khufu is you become more open to considering other explanations.

2.4 The construction itself is stupendous. The mass of the Giza pyramid is estimated at 5.9 million tonnes and its volume at 2.5 million cubic metres. Based on these estimates, construction within the 20 years of Khufu's reign, would require installing 800 tonnes of stone every day of his reign. Based on the calculated number of blocks, 2.3 million, that means placing 12 blocks into place ***every hour*** - 24 x 7 x 365 for 20 years. The above is based on calculations by Sir Flinders Petrie, from *The Pyramids and Temples of Giza, 1882*. And despite such a sustained pace of work, many of the casing-stones and inner chamber blocks of the Giza Pyramid fit together with extremely high precision. Based on measurements taken on the north-eastern casing stones, the mean opening of the joints is only 0.5 millimetres wide. The sides of the base are 230m long with the maximum difference in the length of any side being 58mm whilst the error from perfect square alignment of the four sides is only 12 seconds of arc. Such accuracy seems beyond what could be achieved by simple eye sight – some kind of equipment must have been used to achieve such accuracy. The requirement to deliver precisely cut and smoothed blocks to fit positions tens of metres up in the structure and often deep within the structure around the galleries implies the existence of an accurate and detailed three-dimensional model available at the quarry or stone preparation site – as in-situ stone cutting would seem impossible. The more one ponders the task, the greater the gap in our knowledge appears. Even the management challenge of such a project seems incredible – how to recruit, train, sustain, house such a labour force and how to set up and manage the supply chain for the materials, quarrying, cutting, polishing and transport of 15 million odd blocks, many of which show individual shaping. And, this was supposedly accomplished not only without any computers but utilising the clumsy Egyptian numbering system, cubits (measurement by palm widths!) and on-site measuring using ropes and sticks!!

2.5   It is also agreed that, based on some remaining blocks, when it was first built the entire pyramid was encased in polished white limestone capping stones to finish it with smooth sloping sides. Quite how these were put in place is just another mystery.

2.6   There are a number of other fundamental problems with the attribution to Khufu:- there are many references to the Great Pyramid in both Egyptian and Sumerian records pre-dating Khufu and the lack of any official inscriptions anywhere in the pyramid whatsoever. The ostensible purpose of providing a tomb also lacks any evidence – internal spaces have just been named by archaeologists as the 'Kings chamber' and the 'Queens chamber' on a hunch. Whilst tomb raiders could have ransacked the pyramid over a long period, not the slightest trace of any mortuary materials or gifts and personal possessions have been recovered. There is no evidence whatsoever that Giza was ever used as a tomb. No one has explained why Khufu would devote probably his entire revenue to such a construction if it was not intended as his tomb. It seems that the dubious conventional history will only be finally debunked when Khufu's real tomb is discovered in the Valley of the Kings!

2.7   The Great Pyramid is the largest of the three pyramids forming the Giza complex which share a perfect north – south alignment. The second largest, traditionally associated with Khufu's son Khafre, is only 3m shorter than the 139m tall Great Pyramid – but staggeringly, it was built on slightly higher ground and its capstone was at exactly the same altitude above sea level. Quite how Egyptian builders achieved this remains unexplained. These pyramids and the Sphinx are built on a scale quite different to any other Egyptian monuments – and appear older than any other major Egyptian constructions. Again, it appears that incredible construction skills are apparent in the earliest works and later efforts are less impressive.

Dogged defence of the accuracy of Biblical history

2.8   This is a huge problem whereby many are torn between their principles regarding their religious faith and truth based upon hard evidence. The Catholic church entered the Renaissance sternly defending belief that the Earth was flat – an extraordinary position given the clues in a number of Old Testament books and in particular the Book of Jubilees which they had tried so hard to destroy all copies of.

2.9   Today, in the same way that some fringe types still proclaim that the Earth is flat, there are many who follow what is known as an 'Inerrant' viewpoint. The Inerrants start by insisting that the Bible is the 'Word of God', derived from believing that every book included (in the Protestant version, ignoring all other denominations) was written by authors who were inspired by God. Naturally, this quickly became an absolutist standpoint, it would be difficult to argue that these verses were wholly inspired, these were a bit inspired and those verses were just made up by the author – no, the line adopted is that every word, at least in the original autograph, was individually inspired by God. With this logic, the Inerrantists have constructed an edifice offering stout defence – you cannot say anything in the Bible is wrong because it was effectively written by God. If anyone has evidence that contradicts anything stated in the Bible it must be a mistaken attribution, errors in the measurement or methodology or simply fake. This leads to such mind altering attitudes such as: (i) all 'science' (a major bogeyman) is only theory and all theories change, eventually 'science' will find a theory which confirms the stance on something as stated in the Bible; and (ii) we have to defend all the objectively observable statements in the Bible, such as Joshua destroyed Jericho, because how else can we defend the totally unprovable statements, such as Jesus is the only and unique son of God?

2.10 It is not very difficult to arrive at the conclusion that the books contained in each Christian denominations' version of the Bible (there are many variations) were written by well intentioned but often woefully uninformed men who may have felt that they were inspired by devotion but were indisputably not inspired by God. I can say this for the simple reason that God, whom I think all would agree is the moniker appropriate for the supreme intelligence that designed the laws that rule our universe, would not inspire such writers to make so many mistakes, contradictions and flip flopping on key issues. These arguments are addressed in detail in a few sections of later Parts of this series of booklets – hopefully I have wetted your appetite!!

The explorations of Chinese Admiral He

2.11   When China was first unified, the Yongle Emperor (Zhu Di, who reigned AD1402 to 1424) decided to relocate his capital from Nanjing to Beijing, building the huge complex known as the Forbidden City. To celebrate his new palace complex, Yongle invited leaders of all foreign lands who recognised his overlordship to a long celebration. These foreign dignitaries, from all the kingdoms of south east Asia, the Indian sub-continent and coastal East Africa, were then carried home laden with lavish gifts by a huge fleet numbering in excess of 2000 ships. The fleet, under Admiral He, was tasked with three additional objectives: (i) locate and inform the leaders of all other nations of the grandeur and pre-eminence of the Emperor; (ii) to chart these new lands and (iii) to identify a southern hemisphere star to serve as a southern pole star for navigation purposes, to match the northern Pole Star. In 1421, the Chinese clearly had no silly ideas of the Earth being flat !!

2.12   We are in debt to Gavin Menzies, a retired British nuclear submarine captain, for his careful research of Admiral He's main voyage, which has traced the voluminous evidence of wreaks, monuments, Chinese Han DNA in the genetic makeup of many Peruvian tribes, widespread Chinese place names found in Peru, strains of chicken and pigs around the world's coasts, the solving of the Bimini Roads enigma, etc, that enabled the explorations of He to be re-discovered. As an ardent sailor and knowledgeable of both prevailing winds and currents as well as ancient Chinese naval designs, Menzies has been able to join the dots between the far-flung evidence and identify where He's fleet sailed. Admiral He clearly split his fleet, tasking elements to navigate and map both coasts of the entire Americas – as they left widespread evidence along the entirety of both coasts. For me, Menzies work also solves two enigmas documented by Erich von Daniken – the origin of the Piri Reis map captured by

PREQUEL – YOUNGER DRYAS METEOR IMPACTS, THE FLOOD & ATLANTIS

Venetian fleet in 1513 and the origin of the Bimini 'Roads'.

2.13   Whilst Admiral He was away, Yongle was killed fighting Mongols. His successor, Hongxi, started some reforms, and was persuaded by his key advisors to curb the hugely expensive foreign trade and explorations that had been sponsored by his father. The trade was seen as deeply unequal – giving silks and porcelain in return for exotic animals and fruits. Orders were given to burn down the shipyards and He was ordered to return home, even the Forbidden Palace was to be abandoned and the capital moved back to Nanjing. However, Hongxi died suddenly after ruling for only 12 months. Hongxi's son, Xuande, seems to have relented, allowing He a final voyage during which He appears to have died. Following He's death, the Eunuch faction which denounced foreign trade managed to remove the influence of the scholar bureaucrats who had supported He – and as a consequence, He's achievements were written out of the records and all his papers and charts burned. The vitriol which greeted Menzies painstaking work only proves the stubborn resistance that greets any upstart who challenges smug tenured academia. There is no need to rely on my judgement, Gavin's book *1421* is well worth reading, afterwards read the academic criticisms easily found on the internet - I guarantee you will then share my conclusions.

Columbus discovery of America

2.14   The attachment of many Americans to the idea that Columbus discovered their continent in 1492 may be linked to a desire to hang on to the eponymously named public holiday. But school textbooks lag knowledge available for decades – even centuries. Columbus, in reality a Genoese named Cristoforo Columbo, lived in Lisbon for many years where he was known as Cristóvão Colombo and later referred to by the Spanish as Cristóbal Colón. Seen by Portuguese as a traitor, Columbus is now understood to have stolen charts from the Sagres School of Navigation and then sold these Portuguese state secrets to the Castilian crown. In return, Castile funded his expedition to explore the western Atlantic ocean. He made use of the Portuguese discovery of the 'Volta do Mar', the 'turn of the sea' which enabled easy passage from Iberia westwards utilising the Easterlies and returned by using the curving north-easterly trade winds until out in mid Atlantic and then picking up the Westerlies back to Europe. His recently available secret diary reveals his primary mission was to bring back the elusive Elixir of Life water from a specific Caribbean island for King Ferdinand. It also notes Columbus set off with a stolen Portuguese map and that he reported back to Ferdinand that he had found a Portuguese settlement that had already been established (possibly on Haiti) for over 60 years.

2.15   The British Royal Navy museum at Greenwich, on the east side of London, holds 7 maps showing parts of the Caribbean and of continental America - each dated prior to 1492. These are now thought either to have been the fruits of England's already long standing alliance with Portugal or to have been derived from charts created by the Chinese Admiral He's explorations between 1421 and 1424 as noted above – which are also likely to be the origin of the famous Piri Reis map – the same map that Erich von Daniken attributed to extra-terrestrials.

2.16   As this edition is being updated, I await new DNA research being conducted on the remains of Columbus and known close relatives which it is speculated might prove he was originally Pedro Ataíde, using a pseudonym to protect his name and estates in Portugal. Early in his sailing career, Pedro Ataíde had joined with a French privateer named Colon and adopted the name Pedro Colon in his honour. When first arriving at the Spanish court, the courtier later known as Columbus was originally known as Pedro Columbus. The body of Pedro Ataíde's cousin has been disinterred and DNA tests are being conducted to compare with Columbus.

2.17   The examples above teach us that new truths take time, sometimes a very long time, to displace older false conclusions even when the falsity should be obvious to anyone.

3

Mars – sustaining life 4 billion years ago?

3.1 Images of Earth shot from space show an instantly recognisable view of a blue white pattern indicating plentiful water. But it was not always so. Early in Earth's existence, 4 billion years ago, another planet would have looked like the life sustaining Earth does today - whilst, at that time, Earth was inhospitable and toxic to all life.

3.2 Evidence from soil and rock analysis by the Curiosity Rover based on the surface of Mars, indicates that 4 billion years ago it was Mars that had plentiful surface water. We see clear evidence of water courses, water erosion patterns, smooth water polished pebbles and dried out waterfalls. Martian soil samples reveal that the soil of Mars contains all the key nutrients to sustain life. Indeed, the soil samples analysed by Curiosity comprised 2% H_2O. The composition of the rocks indicates a plentiful atmosphere existed with sufficient oxygen to make it breathable and average global temperatures are estimated to have been around 20C. The Curiosity Rover has also found clear evidence of thermal vents on Mars, exacly the kind of internally heated liquid flows bubbling to the planetary surface which are seen as highly probable feature leading to the emergence of life on Earth. Indeed, it seems the conditions on Mars were at that time significantly more conducive to the emergence of life than the conditions on Earth.

3.3 Mars has always been known as the Red Planet, its red appearance reflects the dominant surface colour created from minerals having oxidized during its existence. This proves that at one time, before the atmosphere was lost, Martian air was rich in oxygen.

3.4 Earth, 4 billion years ago, had an atmosphere comprising mainly methane and ammonia with small proportions of carbon dioxide, nitrogen and water vapour but only trace oxygen. The surface of the Earth was comprised substantially of active volcanic landmass. These greenhouse gases kept average global temperatures very high, at a time when our relatively young star only emitted around 70% of its current energy output. As our planet cooled and average temperatures fell, the clouds that formed brought rain to enable oceans to start accumulating - assisted by multiple impacts of ice meteorites. With plunging temperatures, Earth evolved into 'snowball earth' - a state endured for very long periods. Oxygen only appeared once plant life emerged and photosynthesis started to absorb carbon dioxide and pump out oxygen, starting about 2.3 billion years ago.

3.5 Two factors seem to have acted to dramatically change the fortunes of the respective planets. For reasons not yet determined, there appears to have been very heavy bombardment of (at least Earth and Mars) for a period of around 100 million years from 3.9 billion years ago until about 3.8 billion years ago. Rock samples taken from impact craters on both Mars and our Moon indicate an intense period of impacts. Without surface liquids or any atmosphere to erode surface features, our Moon shows the cumulative coverage of such impact creators – showing hardly a single square kilometre which did not suffer an impact.

3.6 As we shall review in the following few chapters, extraterrestrial impacts can result in dramatic changes in planetary climate. The cumulative effect on Earth eventually created a benign climate to sustain humanity but Mars suffered badly. Over the next 300 million years (between 3.8 billion and 3.5 billion years ago) it appears that Mars cooled, its surface water froze and worse, it begun to lose its atmosphere.

3.7 With Mars orbit lying further out from the Sun, its planetary composition contains less metallic components – suggesting its original molten core contained less iron thereby generating a weaker magnetic flux around the planet. Being half the diameter of Earth, Mars core is a fraction of the mass of Earth's core – also resulting in a weaker magnetic field. As a planet ages, its inner core cools – gravitational forces from other orbiting objects can delay this by pulling the core in different directions – an effect similar to constantly stirring it! One solution would be to trace a highly elliptical orbit around one's star – which would provide a strong internal current stirring your molten core – but such a highly elliptical orbit might also lead to wild swings in planetary climate, so extreme as to make it uninhabitable. The next most effective solution would be to have a large Moon, or a few moons. An orbiting moon will create tidal forces within the planet – affecting a molten core as well as surface liquids. Here again, Earth benefits from having an outsized Moon – by far the largest of any planet in our Solar System when comparing the relative sizes of moon and planet. But whilst Mars has two moons – they are both miniscule. These factors inevitably led to Mars already small inner core cooling to the point where it froze solid and Mars lost the magnetic flux which held on to its atmosphere. This may have happened as long ago as 3.5 billion years – as we have found no rocks younger than that, indicating volcanic activity ceased around that time. As Mars magnetic field died, so its atmosphere started to vent away into space, stripped away by the solar wind.

3.8   So, we have the tantalising prospect that further visits to Mars may well turn up evidence of life having evolved there many billions of years ago, even though it later died out as conditions became harsher. Given how tenacious we have found life to be on Earth, it seems highly likely that if it had been established on Mars when conditions were benign, life would have surely evolved as conditions worsened to retain a hold somewhere on, or more likely beneath the surface of, the red planet!!

3.9   Research at the SETI Institute led by Kaveh Pahlevan points to early Mars enjoying warm oceans for millions of years. The atmosphere would have been dense, with a high proportion of hydrogen, serving as a heat-trapping greenhouse gas that eventually was transported to higher altitudes and lost to space as the magnetosphere faded.

3.10 A French team studying the likely chemical composition of the early Martian atmosphere came up with a novel theory that the life which may have evolved on the Red Planet may also have contributed to its own demise. A team led by Boris Sauterey of Sorbonne University, publishing in the journal *Nature Astronomy* in 2022, explained how microbial life may have flourished only to change the composition of the atmosphere and doomed itself to extinction. The study used climate and terrain models to assess the habitability of the Martian soil 4 billion years ago.

The widespread presence of water would have made the planet potentially habitable for organisms consuming hydrogen which would have likely produced methane. Such organisms could have flourished in the regolith covering Mars. But the presumably moist, warm climate of the young Mars would have been jeopardized by so much hydrogen being sucked out of the thin, carbon dioxide-rich atmosphere. This change in the composition of the atmosphere would have led to a plunge in temperature, of more than 100C, with any organisms at or near the surface moving deeper in an attempt to survive.

3.11   Based on their modelling, the Sorbonne study suggested the best places to look for traces of ancient lifeforms would be unexplored Hellas Planitia and Jezero crater on the north-western edge of Isidis Planitia, where Nasa's Perseverance rover is collecting rocks - for eventual collection and return to Earth in the early 2030's.

3.12   By comparison, Earth's atmosphere was dominated by nitrogen when its first microbes are believed to have evolved – and their biology appears to have helped maintain temperate conditions.

MARS - SUSTAINING LIFE 4 BILLION YEARS AGO ?

4

Earth – violent events enabled life but caused extinctions

4.1   Most of us wake up every day and survey the view from our window and conclude it remains unchanged – but our personal experience is very misleading.

4.2   During its 4543 million year existence, Earth has witnessed a wide range of catastrophic events. The most violent, believed to have occurred during the first 50 million years of Earth's existence, resulted in Earth gaining a moon. This event is the key to any form of life existing on our planet. Small rocky inner planets don't seem to capture moons – neither Mercury nor Venus have captured any all. Neither did Earth in the conventional sense – the consensus view now is that we gained our moon as a result of a collision with another smaller planet. Apart from that early unusual happening, Earth has not managed to capture any moons. Mars has managed to capture two – but both are very small and far too small to do what moons are supposed to do if an ecosystem is to develop. Compare this record with the gas giants – Jupiter currently has 95, Saturn 146, Neptune 15 and Uranus 27. These giant planets seem efficient at hoovering up any bodies wandering near their orbits – indeed given the sheer numbers, the total captured is definitely higher - as some will have been sucked into ever closer orbits and have disintegrated long ago. Suffice to say, without our moon, life may not have emerged on Earth at all. If it had, life on Earth would have remained very basic. Again, in the relatively near future, we shall see what life, if any, managed to develop before Mars molten core solidified. Mars is considerably further from our sun, at 245 million kms versus 151 million kms – meaning that solar

4.3 The previous chapter explored why capturing a moon is so critical to the emergence of life. Without a moon of sufficient mass to maintain strong gravitational tides from regular orbiting, the inner core of a rocky planet will cool and solidify. The process of planetary accretion, when a planet forms from frequent collisions, causes heat and pressure resulting in a liquid magma core. Without a moon to keep stirring the molten core, it will slowly cool and unstirred the core will solidify. The magnetosphere created by the swirling liquid core is crucial to life as it shields the planet from a wide range of radiation. Without a magnetosphere, the radiation from our sun would mutate all lifeforms into extinction. A magnetosphere is also essential for retention of a planet's atmosphere – without it, Earth's atmosphere would slowly bubble away into space, as Mars did.

4.4 We remain open to the possibility of very alien lifeforms but we regard the existence of liquid water as a pre-requite for life. One mystery, so far unresolved, is the origin of Earth's vast treasure of liquid water. During the first 100 million years after Earth's formation, the surface temperature is estimated to have been around 2000C. At this temperature, there would be little water vapour but hydrogen and oxygen would mostly exist in the form of plasma. However, our current understanding is that water appeared within a few hundred million years of Earth's formation – this is surprising given the extensive volcanic activity at that time and the composition of the early atmosphere. Given the high frequency of impacts during the initial phase of planetary formation, it is suggested that any surface liquid would have been liquid magma. A surface temperature of around 2000C would mean that there would be no land – the entire planetary surface would comprise a lethal cocktail of liquid minerals and metals, including:

- lead - melting point 330C
- silver - melting point 960C
- copper - melting point 1085C
- iron - melting point c1500C
- and even liquid granite - melting point c1250C, and,
- liquid basalt - melting point between 1000C and 1260C

hardly conducive to the formation and development of lifeforms!

4.5 The largest single impact is thought to have occurred within 20 to 50 million years of Earth's formation - resulting in the creation of Earth's moon. Given that numerous rock samples recovered from the Moon present very similar chemical and isotopic compositions to ancient rocks found on Earth, it is believed that they must have been formed from the same material. The most popular theory is that an object (dubbed Theia) almost the size of Mars collided with the proto-Earth. Depending upon the nature of the impact, a direct blow or a glancing blow, it is possible that the remains of Theia form a significant part of Earth's surface and our Moon; or that the impact drove Theia deep into Earth's outer mantle and the violence of the impact resulted in a chunk of proto-Earth being displaced from the far side of our planet and forming the Moon. Modelling of theoretical impacts has led to the estimated size of the two colliding bodies and the resulting Earth and Moon which resulted – and accounts for the close similarity of rocks found on both bodies.

4.6 In October 2023, Dr Qian Yuan of the California Institute of Technology and Professor Hongping Deng of the Shanghai Astronomical Observatory published an article in *Nature* reporting that they had identified evidence of the very early planet sized Earth impact. Two massive continental sized shapes, around 2900kms below the Earth's surface and close to the boundary with Earth's core have long puzzled seismologists. These two 'blobs' are somewhat denser than surrounding material and are known as LLVP's (large low velocity provinces). The researchers propose that these LLVP are remnants of the planet sized body which impacted Earth – an impact which carried these bodies a huge distance beneath the Earth's surface and the shock of the violent impact may have been instrumental in displacing material from the far side of Earth - which went on to form our outsized moon. This not only explains Earth and Moon appearing to have near identical rock compositions but the vast surface depression that would have resulted from the impact explains the initial distribution of Earth's surface with a vast continent on one side and a vast ocean covering the impact site - of which the Pacific Ocean is a distant echo.

4.7 The sheer size of our moon relative to the size of our planet is far greater than any other in our solar system. Indeed the relative size makes it almost impossible for Earth to simply have captured the moon during a close encounter – Earth's gravity is simply not great enough to have exerted sufficient pull on the moon to capture it if it was sweeping by.

Hence the high probability that two bodies collided and a large chunk of one of the original bodies separated and became our moon.

4.8 This understanding is not that different from the ancient Sumerian understanding that Earth was formed when the planet that formally orbited between Mars and Jupiter, referred to as Tiamat, collided with another planet, Nibiru, which had a highly eccentric orbit. According to Sumerian history, Tiamat was largely covered with deep water. Tiamat was rent asunder by the collision, with the largest part becoming Earth whilst the remaining debris from the collision became what we call the Asteroid Belt and the ancients called the Hammered Bracelet. Tiamat then collided with the proto-Earth, ejecting a large chunk which became our moon – hence the identical rocks found on both bodies. The large part of Tiamat which collided with the proto-Earth brought our large mass of water, and recent evidence, see below, seems to confirm this former planet orbiting between Mars and Jupiter was indeed a major source of our seawater.

4.9 Three aspects stand out from the ancient Sumerian understanding:

- Earth should have inherited a large volume of water;

- It explains the current understanding that Earth originally had a single giant continent with all the land mass concentrated on one side of the planet;

- It explains what happened to create the Asteroid Belt and why the water found on some asteroids share the chemical signature as our seawater;

But, from where did such a sophisticated, and now seemingly plausible, explanation originate from – it seems hardly likely to have formed the basis of oral myths concocted by hunter gatherers?

4.10 Lunar rock samples contain very little evidence of water, suggesting that water was largely absent from either the body that collided with the proto-Earth or proto-Earth itself. If a large part of Tiamat brought large amounts of water then it would suggest the moon formed from a chunk of the original body orbiting as the proto-Earth – and Earth gained a large amount of water at a very early age.

4.11 If Earth's water supply did not largely originate from Tiamat colliding with the early Earth then where did Earth obtain its generous supply of water? Setting aside the Sumerian understanding, the current explanation is that Earth gained its vast supply of water from meteor impacts. Certainly many meteors have been found to contain water in various forms. We even have two recent examples which has yielded amazing results to support this contention.

4.12 On 11th August 2020, The Guardian reported on the first analysis of data collected by the Nasa spacecraft Dawn - obtained from only 35km above the surface of Ceres. Ceres, with a diameter of 940km, is now designated a 'dwarf planet', same as Pluto, and constitutes the largest remnant of Taimat remaining in the asteroid belt. Previously believed to be a barren space rock, Ceres is now found to be an ocean world with reservoirs of sea water beneath its surface. Infrared imaging has revealed the presence of hydrohalite – a material common in sea ice but has never before been found except on Earth. Maria Cristina De Sanctis, from Rome's Istituto Nazionale di Astrofisica said hydrohalite was a clear sign Ceres used to have sea water. This further supports the theory that (at least) part of Earth and Ceres share a common parent body – Tiamat.

4.13 In 2021, a meteorite crashed in Winchcombe, Gloucestershire, UK, containing water which was a near perfect match for water found on Earth. The meteor comprised mainly carbonaceous chondrites. More than 500gms of material from the impact was quickly collected from surrounding gardens and fields. Analysis found an 11% water content containing a very similar ratio of the different types of hydrogen atoms to water on Earth.

4.14 Fortunately, camera footage of the meteorite's fireball allowed researchers to calculate a very precise trajectory. Backtracking the data, indicated the meteorite came from the asteroid belt between Mars and Jupiter – i.e. the remnants of the planet that the Sumerians referred to as Tiamat, the watery planet. The meteorite also contained carbon and nitrogen bearing organic compounds, including amino acids. If Earth's oceans have been formed from, or at least topped up by, asteroids which were remnants of Tiamat then not only does it confirm Tiamat was a watery planet but life may already have emerged there prior to its destruction. Further, the building blocks for DNA might have already been on Earth when it was formed from the destruction of Tiamat or have been carried to Earth riding on asteroid remnants of Tiamat.

4.15   Apart from the unique mega collision with another planet very early in Earth's existence, the conventional understanding is that meteor impacts, some severe, were common in the early life of the solar system but have more or less ceased as the passage of time has resulted in all the big meteors having collided with one or other planet billions of years ago. However, as we shall see, the frequency of meteors large enough to cause at least regional or continental extinction level events is still happening - with a frighteningly high number of impacts over the past 12,000 years. Moreover, meteor impacts are far from the only extinction level events humanity faces (even excluding nuclear war, pandemics and AI). Indeed our continued existence seems to be miraculous.

4.16   Broadly speaking there are four types of natural events which can radically change the ability of our planet to sustain life, most of which will result in extinction of some, even a majority of species. Some events are interrelated:

(i)   A 'local' supernova, the deadly effect of radiation from a nearby star going supernova at the end of its life. 'Nearby' means anything within 25 million light years would be an extinction level event for Earth. We have evidence of at least 14 such events in the past 8 million years – i.e. almost yesterday for a planet 4543 million years old, indicating a disturbing level of recency, frequency and severity.

(ii)   Life itself fundamentally changing the climate by changing the composition of the atmosphere – we have evidence that this happened in a benign way as early life absorbed carbon dioxide and replaced it with oxygen. Humanity is also changing the composition of our atmosphere right now, probably with fatal consequences.

(iii)   Impacts by other celestial bodies – our planet has experienced a wide range: from an impact with another planet (widely believed to have resulted in our proportionately huge Moon); meteors of varying sizes (being sub-planetary bodies usually with highly elliptic orbits around the sun); asteroids (referring to fragments from the asteroid belt between Jupiter and Mars); comets (usually dust held together by ice); and, small stuff generally referred to as meteorites. Everybody now knows a meteor impact wiped out the dinosaurs but the record of the frequency and severity of such impacts makes grim reading.

(iv) Gravitational forces from the changing proximity of other bodies – causing earthquakes and volcanic activity – which can sometimes be so devastating as to rank as an extinction level event. It is clear that some larger meteor impacts also triggered significant volcanic activity.

Supernovae impact life on Earth

4.17 Our Solar System is travelling through the outer reaches of our Milky Way galaxy, in what is known as the Orion Arm. Very recently, for the past 5 to 10 million years (of our planets 4,543 million year existence), Earth has been traversing what is termed the Local Bubble or Local Cavity. This is an area of extremely low density, around 1/10th of the general density of the Milky Way. This low density is attributed to the occurrence of one or more supernova 'evacuating' the region between 10m to 20m years ago. Writing in the May 2019 edition of the *Journal of Geology*, Brian Thomas (Washburn University, Kansas) and Adrian Melott (University of Kansas) report finding that between 14 and 20 supernovae have occurred in Earth's vicinity over the past 8m years. These explosions, of young, massive stars, are believed to have happened in the Tucana-Horologium stellar group, currently about 130 light-years from Earth. Other potential candidates identified include Geminga in the constellation Gemini and multiple supernovae in sub group B1 of the Pleiades. Earth's proximity to these supernovae would have meant life here would have been bathed in deadly radiation – leading to mutations and death.

4.18 A supernova occurring within say 25 light-years of Earth would be catastrophic - the resulting bombardment of fast-moving atomic nuclei, known as cosmic rays, would destroy the layer of atmospheric ozone that stops most of the sun's harmful ultraviolet light reaching Earth's surface. In combination, these two kinds of radiation, cosmic and ultraviolet, would then kill most forms of life.

4.19 We have both terrestrial and astronomical evidence of the past occurence of supernovae. Firstly, the shock waves from the supernovae created a large void through which we are currently travelling - a peanut-shaped feature 300 light-years long. This near void, known as the Local Bubble has only around 10% of the density of interstellar gas elsewhere in our galaxy and is almost devoid of the magnetic field that normally threads through that gas. The boundary of the Local Bubble presents a wall of somewhat denser gas and stronger magnetic fields. Once the Local Bubble was established, any cosmic rays created by a supernova within it would have kept bouncing off this magnetic wall and back into the bubble. They would thus have strafed every object within it, including Earth, for tens, or even hundreds of thousands of years after the explosion that created them.

4.20　We have terrestrial evidence in the form of the nuclei of a radioactive isotope of iron (iron-60) that is created almost exclusively in supernovae. These unstable nuclei, together with their decay products, have been found in the ocean floor on Earth and in rock samples brought from the Moon. Those isotopes found on Earth can be dated from the sediment they are in. The strongest signal is from only 2.58m years ago, indicating that this explosion was the closest. This peak in the iron-60 isotope reading coincides with the extinction level event denoting the end of the Pliocene Epoch – when early forms of hominoids existed. The significance of evidence of serious events at this boundary led the two leading international authorities who determine the chronological ages of Earth's history, the International Union of Geological Sciences (IUGS) and the International Commission on Stratigraphy (ICS), to change the classification of when the Neogene Period ended and the Quaternary Period began. The result was that in 2009, ten years prior to Dr Melott's work (identifying the most powerful recent supernova occurred 2.58 million years ago), the Gelasian Age was reclassified as Quaternary and the end of the Pliocene Epoch, dated to 2.588 million years ago, recognised as even more significant.

4.21　In an earlier article in the journal *Astrobiology*, Dr Melott suggested that the cosmic particles showered the planet's surface at such high levels that they may have caused cancers in large marine creatures to spike. Among the apparent casualties was the Megalodon - a shark the size of a bus - that vanished from the fossil record at this time. Following a 'nearby' supernova, muon particles would have fallen in large numbers onto the surface of the planet.

4.22　Muons, elementary particles similar to very heavy electrons, penetrate deep into all living creatures (including humans) and are responsible for around a fifth of the radiation dose we receive. Normally our background level exposure is not a problem, but with muon exposure increased by a factor of hundreds, Melott concluded that rates of mutation and cancer would rise sharply. Larger animals would have been particularly susceptible, as they would have caught a greater dose of radiation. This could explain why the Megalodon, as well as a third of other large sea creatures, failed to survive into the next epoch of Earth's history, the Pleistocene. Previous work has suggested supernovae around this time could also have killed off small creatures crucial to ocean health by damaging the ozone layer and allowing a surge of UV light through to Earth's surface.

4.23 A geological feature that coincides with the period when Local Bubble supernovas were going off is an increase in traces of charcoal in oceanic sediment. That is evidence of wildfires on land. This increase starts about 7m years ago and in turn coincides with a period when much of Earth's vegetation shifted from forests to grasslands. The fires recorded by the oceanic charcoal could explain this shift, because grass is more resilient to fire than trees are. Precisely what caused regular and extensive fires remains unknown – although the most likely culprits are obviously lightning strikes, volcanic activity and meteor impacts, particularly in any era when the climate was hotter and drier.

4.24 Dr Thomas and Dr Melott identify a different precursor for the charcoal - cosmic rays from the local supernovas. The main arsonist of wildfires is lightning and it is suggested that intense cosmic rays caused more lightning. The rays would smash into atmospheric molecules, separating electrons from their atoms. These liberated electrons would in turn knock loose other electrons, creating cascades that would make the air electrically conductive. This would generate numerous lightning strikes.

4.25 Observations made recently on a mountain in Armenia, of electron cascades caused by normal cosmic rays, showed that many of these did indeed end in a lightning flash, so the idea is plausible. The Kansas team estimated the incidence of such cascades could have increased 50-fold.

4.26 The replacement of forests by grassland is thought by some anthropologists to have encouraged the evolution of humanity's ancestors away from tree-climbing and towards bipedalism. It was this change in locomotion that freed human hands to get up to all the mischief which distinguishes people from other species.

Life itself has changed the composition of the Earth's atmosphere

4.27 Around 2500 million years ago, organisms evolved deploying photosynthesis to convert CO_2 into O_2. This emergence of cyanobacteria resulted in increasing oxygen levels, causing widespread extinction of previous anaerobic bacteria. The removal of bacteria emitting methane and carbon dioxide resulted in a global cooling – and the start of the snowball Earth eras.

4.28 Earth did not remain a snowball continuously, one abrupt warming occurred 2.2 billion years ago and the cause has recently been identified as a massive meteor impact. Due to its age, there is no visible evidence but distortions to the local magnetic field and the decay of radioactive uranium isotopes in the shocked quartz allow mapping of the impact site and enable accurate dating. Reported in *Nature Communications* in January 2020, the site is Yarrabubba, Western Australia and the crater would have been 70km wide. An impact of this size into ice kilometres thick would have vapourised vast quantities producing water vapour and downpours of warm rain raising global temperatures many degrees. This, in turn, would have helped the new emerging cyanobacteria to boost oxygen levels and allow the later emergence of complex organisms on Earth.

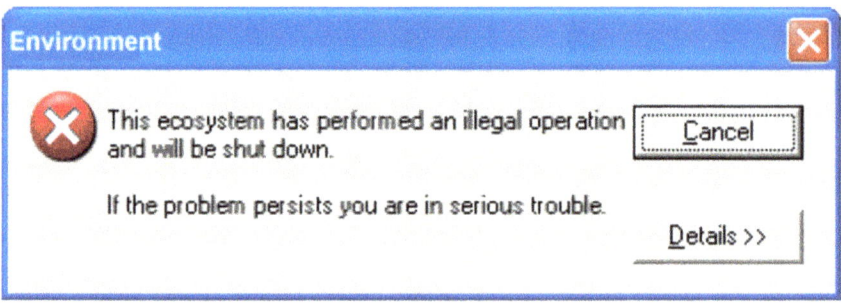

4.29 From around 500 million years ago, global temperatures rose to levels similar to today but 251,941,000 years ago (+/-37,000) there was a mass extinction event linked with dramatic changes to the Earth's climate, now known as "The Great Dying" when global temperatures soared causing oxygen levels in the oceans to drop sharply. With our current knowledge it seems most likely that this abrupt extinction event (70% of all land species and 96% of all ocean species went extinct) was almost certainly caused by one or more meteor impacts.

EARTH - VIOLENT EVENTS ENABLED LIFE BUT CAUSED EXTINCTIONS

Meteor impacts

4.30   Earth is constantly showered with extra-terrestrial objects on a daily basis. The vast majority either burn up during their passage through the Earth's atmosphere or are so tiny that they are barely noticed. However, these projectiles can be much larger and we have identified several impacts which were so massive that life almost became extinct.

4.31   Some scientists suggest that the size and frequency of meteor impacts has been declining with the advancing age of our solar system, as all the wild rogue elements 'left over' from the early formation of our system finally fall prey to the civilising motion of the planets spinning purposefully in their rightful orbits.

4.32   Whilst the record does support this thesis to some degree, the frequency of (what in historical terms) might be regarded as minor asteroid impacts is still pretty staggering. The Earth Impact Database ("EID") maintained by New Brunswick University contains 44 confirmed impact creators ranging between 160km and 20km in diameter which have occurred in the past 600 million years – i.e. whilst multicellular life was evolving. Ominously, the last 600 million years represents the youngest 13% of the life of our planet – i.e. long after all the debris of the early solar system should have been cleared away! Whilst Chicxulub, with a diameter of 150km, exterminated the dinosaurs and would have similarly exterminated humans if we had been around in that era, even the smallest of these confirmed impacts would have devastated any human civilisation.

4.33   Traces of the earliest impacts have largely been weathered away, eroded, blanketed by lava flows or buried under ice – so our current knowledge is based upon evidence from only around 20% of the Earth's surface – and surely understates the full horror of what we have faced in the past. If you examine large scale images of the surface of the Moon, it shows the entire surface pock marked by impact craters – indicating that Earth's history was probably very similar. In addition to the 44 confirmed major impacts recognised by the EID, a further 10 huge impact craters have been identified as 'probables' but confirmation is hampered by these being located under the ice caps or under sea or due to very extensive age and/or weathering which hinders verification. Each of these 10 would have rendered Earth uninhabitable, save for microbes, as the diameters of the craters are estimated between 250km and 600km. The number of less massive but still devastating impacts probably runs into hundreds – for example the Lairg Gravity Low in the Scottish Highlands suggests a crater 40km wide from an impact some 1200 million years ago – a third wider than Hiawatha, it would have devastated the entire European and North American continents.

Gravitational forces drive volcanic activity

4.34 Earth's elliptical orbit around our Sun and the irregular orbits of our moon and other planets mean constantly changing gravitational forces are exerted on our planet – which helps keep our molten core churning. This in turn causes continental drifting and results in volcanic activity along the fault lines of the tectonic plates.

4.35 Our continents float on the mantle of our upper crust – the plates are continually moving, creating pressure as they move against each other. Weaknesses in the crust allow magma to vent, as well as "normal" volcanoes, these can lead to mega-volcanoes creating extinction level events. The most violent known mega volcanoes since humans have walked the Earth have been those at Yellowstone National Park - 2.1million years ago, 1.2 million years ago and c639,000 years ago and also at Toba c74,000 years ago.

4.36 Major meteor impacts are also suspected of having triggered volcanic activity, certainly the impact force makes it highly likely – adding to the firestorms, tsunami and waves of liquefied landmass created by a major impact.

Snowball Earth

4.37 These most extreme of these events probably triggered the dramatic changes in climate which led to the Snowball Earth epochs. Geological work continues to identify more and more periods of extreme glaciation but the first three stand out as being of global extent and long duration:

- Pongola   c2900 million years ago to c2780 million years ago
- Huronian   c2400 million years ago to c2100 million years ago
- Sturtianc   c715 million years ago to c680 million years ago

These were periods when the entire planet was enveloped in ice and single cell organisms clung on, living under ice in the oceans. Some attribute the explosion in the variety of lifeforms during the Cambrian period following the Sturtian ice age as a response to the most severe ice age.

Conclusions

4.38   Earth is 4543 million years old and whilst traces of single cell life forms have been found back as far as 3500 million years, multicellular life first emerged only 600 million years ago, the first mammals around 220 million years ago and the first primates only 63 million years ago. Modern homo sapiens sapiens (us) only emerged c175,000 years ago. The struggle for life to evolve took place through hundreds of millions of years marked by numerous catastrophic events.

4.39   Earth has been transformed by impacts. Four types of events have determined the existence and evolution of our ecosystem and the types of lifeforms it sustains:

- the most rucial was the early capture of a massive moon;

- the accretion of water, probably from impacts by various remnants of Tiamat;

- cyonbacteria, absorbing CO_2 and emitting O_2, winning the evolutionary battle over anaerobic bacteria which absorbed hydrogen and emitted methane and CO_2;

- numerous impacts causing extinction level events which eventually gave mammals a lucky break.

4.40   Without these lucky breaks, Earth would probably be very similar to Venus – totally inhospitable for life. The contrast with Venus is instructive. Venus is a similar size planet but orbits closer to the Sun. Crucially, without a moon, it's molten core has solidified and it has no magnetosphere to speak of. The effect of the solar wind blowing around it does create a weak induced magnetosphere but it does not provide much protection from solar radiation. Venus does retain a shallow but thick atmosphere but the weak magnetosphere has allowed all the lighter gases to bleed off into space. So the Venusian atmosphere has no hydrogen, oxygen or water vapour but comprises heavier gases such as carbon dioxide, methane and sodium dioxide – replenished by continuing bouts of widespread volcanic activity.

5

Earth - major extinction level events in the past 600 million years

5.1 When we look at the surface of Mars or of our Moon we see almost the entire surface pock marked by craters – the likelihood is that Earth suffered from just as many impacts. In addition, with a molten core and constantly stirred by the gravitational forces of its proportionately large moon, Earth also experienced large scale volcanism. The largest impacts and most violent eruptions have caused many extinction level events for life battling to colonise our planet. We are only recently learning just how alarming the severity and frequency of these events has been.

5.2 This chapter focuses on major events which threatened the very existence of life on earth, the following chapter focuses on more recent threats to humanity.

5.3 Earth is constantly showered with extra-terrestrial objects on a daily basis. The vast majority either burn up during their passage through the Earth's atmosphere or are so tiny that they are barely noticed. However, these projectiles can be much larger and we have identified several impacts which were so massive that life almost became extinct.

5.4 Some scientists suggest that the size and frequency of meteor impacts has been declining with the advancing age of our solar system, as all the wild rogue elements 'left over' from the early formation of our system finally fall prey to the civilising motion of the planets spinning purposefully in their rightful orbits.

5.5 Whilst the record does support this thesis to some degree, the frequency of (what in historical terms) might be regarded as minor asteroid impacts is still pretty staggering. As noted in 4.32 above, the Earth Impact Database ("EID") maintained by New Brunswick University contains 44 confirmed impact creators ranging between 160km and 20km in diameter which have occurred in the past 600 million years – i.e. whilst multicellular life was evolving. Ominously, the last 600 million years represents the youngest 13% of the life of our planet – i.e. long after all the debris of the early solar system should have been cleared away! Whilst Chicxulub, with a diameter of 150km, exterminated the dinosaurs and would have similarly exterminated humans if we had been around in that era, even the smallest of these confirmed impacts would have devastated any human civilisation. In section 7, we examine the Hiawatha impact (31km) in more detail – and see how this almost wiped human life from North America and Europe whilst the ejecta thrown up into the atmosphere may have created a nuclear winter for at least 5 years – and that was terrifyingly recent – c10765BC.

5.6 Traces of the earliest impacts have largely been weathered away, eroded, blanketed by lava flows or buried under ice – so our current knowledge is based upon evidence from only around 20% of the Earth's surface – and surely understates the full horror of what we have endured. If you examine large scale images of the surface of the Moon, it shows the entire surface pock marked by impact craters – indicating that Earth's history was probably very similar. In addition to the 44 confirmed major impacts recognised by the EID, a further 10 huge impact craters have been identified as 'probables' but confirmation is hampered by these being located under the ice caps or under sea or due to very extensive age and/or weathering which hinders verification. Each of these 10 would have rendered Earth uninhabitable, save for microbes, as the diameters of the craters are estimated between 250km and 600km.

5.7 Earth is 4543 million years old and whilst traces of single cell life forms have been found back as far as 3500 million years, multicellular life first emerged only 600 million years ago, the first mammals around 220 million years ago and the first primates only 63 million years ago. Modern homo sapiens sapiens (us) only emerged around 175,000 years ago. The struggle for life to evolve took place through billions of years marked by numerous catastrophic events.

5.8 We have identified two massive impacts which occurred when only single cell organisms had evolved. The oldest, at Vredefort in South Africa, estimated at 2 billion years ago, left a crater 300km wide – almost twice the size of Chicxulub, the dinosaur killing impact 66m years ago. Relatively soon afterwards, 1.85 billion years ago, the amoeba were hit by another huge impact creating the Sudbury Basin in Ontario. This has left a crater 130km wide with rocks ejected from the impact found up to 800km away.

5.9 We know of six extreme extinction level events which caused more than 75% of all species living at the time to become extinct – each time, life was almost reset and a completely new range of species emerged during the ages that followed. Not all of these events have been directly linked to identified meteor impacts but such an event remains the most likely explanation for each extinction.

550 & 538.8 million years ago, the Eriacaran-Cambrian Events

5.10 The Ediacaran period from 635 million years ago to 538.8 million years ago ended with two events which saw almost all species become extinct. Most organisms in the Ediacaran period were soft tissue eukaryotes, without bones, teeth or nails. 550 million years ago an event caused 80% of the extant genera to disappear from the record. The event is believed to have resulted in a massive reduction in oceanic oxygen levels. The number of genera fell abruptly from 80 to 14 and the diversity of other lifeforms greatly reduced. A second event, 538.8 million years ago, has been adopted as marking the boundary between the Ediacaran and the Cambrian - barely any species have been found existing both sides of this boundary.

5.11 The Deniliquin impact, in New South Wales, has been identified as a potential cause. So far, this is the single largest impact identified, creating a crater 520km in diameter. It is also thought to have been responsible for cleaving asunder the ancient continent of Gondwana. However, the dating is not yet resolved – it was estimated at 514 million years ago but new research in August 2023 placed the impact at 443.8 million years ago – the later date fitting nicely with the Ordovician-Silurian Boundary Event (details below). Something biologically significant changed, presumably in the atmospheric composition or in the climate, which then led to the explosive growth in the variety of species for which the Cambrian period is famous.

485.4 million years ago, Cambrian-Ordovician Event

5.12 The Ordovician Period started and ended with major extinction events. This event, marking the end of the Cambrian period wiped out 60% of all species, the range and diversity of which had blossomed during the Cambrian period. This extinction event has not yet been linked to a specific meteor impact but there are some tentative candidates.

443.8 million years ago, Ordovician-Silurian Event

5.13 The Ordovician Period ended with an even more intense extinction event, which resulted in 86% of all existing species abruptly disappeared from the fossil record. No direct cause has been established but the tentative dating of the Ishim impact in the Akmola Region of Kazakhstan at 445 (+/-15) million years ago is a potential candidate and was certainly massive. The Earth Impact Database lists Ishim at 300 km diameter, which is roughly double that of the dinosaur killer meteor impact and therefore at least 4 times as powerful. However, Frank Dachille of Penn State University, noting that the shape of the impact crater has been folded by subsequent tectonic movements, estimates the impact crater had a diameter of 700km – implying a near total life extinction level event. Other research has identified a severe glacial period from 445.2 to 443.8 million years ago, known as the Hirnantian Glaciation Event – which could have been triggered by an impact creating a crater 300km wide or massive volcanic ejecta causing a nuclear winter. The two Ordovician events are linked to the creation of extensive oil and gas deposits. The climate in the Ordovician Period had oxygen levels c68% of current and CO_2 at 15 times current levels with mean sea level 190m higher than today.

375 & 360 million years ago, the Kellwasser and Hangenberg Events

5.14 A series of eight major events occurred late in the Devonian Period over a relatively short period of 15 million years, with the most significant events being the first and the last. The first is known as the Kellwasser Event when 75% of all species identifed prior tot he event suddenly disappeared from the record, and the last is known as the Hangenberg Event. The climate in the Devonian Period had oxygen levels c75% of current and CO_2 at 8 times current levels with mean sea level averaging

155m higher than today.

252.8 million years ago, the 'Great Dying' ending the Permian Epoch

5.15 This event, at the end of the Permian Epoch, is the most extreme extinction yet identified, when an estimated 96% of all species of life became extinct. The evidence from rock strata indicate a cataclysmic eruption near Siberia which blasted huge volumes of CO_2 and SO_2 into the atmosphere. Methanogenic bacteria responded by belching out methane, a potent greenhouse gas. Global temperatures surged while oceans acidified and stagnated, belching poisonous hydrogen sulphide. Seeds preserved from pine cones during this period show severe mutations causing some to conclude that the huge increase in atmospheric CO_2 and SO_2 from the eruptions would have severely damaged the ozone layer. Loss of the ozone layer would have resulted in Earth being bathed in deadly solar radiation intensifying the extinction.

5.16 Two massive impact events have been provisionally dated to c250 million years ago – one offshore Western Australia (the Bedouf anomaly) and the Wilkes Land mass concentration anomaly under the Antarctic ice sheet which, without direct sampling, is difficult to date accurately. However, gravitational readings indicate this anomaly cannot be more than 500 million years old whilst it carries the scars of more recent geographic events making it more than 200 million years old. The NASA mass concentration readings show a collapsed ring 300km wide and the outer impact depression is estimated to be 480km wide. Frank Dachille of Penn State University has linked the Wilkes Land anomaly to the Siberian Traps – which are exactly antipodal. The sheer size of the impact forming such a crater, 2.5 times wider than Chicxulub, indicates an extinction level event took place. Some researchers have also concluded that the Bedouf anomaly, also dated to 250 million years ago and itself significantly bigger than Chicxulub, could have been responsible. Gregory Retallack, a geologist at the University of Oregon, has discovered tiny quartz crystals marked with microscopic fractures in rocks from the time of the extinction in Australia and Antarctica. Retallack notes that staggering force is required, many times greater than a nuclear explosion, to create this shocked quartz, only a meteor impact could create such deformations.

5.17 The antipodal feature, the vast lava field known as the Siberian Traps, is a 2.6 million square kilometre covering of lava up to 4km thick. Expelled from dozens of volcanic vents, hundreds of cubic miles of lava were spread across Siberia —enough to cover the entire Earth to a depth of about 6 metres. For decades, scientists have known the Siberian Traps were formed around the time of the Permian extinction. Could the greatest extinction be related to the greatest volcanic eruptions? Paul Renne of the Berkeley Geochronology Center, an expert at determining the ages of rocks, has been trying to work out the timing of the events, dating the rocks by measuring the decay of radioactive isotopes within them. Renne secured chunks of lava from the Siberian Traps and Permian-Triassic boundary rocks from China. He determined that the two events occurred within 100,000 years of each other. That is unlikely to be a coincidence. The force of the impact shock in Antarctica could perhaps have disturbed the mantle of the other side of our planet – triggering the vast outpouring of volcanic magma.

5.18 Given the global destruction caused by the Chicxulub Event (described in section 5.23 below) which created a crater 150km wide, the Wilkes Land crater estimated as up to 480km would indicate a truly global cataclysmic event from which very little would have survived.

201.3 million years ago, the Triassic-Jurassic Event

5.19 This event marks another epochal boundary but the cause remains an enigma. The event was very serious, with an estimated 80% of all species made extinct. The ecological niches that became empty permitted the rise to dominance of the dinosaurs. Plant species also suffered very heavy extinction rates. No coincident meteor event has been identified, so far, but the scale of the extinction and the level of climatic change point to a major impact. The Manicouagan Impact in Quebec, resulting in a 100km wide creator, has radiometric dating to 214 million years ago (Hodych & Dunning, 1992) and is associated with a relatively minor extinction but is too early to account for the major Triassic-Jurassic extinction. The Manicougan impact did have a widespread effect – its ejecta blanket of shocked quartz has been found in strata as far away as England and Japan. Possibly it triggered long term climate change which led to a tipping point mass extinction 13 million years later.

5.20 An alternative explanation has been proposed, linking various smaller impacts which did occur right at the extinction period. But other Triassic craters dated to the boundary date are much smaller than Manicouagan: the Rochechouart crater in France, 25km and possibly up to 50km, and the Puchezh-Katunki crater in Eastern Russia (80km); the Saint Martin crater in Manitoba (40km); the Obolon crater in Ukraine and the Red Wing Creek crater in North Dakota (9km). John G. Spray of the Geology Department, University of New Brunswick and others, published an article, *Evidence for a late Triassic multiple impact event* in the journal *Nature* in March 1998, in which it was noted that the Manicoagan, Rochechoart, and Saint Martin craters all seem to be at the same latitude, and that the Obolon and Red Wing craters form parallel arcs with the Rochechoart and Saint Martin craters, respectively. Spray and his colleagues hypothesized the Triassic experienced a "multiple impact event", a large fragmented asteroid or comet which broke up and impacted the earth in several places at the same time. Just a few years earlier, Earth bound observers had witnessed multiple fragments of the Shoemaker-Levy comet slamming into the face of Jupiter.

5.21   Recent research, led by Manfredo Capriolo of the University of Padova, Italy, with summary findings published in *Nature Communications* on 7 April 2020 (Article number 1670 of 2020), identifies an alternative or complementary cause for this extinction event. This work has shown vast amounts of carbon dioxide were emitted in large scale volcanic eruptions which are estimated to have taken place over 500 years marking the end of the Triassic Epoch. Samples taken from rocks in North America, Portugal and Morocco reveal bubbles of carbon dioxide trapped in the igneous rocks. From this it is estimated that around 100,000 gigatons of CO_2 may have released into the atmosphere as around 100,000 cubic kilometres of lava vented over a vast area named as the Central Atlantic Magmatic Province. These eruptions caused the break-up of the Pangea super-continent and the emergence of the Atlantic Ocean.

5.22   In addition to CO_2, analysis indicates the eruptions also released vast quantities of other poisonous volcanic gases. The effect would have been a rise in global temperatures on a scale similar to that forecast for the coming 100 years and very strong acidification of the oceans. This comparison draws attention to the potential impact of current human activities in leading to widespread species extinction. Certainly, this research provides strong evidence of a likely extinction level event ending the Triassic Epoch. The coincidence of several meteor impacts around the same time would have exacerbated the jolt to Earth's climate.

65.76 million years ago, the Chicxulub meteor, ending the Cretaceous Period

5.23   Probably the best known major meteor impact, Chicxulub 65.76m years ago, in the Gulf of Mexico, is blamed for the demise of 75% of all plant and animal species, including the dinosaurs. The initial impact punched a hole in the Earth's crust 30km deep and 80 to 100km wide. For Earth's ecosystem the impact site was very unfortunate – the 12km wide asteroid vaporised billions of tonnes of sulphur containing rocks such as gypsum and anhydrite plus carbonates. According to Julia Brugger of the University of Potsdam, global climate temperature models indicate that injecting 100 billion tonnes of sulphur and 140 billion tonnes of carbon dioxide into the atmosphere would reduce average global temperatures by 26C, with between 3 and 16 years spent below zero. However, recent estimates of the rocks vaporised have been increased sharply upwards. It has been estimated that the impact threw an estimated 325 billion tonnes of sulphur and an estimated 425 billion tonnes of carbon dioxide into the atmosphere which would have reduced average global temperatures below zero for several decades. Ocean temperatures would have been markedly lowered for a few centuries.

5.24   Thus we learn that destruction from a meteor impact comes in a variety of forms. The immediate shock and awe, as assessed by a panel of 41 experts in 2010, estimated the Chicxulub meteor was 15km in diameter and travelling at around 20km per second, upon impact it created a hole 30km deep and released one billion times more energy than the Hiroshima bomb. The manner in which fossils in North Dakota have been found indicates a pressure wave emanating from the impact site would have liquefied the continental crust for thousands of miles in every direction.

5.25   The shock wave from an impact on the scale of Chicxulub would also create a tsunami with a global reach. In recent years we have seen devastating tsunamis in Asia with waves of between 10 and 20 metres. Molly Range of the University of Michigan, headed a team that has modelled the Chicxulub tsunami as being 1500 meters high, which would have raced completely around the globe. The team estimated the tsunami would still be 10 meters high when hitting New Zealand and mashed up rocks have been identified along that coast as dating from 66m years ago. Excavations in North Dakota reveal fossils of fish and trees that were sprayed with rocky, glassy fragments from the sky. The deposits also show evidence of having been swamped with water - the consequence of the colossal sea surge that was generated by the impact reaching 2500 kms inland from the Gulf of Mexico.

5.26   The debris thrown up by the impact would cause a nuclear winter, blocking out sunlight for years threatening any surviving lifeforms whilst causing a sharp drop in temperature – globally. Evidence from the KT boundary layer strata of iridium and shocked quartz mineral grains indicates that the ejecta from such an impact created continental scale firestorms.

5.27   Certainly we are discovering evidence of numerous ice ages, some quite severe and prolonged, the Karoo (360 million to 255 million years ago) lasted up to 105 million years, denying large parts of the planet to most lifeforms and generating stress for survival. This culminated with a mass extinction event known as the Capitanian mass extinction event 259m years ago, with 35% of allextant species becoming extinct.

5.28   In conclusion, it seems reasonable to attribute evidence of sudden mass extinctions of species to climatic changes caused by large meteor impacts. In the next few chapters we shall take a closer look at some smaller but **very recent impacts** that had a devastating impact on humanity and whose memory is indelibly seared in our collective memory.

6

Catastrophic events impacting hominids in past 1 million years

6.1 Now we change gear – from looking at events measured in tens of millions or hundreds of millions of years to examine just the past one million years and look at events affecting our immediate hominid ancestors and early homo sapiens sapiens.

6.2 The study of ancient human like fossils points to a variety of strands evolving amongst early hominids over the past 5 million years with recent discoveries of even more sub-species. However, modern humans seem to have evolved from one main species, albeit with some interbreeding with, for example, Neanderthal populations in Europe. DNA analysis, specifically of mitochondria, show what seems to be a single point of origin for our species a mere 175,000 years ago. Mitochondria is passed down the female line and exhibits a single change between each generation – in theory enabling analysis of mitochondria from any two humans to be used to determine the number of generations since the two humans shared a common ancestor. By applying an assumed value to the number of years between each generation, one arrives at an estimated date for the first human – our Adam.

An event c930,000 years ago which almost wiped out all our ancestor species

6.3 Throughout the 5 million or so years that hominids were evolving on Earth, geological data indicates a cyclical pattern of alternating mild ice ages and warmer periods with an average duration of 41,000 years.

Suddenly, for reasons unknown, the pattern changed into longer and more extreme cycles averaging 110,000 years up to the present day. This change is known as the Mid-Pleistocene Transition.

6.4 The new regime started with a prolonged ice age estimated to last from 930,000 years ago up to 813,000 years ago. This severe and prolonged climatic cooling almost wiped out the ancestors from which homo sapiens evolved. Based upon analysis of the diversity of our genetic variations it is possible to identify 'population bottlenecks' (periods when the population fell dramatically) and even calculate the estimated total population. Genetic analysis indicates c99% of the population of our ancestors died out - exposing them to a high risk of extinction.

6.5 The stress on the population appears to have triggered the genetic change separating homo erectus from other hominids and apes – the fusing of two of our chromosomes into a much larger single chromosome, our No 2. This resulted in future types of humans having 23 pairs whilst all other members of the ape family retained 24 pairs. This change has been linked to evolutionary changes in the structure of our brains.

6.6 Research led by Prof Giorgio Manzi, an anthropologist at Sapienza University of Rome and published in Science magazine found humanity's ancestors came perilously close to extinction. Genomic sequences were analysed from 3,154 people alive today, from 10 African and 40 non-African populations. By looking at the different versions of genes across a population, it is possible to roughly date when specific genes first emerged – the more time that has elapsed, the more chance for different variants of a gene to crop up. By estimating the frequency with which genes have emerged over time, scientists gain insights into how ancestral populations grew and shrank over time. The results suggested that our ancestors' total population plummeted from around 1 million prior to the sudden ice age to stabilise at only about 1,280 breeding individuals for the 117,000 year duration of the ice age. Scientists believe that an extreme climate event could have led to the bottleneck that came close to wiping out our ancestral line.

6.7 The analysis found evidence for the bottleneck in all the African populations, but only a weak signal of the event was detected in the 40 non-African populations. This is probably due to the ancestors of those of non-African heritage having in effect undergone a more recent population bottleneck, such as Toba 74,000 years ago, during the out-of-Africa migration, which would be expected to mask the earlier event.

6.8 The hominid specimens from that period 800,000 years ago, Homo Heidelbergensis, were our last shared ancestor with Neanderthals and Denisovans. Other descendants led eventually to the emergence of homo sapiens, the first of whom are now thought to have emerged around 300,000 years ago.

6.9 The tiny numbers of breeding individuals, 1,280, correspond to those of species that today we assess as at high risk of extinction. Any sudden major volcanic activity, meteor impact or pandemic could have eradicated any chance for humanity.

6.10 The decline appears to coincide with significant changes in global climate that turned glaciations into long-term events marked by a decrease in sea surface temperatures and prolonged droughts across Africa and Eurasia. This period also coincides with a relatively empty period on the fossil record. Between 900,000 and 600,000 years ago, the fossil record in Africa is very scarce, if not almost absent. The same can be said for Eurasia: in Europe we have a species known as Homo antecessor around 800,000 years ago and then nothing for about 200,000 years. Actually, the absence of specimens is itself evidence of the stress impacting our species.

Mega volcano eruptions threatened humans' immediate ancestors

6.11 Volcanic activity has come close to wiping out the ancestor species which led to modern humans. We have very good data on past volcanic explosions due to the clear evidence left behind – the magma can be dated and the caldera and ejecta underpin estimates of the explosivity and volume of ejecta. The violence of volcanic eruptions is classified under the VEI – Volcanic Explosivity Index. Eruptions are classified from lowest of 1 to the highest at 8.

6.12 The highest explosivity results in the largest volume of ejecta blasted into the atmosphere – with the potential to create a nuclear winter as dust is blown around the world and sunlight blocked, in the worst cases for years. This leads to the loss of vegetation and mass starvation amongst animal species. As a useful reference point, Mount Vesuvius which buried Pompeii and three other Roman towns in AD79 had a VEI of 5 and

PREQUEL – YOUNGER DRYAS METEOR IMPACTS, THE FLOOD & ATLANTIS

is estimated to have ejected 3 cubic kilometres of material.

6.13 At the extreme, we have identified three mega volcanoes with eruptions classified as VEI 8 – the most recent eruption at Yellowstone, 639,000 years ago, which ejected around 1100 km3. When the next eruption of Yellowstone occurs, life as we know it will end.

6.14 The Lake Taupō area of New Zealand has a grim record, over the last million years it has erupted at VEI 8 no less than three times: one million years ago it ejected an estimated 2760km3; 254,000 years ago it ejected 2000km3 and only 24,500 years ago it erupted 1760km3. At least the eruptions are getting smaller!

6.15 Then we have Toba – 74,000 years ago with estimates of its ejecta ranging from 2000km3 to as high as 13,000km3. This makes Toba thousands of times more explosive than Vesuvius and clearly it devastated many species on Earth.

The climate experienced by homo sapiens since we emerged

6.16 Let's look at the climate which Homo Sapiens Sapiens has experienced since its emergence as a distinct species only 175,000 years ago. Fortunately, recent interest in building climate models to simulate the potential impact of increasing levels of CO_2 in our atmosphere has led to far better analysis of our past. Finely grained detail of average global annual temperatures has been built up from numerous sets of data points in order to try to understand the interaction of the key variables.

6.17 We now know that modern humanity came into a world which was experiencing Ice Age maxima roughly every 110,000 years, alternating with warmer periods climaxing with maximum temperatures similar to ours in the 19th Century. Global average temperatures ranged from lows of around 5C during the coldest parts of the Ice Ages to highs of 12C. I am not aware of whether we yet understand why the global climate oscillated between these extremes.

6.18 On the face of it, the two global averages do not seem that extreme but our overall experience of weather can differ a lot from changes of only 1 or 2 degrees. Note, today we fret over the increase of 1.5C in the global average over the past 100 years. At its maxima, the ice sheets covered all of Canada and parts of some northern states in the US, almost the entirety of the UK plus Benelux, half of Germany and most of Poland. The Alps and the Pyrenees contained many glaciers.

6.19 The warmest periods of these cycles were quite short, only 10,000 years or so, followed by quite sharp cooling periods which then became more gradual, with cooling continuing over usually 50,000 years or more. Similarly the ice age maxima were both short lived, usually only around a few thousand years and seemingly always followed by a particularly sharp rebound in global average temperatures from almost the same minimum level of 5C – with increases in global averages of 6C to 7C in a continuous sharp trend over only a few thousand years.

6.20 Clearly some key triggers prompted the onset and soon afterwards the reversal out of Ice Ages.

6.21 The NOAA (National Oceanic and Atmospheric Administration) value for global average surface temperature for 2022 was 14.7C, whilst monthly data for 2023 is pointing to a sharp rise - to a level never before experienced by humanity.

6.22 What caused these dramatic climatic changes? There would appear to be three possibilities:

(i) the regularity of the pattern has been suggested to arise from some sort of self-stabilizing force which was keeping the planetary climate within set boundaries. Whilst there may be as yet undiscovered feed-back loops, perhaps from changes in average temperature diverting or weakening major ocean currents which then act to heat or cool against the trend and reverse the process, another explanation is gaining traction – the Milankovitch cycles, see the next paragraph;

(ii) Meteor impacts – we have evidence indicating many uncomfortably large meteors have impacted Earth in the relatively recent past. During the very unstable period between 13000BC and 9600BC a series of events, most likely impacts, triggered at least six abrupt changes in global average temperatures. These have the potential to raise or lower global average temperatures by substantial amounts. The most recent work on the Chicxulub meteor impact 65 million years ago suggests it could have lowered global average temperatures by a staggering 26C; and,

(iii) Eruptions of mega volcanos. These also have the potential to raise or lower global average temperatures by substantial amounts. Spewing large volumes of ejecta into the upper atmosphere would reduce levels of sunlight reaching the surface and cool temperatures. At the same time volcanic eruptions can inject greenhouse gases into the atmosphere leading to higher average temperatures.

6.23 Milutin Milankovitch (1879 – 1958) was a Serbian astrophysicist who proposed that regular climatic cycles were being caused by perturbations in the Earth's solar orbit. The presence of Jupiter, comprising 4% of the mass of our solar system, exerts gravitational attraction which on a 96,000 year cycle changes Earth's orbit from almost perfectly circular to more elliptical. In addition, Earth is still vibrating from the primordial collision which created our Moon. The angle of tilt, which generates our seasons and results in hemispheres having opposite seasons, itself changes over a 41,000 year cycle, whilst the axial vibration means our magnetic pole wanders around like the vibration following a bell being struck – the nutation cycle. Initially dismissed as the theory of a crank, the Milankovitch cycles have now been widely accepted as a key determinant of global climate.

6.24 A good understanding of glaciation cycles has now been established from ice core samples for the past 500,000 years. The data shows a regularity of ice age maxima occurring very close to every 41,000 years – which fits one of the Milankovitch cycles. Surprisingly the cycle changes around 300,000 years ago to a cycle of approximately 100,000 years – suggesting the other Milankovitch cycle had been adopted by the planetary climate! No explanation for the change in dominant cycle has yet gained dominance.

6.25 Both meteor impacts and mega volcanic eruptions have severely disrupted human development. Increasing evidence is coming to light, some identified in this book, indicating that earlier human civilizations were devastated by cataclysms so severe that mankind was relegated back to a stone age survival lifestyle.

Toba mega eruption 72000BC

6.26 With a volcanic explosivity index of 8, the highest rating of any volcano known on Earth, the Toba mega volcano is estimated (based on potassium argon dating) to have erupted 74,000 years ago (+/-900 years).

Toba, now a large lake, is on Sumatra in Indonesia. The mass ejected in the eruption is estimated to have been 100 times greater than the next most violent volcano since, Mount Tambora, also in Indonesia in 1815, which caused the 1816 'year without a summer'. The Toba caldera is 30 x 100 km wide. Michael Rampino, a geologist at NYU, and Stephen Self, a volcanologist at UC Berkeley estimate that the Toba eruption lowered global temperatures by between 3C and 5C for a few years as dense ash in the upper atmosphere blocked sunlight, followed by around 1000 years of a cooler climate. Others have variously estimated the immediate fall in global temperature in a range between 1C to 15C. A layer of ash 15cm thick appears to cover the whole of South Asia and is linked to the Toba eruption.

6.27 Studies of the human genome identified strange patterns indicating ancient population bottlenecks – periods when the human population appears to have fallen to dangerously low levels suggestive of having survived an extinction level event. Differences in DNA amongst today's human population is surprisingly small compared with other primates for example. This and other genetic evidence implies that today's humans are descended from a very small population of between 1,000 and 10,000 breeding pairs that existed about 70,000 years ago. Ann Gibbons, a graduate of UC Berkeley active in DNA analysis and a regular contributor to Science magazine, estimates that 1.2 million years ago the population of early humans was between 18,500 and 26,000 – levels we classify as endangered species today. After the Toba eruption, Gibbons estimates the surviving population was around 15,000.

6.28 Europe is likely to have been disproportionately affected by the nuclear winter and overall drop in temperatures – with other DNA analysis indicating that all Europeans are descended from only 7 females. A large volume study of around 300,000 samples of Caucasian mitochondria concluded that the entire sample were surviving descendants of only 7 females alive 74,000 years ago. It may be that relatives of other breeding age females survived the event but all their descendants later died out.

The Dryas Periods 14000BC to 9600BC

6.29 What we term 'recorded history' stretches back only to the first dynasty of Egypt and the crowning of Etana of Sumer in 3760BC. The last major ice age ran from around 110,000 to 20,000 years ago. This was followed by the normal cyclical warming but from around 14000BC to 9600BC the Earth's climate suffered a series of rapid and violent changes in climate. These are seen as three sudden coolings relatively quickly followed by equally sudden warmings back to or even ahead of the normal warming trend. These three oscillations are known as the Dryas periods – the Oldest, the Older and the Younger. Until very recently we had no clue as to what caused each of these traumas and recoveries. Now, lots of evidence is emerging of both the event which triggered the Younger Dryas cooling and the event which ended that period - essentially the research embedded in this book.

6.30 In chapters 7 and 8, we examine in more detail the Hiawatha impact (31km crater) which triggered the Younger Dryas period – and see how this almost wiped human life from North America and Europe – and that was terrifyingly recent – c10765BC.

6.31 In chapter 9, we shall look at evidence of an even bigger impact - a twin impact creating adjacent craters of 50km and 25km, in the Mediterranean. This has not yet been dated but other evidence points to c9600BC being the likely date.

Major events during 'recorded' history

6.32 Beware of taking comfort from the dating of the last eruption of Yellowstone National Park, 639,000 years ago or of Toba being 74,000 years ago – a major eruption, severely threatening human life worldwide, occurred only 1,500 years ago.

6.33 You may be surprised to hear of cataclysmic events have occurred in the past 5,000 years which would have a devastating effect on modern life. Two of these would almost certainly cause a mass collapse of our civil societies if they had occurred now:

- the Burckle Impact c2900BC
- an event in AD536 widely recorded in Roman annuls

Others would have very serious consequences – including:

- the Mazuma eruption c5700BC remembered by the Klamath people;
- the meteor which simultaneously wiped out Sodom & Gomorrah and

and Jericho c1650BC - the former abandoned permanently, the latter only resettled some 750 years later;

- the Thera eruption near Crete in 1610BC which buried the Minoan civilization;

- the Changbaishan eruption on the border of China and North Korea in cAD1000;

- the Tambora eruption in AD1815 believed to have made the loudest bang ever heard by humans (at least since the Toba eruption); and,

- the Krakatoa eruption in AD1883.

6.34 The Burckle Impact created a 29km crater 4km below the Indian Ocean and a massive tsunami – we look in more detail in Chapter 7. The event in AD536, which may be attributable to a large volcanic eruption or a twin meteor impact, we also look at below - starting at 6.37.

6.35 The serious consequences for the major but less than cataclysmic events listed in 6.33 above would include serious loss of life, a drop in global temperatures of a few degrees, significant disruption to agriculture and cessation of all air traffic for a long period of time due to the huge volume of dust ejected into the atmosphere. One measure, the volume of ejecta from eruptions, gives some idea of the devastating scale of the selected eruptions, again compared to Vesuvius ejecta of only 3km3:

•	Mazuma	5700BC	VEI 6	61km3
•	Meteor over Jordan	1650BC		unknown
•	Thera	1610BC	VEI 7	100km3
•	Changbaishan	AD1000	VEI 7	est. 40km3 to 98km3
•	Tambora	AD1815	VEI 7	160km3
•	Krakatoa	AD1883	VEI 6	10km3

6.36 Most of these discoveries were made only in the past decade. Moreover, we have only just found a smart way of finding undersea impact craters and being able to date the impacts. How many more will we find?

The event of AD536

6.37 Ancient documents record a devastating climatic event affecting the

Roman Empire over a number of years starting from AD536 during the otherwise highly successful rule of Emperor Justinian. Historical texts refer to the sun being dimmed or hidden for a few years and there being persistent cold conditions. David Keys, an investigative journalist, undertook a major project to understand the cause, his research revealed the impact was not limited to the Mediterranean but truly global. His work, *Catastrophe: An Investigation into the origins of the Modern World*, chronicles his massive research effort. Dendrochronology, the study of tree rings has confirmed very widespread and dramatic climatic change affected the year 536 and up to six following years. Tree rings indicated almost zero growth occurred for a number of years – pointing to wintery conditions preventing plant growth. For more details see publications by Professor Mike Bailey of Queens University, Belfast.

6.38   The historical texts are supported by the evidence from tree rings, but what was the cause – a meteor impact or a volcanic eruption. David Keys set about trying to discover the culprit. The evidence of ice cores would indicate whether the event was caused by a meteor, which would deposit metallic residues, tektites and nanodiamonds; or, by a volcanic eruption, which would typically cause spikes in the amount of sulphur contained in the cores. Analysis of ice cores from both Greenland and the Antarctica yielded no evidence indicating a major meteor impact but sharp spikes in sulphur content. The final part of the quest was to identify the volcano responsible. The distribution of evidence suggested a location near the equator which resulted in prevailing winds distributing the ejecta across both hemispheres. The culprit appears to have been Krakatoa, which also erupted in 1883 killing over 36,000 people and which has an older very thick deposit of lava underlying the 1883 deposits. Analysis of samples of carbonised wood found just above and below this thick lava deposit points to a huge eruption sometime in the first millennium AD. More precise dating may be achieved in the future but a plausible cause of the weather disruption had been identified, linked to a suspect volcano.

6.39   The key lesson to be learned here is that our civilisation is highly susceptible to major volcanic eruptions. From the lava deposits and the underwater caldera, it appears that the mid first millennium eruption of Krakatoa was much greater than the 1883 eruption but smaller than the Toba eruption of c74,000 years ago and both much smaller than the last Yellowstone eruption. The 1883 eruption has been estimated to have ejected c20 cubic kilometres compared with the last Yellowstone eruption at some 1000 cubic kilometres.

6.40   More recently, another potential culprit has been discovered which might have triggered the "two years without summer" in Europe. There is clear evidence of a twin meteor impact in the Gulf of Carpentaria, on the north coast of Australia, initially dated as AD572 but +/- 86 years but with more research the date range will be refined. This impact might be linked to the two years without summers (AD536 and 537) recorded in Roman annuals which had a devasting effect on life in Europe. The two craters in the Gulf of Carpentaria lie just off the coast – the 12km wide Kanmare Crater and the 18km wide Tabban Crater. These are thought to have been created at the same time by an inbound object, estimated to have been around 600m wide, breaking apart just before impact. The site was identified after assessment by Abbott of Columbia University Earth Observatory, of coastal sand chevrons orientated to the two sub-sea creators on the assumption that the chevrons had been formed by tsunami generated by the impacts. Evidence found from sub-sea core samples included quench textured magnetite spherules, nearly pure carbon spherules, teardrop-shaped tektites and vitreous material.

6.41   Furthermore, a 2004 paper in the journal Astronomy and Geophysics, suggested that the AD536 global cooling event might have been caused by dust from an impact of approximately the size Abbott has now calculated for the Carpentaria impacts.

6.42   Roman records tell of the devastation during the years 536 and 537, years without summers and with the sun almost hidden - which led to near total crop failure. Urban populations had to fall back on to hunting and fishing. Many cities are recorded to have been destroyed, attributed to social unrest as well as armed conflict, and abandoned. If such an event occurred today, the impact on food production would be devasting for human populations – the very survival of our sophisticated civilization would be threatened.

6.43   Estimates of European population show a pronounced drop between AD400 and AD600. According to researchgate.net the total European population was 36.1m in AD200, falling by 10% to 32.3m by AD400. This decline would have been influenced by the unstable Roman leadership and constant warfare with Germanic tribes during these centuries.

However, the estimate for AD600 shows a further 20% drop to only 26.0m and a modest 10% recovery to 28.6m by AD800. The 20% fall in population spans the first centuries after the collapse of the European part of the Roman empire – so a significant proportion might be attributable to the climate catastrophe caused by the meteor impact in AD535.

Conclusions

6.44   Apart from the mega volcano eruptions classified as VEI 8, there have also been dozens of volcanic eruptions classified VEI 6 or 7 over the past million years – these are estimated at ejecting between 10km3 and 1000km3. Remember, the eruption of Vesuvius, which smothered four Roman towns, including Pompeii, ejected only 3km3. So, humanity has experienced many devastating eruptions as it evolved - and many more will occur in our future.

6.45   Then we have meteor impacts and radiation from 'nearby' supernovae. The former have been uncomfortably common but thankfully the latter far less so. Both volcanic eruptions and meteor impacts can cause abrupt climate change – as abrupt as what today we term the nuclear winter that would follow an exchange of nuclear missiles.

So, what events await us?

6.46   Arguably the most predictable and certain future extinction level event will be the next eruption of the Yellowstone National Park caldera. The United States Geological Survey (USGS) estimates previous eruptions of this mega volcano occurred 639,000 years ago, 1.2 million and 2.1 million years ago. Based on the last two eruptions we are already overdue, based on averaging the last three eruptions we might have 90,000 years to go. Either way, the USGC believes we shall get plenty of warning from elevated activity producing earthquakes, ground uplift and volcanic rumblings. Ominously over the past 100 years there is clear evidence of ground uplift in parts of the Yellowstone NP area. Sonic surveys detect a huge magma chamber has built up since the last major eruption. A full scale release of this magma would trigger significant climate change, with global food production devastated for a few years and with US agriculture (and much else) effectively shut down.

6.47   As well as meteors (that we might become technically able to deflect) and mega volcanoes (that we almost certainly will never be able to stop), there is another looming and deadly threat – another supernova.

6.48 If the last significantly destructive supernova occurred 2,588,000 years ago and is now marked as the end of the Pliocene Epoch, what risks do we face in the future. Have we identified stars in our neighbourhood that are approaching the state where they will soon go supernova? Actually yes, we know of a red supergiant around 20 times the size of our Sun and usually the 7th brightest star in our sky. Known originally as Yad al Jawza, medieval monks translated it as Betelgeuse, the biggest star in the constellation of Orion. Its colouration and chemical composition point to a star nearing the end of its life and of a size that will end in a massive supernova.

6.49 Until a few years ago, it had been thought that Betelgeuse would only reach supernova in thousands or even tens of thousands of years. But it started dramatically dimming in 2020 and 2021, becoming 40% dimmer, and some analysts warned that having long ago converted all its hydrogen to helium, then burnt its helium to create oxygen and carbon – it is now fast approaching the end of the final stage of carbon being fused into iron. Once all the carbon has been used, Betelgeuse is expected to turn supernova. Suddenly during 2023, Betelgeuse has grown much brighter, at the time of writing 50% brighter than before it started dimming. This sudden and substantial variation in brightness has led some to theorise it is about to go supernova in just a few tens of years. Indeed, as Betelgeuse lies some 640 light years from Earth, some now believe that it might have already gone supernova.

6.50 Ah, you may think, being 640 light years away from us means we are safe - as only those nearer than 25 light years would be catastrophic. Unfortunately, Betelgeuse is of a size and type that will radiate a vast wave of gamma radiation that even from that distance may deplete our ozone layer enough to allow solar radiation to cause an extinction level event here on Earth. Gamma radiation travels at the speed of light – so, at some future time, as we see Betelgeuse become the brightest object in our sky, we shall be witnessing the total destruction of our ozone layer. This is tragic, as this type of supernova is thought to be extremely rare, estimated as occurring in our galaxy only about once every billion years.

7

The Hiawatha impact 10765BC & the Younger Dryas Period

» *Direct impact evidence – nano-diamonds, etc*
» *Continental firestorm destroying vegetation and extinction of megafauna*
» *Massive flooding from meteors unfreezing huge volumes of the ice cap*
» *Global rise in sea levels*
» *Sudden and dramatic climate change*
» *Oral traditions of surviving North American native tribes*
» *Traditions of refugees arriving in less affected areas*

7.1 In November 2018, NASA discovered a huge impact crater under the almost 1 km thick Hiawatha glacier in north west Greenland. The crater is 31km wide and comprises a depression 300m deep. It is estimated that it was created by a 1.5km wide iron meteorite weighing around 10 billion tonnes impacting at 18km per second. The impact would have unleashed a force equivalent to a 700 megaton nuclear bomb, by comparison the Tunguska event in 1912 which flattened 800 square miles of Siberian forest is estimated at 10 megatons and Hiroshima was a baby 0.15 megatons.

7.2 At 31 kilometres wide, the crater ranks among the 25 largest known on Earth and is the first to be found beneath an ice sheet.

7.3 Scientists first suspected a crater in 2015 when they spotted a huge depression in NASA radar images of the bedrock beneath the Hiawatha glacier in north-west Greenland. Researchers at the Alfred Wegener Institute in Germany were planning to test a powerful new airborne ice-penetrating radar system. In May 2016, the scientists flew over the Hiawatha glacier and used the radar to map the underlying rock in unparalleled detail. The images revealed all the hallmarks of an impact crater.

7.4 To establish proof, the researchers flew out to the glacier and collected sediments that had washed from the crater on to a nearby floodplain. Among the gathered grains, the scientists found particles of shocked quartz and other materials that are typically produced by the violence of an extra-terrestrial impact. Geochemical tests of the grains indicate that the meteorite was predominantly iron.

7.5 So far it has been impossible to put a firm age on the crater, but its condition suggests it formed very recently. The radar images show that while the surface layers of the glacier immediately above the crater look normal, deeper layers that are older than 12,000 years are badly deformed and strewn with rocks, with some lumps as big as trucks.

7.6 In February 2019, NASA published findings of a second even larger impact creator only 183 kilometres south east of the Hiawatha crater. The second crater was found using the same technology and also lies under 1km of ice cap. This crater is less circular than Hiawatha, which suggests a longer period of erosion and thus unrelated to the Younger Dryas period, but with a dimension of 35km rates as the 22nd largest impact crater yet discovered. Features detected under the ice reveal a complex impact crater: a flat bowl shaped depression in the bed rock surrounded by an elevated rim and centrally located peaks, which form as the floor of the crater achieves equilibrium after the impact. The crater area also registers a negative gravity anomaly typical of an impact crater. From ice cores collected nearby, the age of the overbearing ice is up to 79,000 years old formed in smooth layers indicating the ice had not been disturbed during that period, although the original ice coverage may have moved and been replaced by older ice from further inland. The researcher also considered possible erosion rates, based on the diameter of the crater it would be expected to show a depth of about 1km between the floor and the rim – a multiple of the current depth. Accordingly, the age of the crater is initially estimated at between 100,000 years and 100 million years determined by the rate of glacial erosion.

7.7 Whilst the dating of the Hiawatha impact is yet to be fully confirmed, it does provide the missing causation event which all the evidence points to as the principal cause of the onset of the Younger Dryas period.

7.8   What kinds of evidence have been identified:

- Direct impact evidence – nano-diamonds and a range of special minerals, the formation of which requires temperatures in excess of 2500C, arising only from meteor impacts together with plentiful extra-terrestrial isotopes carried from deep space

- A continental firestorm destroying vegetation and the extinction of megafauna

- Massive flooding from meteor ejecta melting huge volumes of the ice cap

- Global rise in sea levels

- Sudden and dramatic climate change

- Oral traditions of passed down by native North American tribes

- Traditions of refugees arriving in less affected areas in South America and the Middle East

Direct impact evidence – nano-diamonds, etc

7.9   The biggest single clue as to the timing and location of the event has been the boundary strata – the same rare mix of deposits as found marking the Chicxulub event. The 22 May 2007 edition of the *New Scientist* first reported extensive nano-diamonds being found in Younger Dryas boundary deposits. It noted that the thickest deposits were along the ancient margin of the North American icecap and that nano-diamonds had also been recovered from samples excavated at all former Clovis culture settlements. The *New Scientist* article concluded a meteor had either exploded whilst still airborne or had impacted the 2km thick Laurentide icecap – which had removed all traces upon melting.

7.10 The Proceedings of the National Academy of Sciences for 9 October 2007 confirmed the findings. The proceedings noted that a carbon rich layer had been found at Clovis age sites across America contemporaneous with the onset of the cooling Younger Dryas period – with extinct Pleistocene megafauna and Clovis tools found below this layer but none in or above the layer. Clovis era sites were reported as overlain by a thin layer comprising magnetic grains of iridium, magnetic microspherules, charcoal, glass like carbon containing nano-diamonds and fullerenes containing extra-terrestrial helium (H-3) – all of which being consistent with an extra-terrestrial impact combined with mass burning of biomass c.12900 years earlier. The sheer extent of carbon residue from the burning of the vegetation has led to the layer being known as the 'black mat'.

7.11   In 2008, a research team led by R. Muscheler published data in *Nature* from analysis of Greenland ice cores covering most of the past 14,000 years. They reported two distinct and synchronised peaks in the occurrence of Carbon-14 and Beryllium-10 isotopes. It was concluded that such peaks in the readings can only be attributed to previously unknown levels of solar flare activity or a meteor impact. The two peaks appear at the correct interval between the two dramatic climatic changes used to denote the start and finish of the Younger Dryas but seem slightly out of sync – being dated to c500 years earlier than the current best dates for the climate changes. The data does suggest that both climate changes might have shared the same cause – somehow the abrupt and even greater rise in global temperatures at the end of the Younger Dryas might also be attributed to an impact event – we just need to fathom out the sequence of events. It will be interesting to see if further research is able to refine the dating to more firmly link the evidence. Also, surprisingly, these cores do not seem to detect similar peaks coinciding abrupt climate change associated with the Older Dryas event. To me, the absence of these isotopes from Greenland ice core samples suggests the Older Dryas events may have involved deep sea impacts which may have reduced the extent of airborne ejecta being circulated by terrestrial winds. On the other hand, one might think that the volume of ejecta produced by the Hiawatha impact may not have been materially different if it hit 1km thick ice or a 1km thick layer of liquid water?

7.12   The hunt was on to find the smoking gun, a substantial crater showing where such an impact occurred to cause such ejecta. In January 2009, a team from Acadia University headed by Ian Spooner, published in *The Meteoritical Society* details of research carried out at a crater site at Bloody Creek, Nova Scotia. First identified in 1987, the crater is 0.4 km wide and 10m deep, but interpretation is inconclusive. The crater may be very old and have been eroded by the Laurentide Icecap over aeons or quite young and the crater minimised by having lain under a kilometre of ice when created. In July 2015, the team announced they had found evidence of further impact craters adjacent to the original. The findings concluded that impact was at a narrow angle and fragments had broken off at or shortly prior to impact creating some oval craters nearby. Clearly such a modest impact had not caused the Younger Dryas event, but might have been fragments of something much larger and, so far, undiscovered.

7.13   In 2011, M. Higgins and P. Lajeunesse of the University of Quebec published findings relating to the 4.2km Corossol crater found underwater in the Gulf of St Lawrence. Evidence included recovery of tell tale ejecta – including shocked quartz and glassy droplets. Here was evidence of a more significant impact but still not sufficient to cause the Younger Dryas onset and again there was no clear evidence of its likely date.

7.14   Collection and assessment of samples from the Younger Dryas boundary level, the black mat, continued. Proceedings of the National Academy of Science for 4 June 2013, refined the impact date by 100 years (to 10800BC); issued a more detailed map of the strewnfield (see below), showing coverage extended over 50 million square kilometres of North, Central and some of South America, the Atlantic Ocean, most of Europe, North Africa and the Middle East; and, estimated the volume of ejecta thrown up by the impact at 10 million tonnes of spherules. The spherules had been found at 18 sites on four continents and display large abundance peaks only at the Younger Dryas onset, being rarely found above or below this layer – proving the occurrence of a major impact.

7.15   In August 2013, a team from Texas A&M, led by Tony Holcombe, published research on an underwater crater found at the edge of Lake Ontario. Disappointingly, this 1.2km to 1.5km crater was judged to be far older, around 470m years old with evidence that the crater rim had been 80% to 90% eroded away by glacial movements.

7.16   In July 2015, the results of new research were announced by UC Santa Barbara geologist James Kennett that, using data from 354 samples from 30 sites across the strewnfield, his team had narrowed the date of the impact to a 100-year range, sometime between 12,835 and 12,735 years ago – giving the mid point of 10765BC that is used in this book.

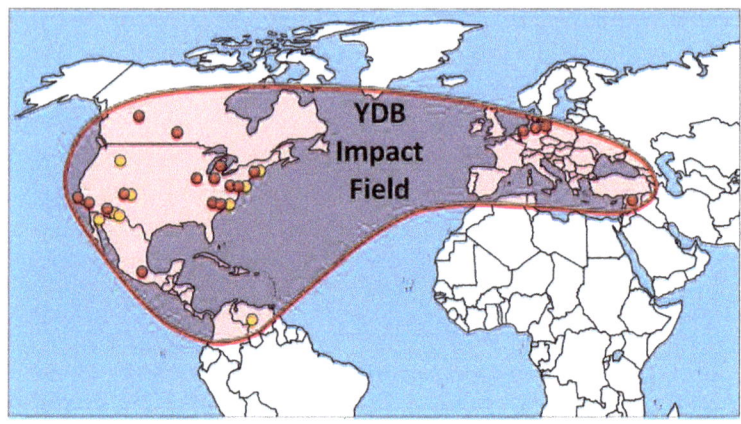

PNAS/naturalishistoria.files
Range of sites for which the spherules have been found at the beginning of the Younger Dryas boundary. The full geographic distribution of spherules has yet to be determined so the map above is the minimum area impacted by a potential meteor explosion.

7.17   By 2019, the number of sites across North America from which black mat samples have confirmed timing and composition of ejecta has exceeded 50. Unfortunately, far fewer samples have been collected across Europe whilst dating glacial moraine deposits in Scandinavia show a somewhat confusing record through the Younger Dryas period. It is estimated that the Black Mat layer covers around 30% of Earth's landmass.

7.18   One of the sample sites indicated on the map of the YDB Impact Field shown above, on its eastern most edge, is at Abu Hureyra in Syria. When the Tabqa Dam was being constructed in the 1970's, archaeologists managed to excavate an ancient Tell which was going to be flooded by the new Lake Assad created by the dam. Excavations during 1972 and 1973 revealed houses, tools and food indicating a Palaeolithic village surrounded by indications of early agriculture. The entire site appeared almost obliterated in a powerful, extreme temperature explosion. Evidence collected included fused glass, nanodiamonds, microspherules, and charcoal. Analysis revealed minerals rich in chromium, iron, nickel, sulphides, titanium and even platinum- and iridium-rich melted iron. Dr. Günther Kletetschka, a researcher from the Czech Institute of Geology, Charles University, and the University of Alaska Fairbanks explained that such intensity could only have resulted from an extremely violent, high-energy, high-velocity phenomenon, i.e. a cosmic impact. He noted that the samples that collected from this location indicated that enormous pulses of heat energy were delivered to the village. The impact has been dated to 10780BC, close enough to confirm it must have been part of the Hiawatha impact event – which very likely involved fragments breaking off the meteor as it entered Earth atmosphere. 250km north of Abu Hureyra lies Göbekli Tepe.

7.19 Thus an explanation was emerging for three puzzles – what caused the sudden megafauna extinctions in North America; what caused the topography indicating massive water flows across eastern Washington State and what caused the sudden onset of the Younger Dryas cooling.

Continental firestorm destroying vegetation and causing extinction of megafauna

7.20 The 'black mat' deposits at the onset of the Younger Dryas period show evidence of massive firestorms covering the whole of North America. The temperature at the impact site was sufficient to melt chromite (melting point 2265C) and to produce huge volumes of nano-diamonds – requiring 15 times atmospheric pressure and temperatures exceeding 2700C. Iron has a melting point of only 1530C, so the impact ejecta would have contained droplets of liquid metal which would rain down over a vast area – the distribution of the Younger Dryas boundary material covers the whole of North and Central America, Western Europe and some deposits in Turkey and Syria. As with the Chicxulub event and the findings in North Dakota of dinosaur fossils riddled with metallic shards, the rainfall of these metallic droplets would annihilate most of the animal and human population. Similarly, the same rain of superheated ejecta would have ignited vegetation wherever it fell and be fanned by the extremely high velocity winds generated by the impact itself.

7.21 The extensive fossil evidence shows 35 genera of mammals suddenly went extinct in North America around 12800 years ago, including all the megafauna. North America saw the instant extinction of its giant sloths, mammoths, lions, tapirs and giant beavers – and the equally sudden disappearance of the Clovis culture which had been widespread across the continental US.

7.22 The Clovis people, so named after the site of the original discovery, Clovis in New Mexico, appear to have migrated from north east Asia around 13000BC. The Clovis people are easily identified by their tool kit – using ivory tools and distinctive spear tips known as Clovis Points. The Clovis were skilled hunters especially of mammoths, bison, mastodon, camelops, sloths, tapir and gomphotheres (elephant like creatures) using specially fluted bifacial stone spear tips. Clovis sites have been excavated all over North America and as far south as Venezuela, however the culture disappears from the record from the onset of the Younger Dryas – most were probably killed by a combination of (i) the superheated metallic projectiles from the impact; (ii) the continental wide firestorm; and, (iii) the resulting loss of both animals and vegetation leading to starvation of most survivors of the initial destruction.

7.23　Some Clovis did manage to survive, as genetic analysis has identified c80% of native American tribes appear to be descendants of Clovis people. It is noteworthy that the successor peoples did not have ivory tools (indicating their source had disappeared) nor the need for such exquisite spear points – as all the megafauna were extinct.

Massive flooding from meteors unfreezing huge volumes of the ice cap

7.24　The earliest evidence that something spectacular had occurred sometime in the past came from the visual geology of Washington State – the eastern half of which mostly comprises the Scablands. The term is descriptive as the terrain looks as though something has ripped away sections of the natural grassy landscape to reveal slashes of bedrock whilst the whole area is littered with 'erratics' – a term used by geologists to describe rocks brought by glaciers or rivers from far away and dumped when gradients flatten and forward momentum is lost. J Harlen Bretz, a professor at the University of Chicago had in the 1920's argued that a huge hydrological event had taken place which could only have been caused by a sudden massive melting of the ice caps which it had been concluded had suddenly retreated sometime between 13000 and 9000 years earlier.

7.25　In a paper published in the *Journal of Geology* in 1923 entitled '*The Channelled Scablands of the Columbia Plateau*', Bretz gave calculations of how he believed the erosion and flood marks visible in the Grand Coulee had arisen. The massive volume of water indicated by the striations high in the gorge, suggested a single massive melting of a significant portion of the ice cap rather than regular seasonal releases of accumulated meltwater from ice damned lakes. Such an event appeared to have carved out an estimated 42 cubic kilometres of basalt from the Grand Coulee creating a gorge 48 kilometres long in little more than a month - as against the estimated 12,000 years Niagara has taken to cut its 11 kilometre gorge.

7.26 A survey of the Grand Coulee area by Graham Hancock and Rendall Carlson describes the scale of the flooding that occurred. For full details, please refer to Hancock's truly excellent book *Magicians of the Gods* (don't judge a book only by its cover!) published in 2015. The Dry Falls, descriptive of what was obviously a massive waterfall in the past but now virtually dry, separates the Upper and Lower Grand Coulee. The Dry Falls are three times the height of Niagara and six times wider. Erosion on the sides of the Coulee show that the floodwaters were running at least 150 metres deep, indeed massive erratics, carried inside floating 'icebergs', have grounded on ridges of the Waterville Plateau – 240 metres above the valley floor. Many erratics are estimated to weigh more than 10,000 tonnes and one sitting high on a ridge above the valley is estimated at around 16,000 tonnes meaning the entire valley must have been overflowing with meltwater – a stupendous sight indeed. Many more erratics can be seen scattered across the Ephrata Erratics Fan of the Scablands below the Coulee.

7.27 In his book, *Environment of Violence*, Hunt estimates that the total volume of the ice sheet required to generate the meltwater to gauge out the Coulee and the Channelled Scablands at 840,000 cubic kilometres, which is estimated to be around 10% of the continental scale Laurentide Icecap, which covered the entirety of Canada at that time.

Global rise in sea levels

7.28 The tribal folk memories of a flood seem to reflect a period of rapid rises in sea level which occurred at the onset of the Younger Dryas period. The last ice age maxima had sea levels at minimum levels some 20000 to 22000 years ago. After that, the ice fields gradually retreated but the pattern was disturbed by a traumatic event which is now dated as c10765BC – marking the onset of the Younger Dryas period and another event occurring in c9620BC seen as the end of the Younger Dryas period. Evidence indicates the meteor impact event triggered a 1m rise in sea level during a single day. It has been estimated that global sea levels continued to rise by circa 5 metres per annum for a few years following the impact – which compares with the current annual rate of 3mm per annum. It seems little wonder that we have tribal traditions from over 500 ethnic groups, scattered all around the world, telling of relentless flooding.

7.29 Even after the immediate post impact decade, sea levels continued to rise at their fastest rate since the last ice age maxima. Indeed, it was only around 6,000 years ago that sea levels almost stabilised – until the effects of industrialisation again started to accelerate the annual sea level rise. In the past century we have raised average sea temperatures, which expands the volume of sea water as well as raising its level and its ability, in conjunction with warmer average air temperatures, to trigger a sustained weakening of the ice caps and shrinking of glaciers worldwide.

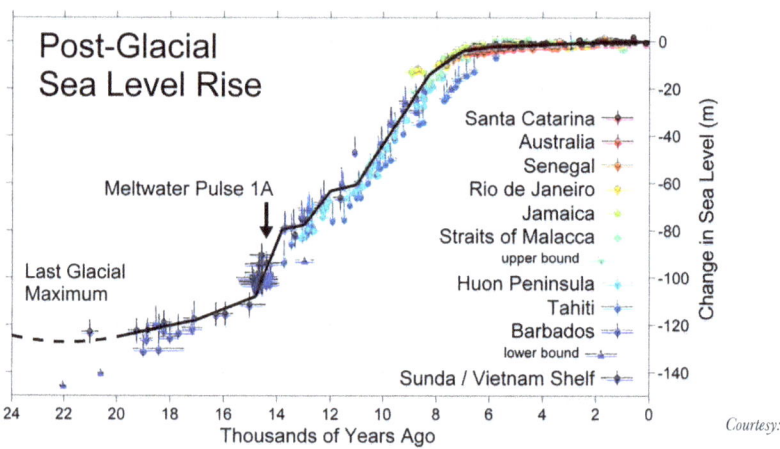

Courtesy: commons.wikimedia.org

Sudden and dramatic climate change

7.30 The Younger Dryas period is so named after a pale yellow arctic wildflower whose pollen distribution was used as an early proxy for changing climatic conditions. As the name implies, there were earlier 'Dryas' periods – the Older and the Oldest Dryas, both were marked by so far unexplained abrupt changes in average global temperatures. Because the culprit for the onset of the Younger Dryas has now been identified, the very abruptness suggests that impact events were probably also involved in the first two Dryas events. The start of the Oldest Dryas period appears to have been a more gradual change in temperature starting no earlier than 17050BC, but the end of the Oldest Dryas is sharply defined: data derived from isotope variations of nitrogen and argon revealed by Greenland ice cores gives a high-resolution date for a sharp temperature rise at the end of the Oldest Dryas of 12650BC. Then in quick succession we see the Older Dryas, which marked two distinct falls and two less extensive recoveries in temperature over a period estimated between 300 and 500 years – with Greenland data giving dates of c12230BC to c11930BC whilst Canadian data suggests c12000BC to c11500BC.

7.31   Whilst recent discoveries and research has focused very much on the Younger Dryas period, two very significant events must have also occurred just a few centuries earlier. As far as I have read, there is only a single 'black mat' layer. What may have been different is possibly similar sized meteors striking the Earth but impacting deep ocean locations. Such impacts would similarly devastate the ice caps through the enormous energy release of the impact being absorbed by the sea, thereby raising its temperature, and by gigantic tsunami of warmed water being launched at surrounding coasts. If the impact was in deep enough ocean, there might be far less ejecta apart from voluminous steam – therefore no continental scale firestorms and no black mat layers created. Sir Fred Hoyle is amongst those concluding that a deep ocean impact was the cause of the sudden end of the Younger Dryas cold snap. As the loss of the Malaysian flight MH370 in 2014 revealed, hardly any of the Southern Ocean floor has yet been mapped. As one would conclude from chapters 4 and 5, huge subsea craters must be awaiting discovery.

7.32   The Younger Dryas started with the sudden melting of a vast volume of the North American ice cap (the Laurentide Ice Sheet) which, running into both Atlantic and Pacific, dramatically cooled sea temperatures and reduced salinity – and recent modelling shows would have greatly weakened thermohaline ocean circulation leading to a sharp reduction in temperatures in northern climes. According to '*The Younger Dryas cold interval*' by Richard B. Alley, average annual temperatures in Greenland fell by 6C in just a few years at the start of the Younger Dryas period.

7.33   The volume of dust and other ejecta from the impact would have blotted out sunshine and taken many years for rain to wash out of the skies. The atmosphere would have been dense with ejecta and dust from the raging forest fires – well above the level rainclouds form. Hence it may have taken a decade for the higher altitude airborne particles to drift low enough to be washed out.

7.34 The dramatic nature of the Younger Dryas events may be measured by the fact that the climatic warming over c10,000 years from the previous ice age maxima was completely reversed in very short order, plunging global temperatures back to the previous ice age maxima in less than a decade. Then, with equal suddenness, global temperatures rose back again at the end of the Younger Dryas period, ending some 5C higher than at its start. Richard B. Alley estimates average annual temperatures in Greenland fell by 6C in just a few years at the start of the period and 1200 years later average temperatures rose by 10C in only 40 years. The dramatic scale of these changes may be judged against contemporary concerns over climate warming – according to the IPCC average global temperatures have risen by 1.3C during the past 100 years – a level we now regard as a portent of environmental disaster during the coming century.

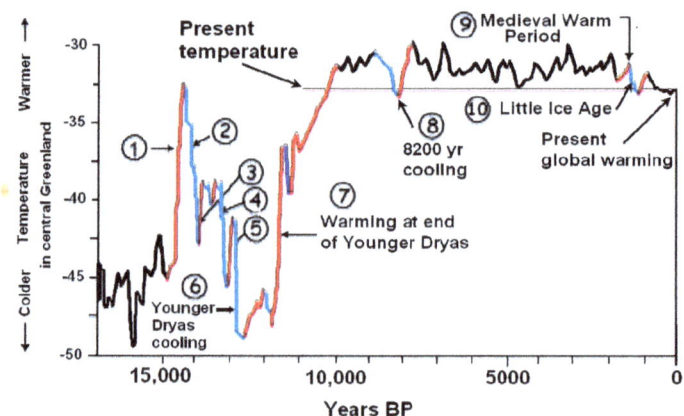

Courtesy WUWT climate change website. NB the chart shows dates as Years before Present.
Temperature fluctuations over the past 17,000 years showing the abrupt temperature changes associated with the three Dryas periods. The Oldest Dryas cooling occurred during the period before the chart and ended sharply with a huge temperature rise about 12650BC (1). The Older Dryas data is less distinct but involves sharp temperatures changes including a 10C drop and a 6C drop with smaller rises of 4C after each fall (2-4). The Younger Dryas starts with temperatures suddenly plunging by 6C (5), remaining cool for 1300 years (6), and ending about 9620BC when the climate suddenly warmed by 10C again (7).

Oral traditions of surviving North American native tribes

7.35 Graham Hancock's research also identified widespread ancient Native American tribal lore, for example the Ojibwa people, whose tribal history remembered a comet with a long wide tail with radiation and burning in its wake. Legend describes its tail burnt the earth and afterwards intense cold made survival difficult. The Ojibwa tell of a comet bringing fire, widespread destruction of megafauna and then persistent heavy rainfall. The Lakota people tell of the gods throwing down fiery thunderbolts with fiery blasts that shook the world and set the forests and the prairies ablaze. The rocks glowed red hot and giant animals and evil people burned where they stood. This was followed by heavy rain and swollen rivers, leaving the bleached bones of the giant animals buried in rock and mud – pretty much as they are found today. We need to recognise the diligence of researchers like Hancock, whose perseverance prepared us for the explanation – with initial indications of the Hiawatha impact being found the same year as his work was published – 2015.

7.36 It is amazing that such ancient tribal memories handed down by oral tradition over 12,000 years remain so informative – these features of dramatic destruction are exactly as the evidence indicates. The number of North American native tribes with oral traditions, many recorded by James W. Lynd whose manuscript was found after his death at the hands of Union soldiers in 1863 and later published in his name under the title *History of the Dakotas*, is astonishing and includes tribes from all over the North American continent:- the Algonquin, the Chickasaws (who talked of two of every animal being saved), the Cowichan of BC, the Inuit of Alaska, the Hurons, the Lakota, the Luiseno of California, the Malisee, the Micmac, the Ojibwa, the Passmaquoddy, the Pima of Arizona and the Quillayute. Many of the traditions also tell of megafauna (lions, giant beavers, giant sloths, mammoths and tapir) which all then disappeared. As noted earlier, 80% of current North American natives have DNA carrying distinctive Clovis markers showing their ancestry as survivors of the skilled hunters that must have been decimated on the day of the impact.

Traditions of refugees arriving in less affected areas

7.37 One intriguing theme of a number of ancient traditions, which is also backed up by various suggestive monumental engravings, is that cultures devastated by the climatic effects of the Younger Dryas impact were assisted by intelligent visitors who provided teaching and guidance.

7.38 In particular, similar engravings record images of hero's carrying 'handbags' with curved handles. One of the Göbekli Tepe megaliths shows a row of three handbags with curved handles. This is remarkably similar to images of Oannes, a civilising hero in Mesopotamia referred to as dating from the time of the flood, which also depict the carrying of a handbag with curved handles. Oannes was revered by all ancient cultures across Mesopotamia for bringing knowledge of writing, mathematics, law, building, planting and harvesting – in short teaching men all the skills supporting civilisation. What was carried in these 'handbags' – ancient laptops?

7.39 Oannes was always depicted with both the scales of a fish and with feathers – maybe representing capabilities of travelling over the sea and through the air? According to Berossos (3rd century BC), Oannes was known as the leader of a group of 7 Sages known as the Seven Apkallu – portrayed as bringers of civilisation from before the Flood. Note that Göbekli Tepe is only 75km from Harran, the ancient northern capital of Sumer – the city to which Abraham's father relocated his family from Ur c2000BC.

7.40 The same handbag design also appears to be carried by the "feathered serpent" engraving of "man in serpent" at La Venta, Mexico, an Olmec site which is conventionally dated around 1000BC, a deity later known as Quetzalcoatl. Whilst Quetzalcoatl is represented with serpent features, he is usually described as a large tall bearded white man who came to teach the ancient inhabitants of Mexico settled agriculture and the construction of temples. According to the 16th century Spanish chronicler of Aztec traditions, Bernadino de Sahagun, Quetzalcoatl also travelled with his own band of wise men, arriving across the sea 'in a boat without paddles' as a great civilising agent who imparted skills, fostered architecture and managed the construction of spacious buildings.

7.41 The Andean legends of Viracocha are remarkably similar. One of the Inca names for Viracocha was *Wiraqocha Pacayacaciq* (the Instructor). After heavy black rain (presumably thick with washed out soot from the huge fires), Viracocha emerged from Lake Titicaca and told of the creation of two races, one of giants who were destroyed by their creator and the other humans whom he came to civilise. Viracocha was described as a bearded man of medium height, white and dressed in a white robe secured round the waist, and that he carried a staff and a book in his hands. Viracocha is remembered as having taught the skills of civilisation – including language, agriculture:- teaching what and when to plant, which plants were edible, which had medicinal properties, and which were poisonous, construction skills and various arts. Viracocha departed across the sea vowing to return – hence the docile welcome afforded by the Inca to the bearded white Spanish conquistadores.

7.42   One must ponder the similarities between occurrences in the Middle East, Mexico and the Andes – and the dating ascribed to the La Venta inscription must be questioned. Other evidence suggests much earlier advanced activities in Columbia and Peru – see chapter 13.

7.43   For such memories of the gifts of teaching great and varied skills to endure over nearly 10 millennia, two points stand out:

- the teaching must have transformative (in terms of the livelihoods of those who received the teaching), and,

- those receiving it must have previously lacked these skills.

One might speculate that these teachers (sages/wise men) were remnants of a comparatively advanced culture that had fled from a catastrophe. A catastrophe which occurred around 10000BC.

7.44   We have two sources which tell of a handful of survivors from a leading power which arrived in a devasted Egypt to direct recovery and teach many skills. One source is the veritable treasury of information contained in inscriptions at the Edfu temple complex, described in sections 9.17 to 9.25 below, and the other source being quotations from the original source of the Atlantis story which, as explained later, not only comes from an impeccable source but has appeared to have suffered from some misleading translations. Further information has come to light since I first wrote this book and this new edition now has a chapter devoted to Atlantis – chapter 9.

7.45   Whilst poor research can easily reinforce claims of quackery and labels like 'myth' or 'legend' are generally applied to tales recorded as having been handed down orally for generations – sometimes surprising evidence of veracity emerges. The Economist of 27 February 2020 carried an article reporting two ancient tribal legends had been largely verified by geological evidence. One had been handed down by a Native American tribe living in Oregon, the Klamath, which tells of god who lived in a mountain who fell in love with a village girl. When the girl rebuffed his advances, Llao (an underworld god) emerged and cascaded fire and brimstone down the mountain onto her village. A sky god, Skell, protected humans and forced Llao back into his mountain – which then collapsed on top of him. The huge whole thereby created was filled with water and became a lake. Today the lake is known as Crater Lake in the midst of a dormant volcano known as Mount Mazama. Geological evidence shows the last eruption took place around 5680BC – providing evidence that 'myths' handed down in oral tradition over thousands of years are sometimes derived from real events.

7.46 The Economist article also reported even more astonishing evidence of the potential reliability of oral traditions. In the Australian state of Victoria, another group of indigenous people, the Gunditjmara, also maintain an oral tradition about a lake in an extinct volcano. However, evidence published by Erin Matchan of Melbourne University in *Geology* indicates this tradition is dramatically older. This tradition concerns an individual whose name is preserved today as the name of the mountain, Budj Bim. The tradition tells of the land and trees dancing as beings came to life deep below the ground, with Budj Bim himself spitting liquid fire from his mouth. Whilst this volcano was known to be relatively young in geological terms, Dr Matchan resolved to date the last eruption. The results are astounding. Argon dating, measuring the gradual decay of a radioactive isotope of potassium, dates the last eruption to 35,000BC – the date of the defining event which has been immortalized in the 'myth'.

7.47 The strong evidence of a factual historical basis for the key elements of such oral traditions surely makes it dangerously presumptive to write off the detailed sober record left to us by an intellectual like Solon.

THE HIAWATHA IMPACT 10765BC & THE YOUNGER DRYAS PERIOD

8

The human dimension of the Hiawatha impact

8.1 No fossilised human remains directly linkable to the impact catastrophe have yet been found. It may be that we will eventually find entombed fossilised remains similar to those at Pompeii. However, whilst the entire North American continent appears to have been covered by the 'black mat' layer, unlike the thick layer of ash at Pompeii, it only averages around 1cm thick.

8.2 Humans that managed to dodge the super heated metallic hailstorm from the initial impact were then faced by raging firestorms that appear to have reduced the entire continent to a cinder. After this, the evidence suggests those close to the former ice cap would have faced sudden cataclysmic flooding, with rivers so swollen as to overflow valleys. From the volume of ice vaporised, it is logical that incessant rainfall continued for many days – which fits both native American legends and Noah type stories of many days of continuous rain. If sufficient water vapour had been ejected high enough by the blast and resultant wind force, it would also account for the numerous references to giant hailstones – which the traditions tell of killing many initial survivors.

8.3 After the pyrotechnics ceased and the heavy rain abated, the next problem would have been food. Much of the meat would have been roasted to a cinder and in large areas it seems there would be no remaining game and no vegetation either – one would need to know where to dig for tubers!

8.4   Even outside of areas subjected to falling ejecta and resulting fires, the experience would have been traumatic. As everyone viewed the night sky daily (no light pollution and no electronic media distractions), everyone would have been aware of the approaching fiery comet – and many traditions tell of a fiery dragon or serpent coming to wreck vengeance upon the Earth, presumed to be punishment for some misdeeds. There are a number of tales describing the tail of a dragon swinging low upon the Earth and smiting it with fire – suggestive of a comet breaking up and at least some fragments impacting Earth. With no cosmological understanding, it is easy to understand ancient peoples deciding to animate the cause of the chaos and see the devastation as punishment for some errors they had committed.

8.5   Even for lands not subjected to falling ejecta, the dramatic scenes of the passing comet would be followed by darkness as the vast dust clouds raised by the impact were carried around the globe, likely remaining for a number of months, if not years, before gravity and rain could once again clear the skies. The sudden overnight rise in sea levels would mean previous high tide levels were suddenly below the new low tide point and water levels continuing to rise persistently year after year for a few decades. It seems likely that the impact vaporised a huge amount of ice resulting in prolonged rainfall, probably globally. The effect of the nuclear winter, making the sun almost invisible, maybe for a few years, would severely damage the growth of vegetation. This would severely limit the availability of fruit and nuts – so far, we have no evidence of agriculture being practised until around 9000BC at the very earliest.

8.6   Looking at the climatic record of the three Dryas periods, we see no less than seven very dramatic rapid changes in average global temperatures occurring over a period of only 5000 years. The Hiawatha impact has given us a good explanation backed by widespread evidence of what caused the start of the Younger Dryas event, and as explained later in this book, only very recently has speculative evidence started to emerge explaining its equally abrupt ending 1200 years later. But we have no explanations or evidence for the sudden onsets and endings of the Oldest and the Older Dryas periods. Given the sheer scale of the global temperature changes which occurred with each period, which dwarf the scale of changes that we fret over today, we must also consider that the most likely cause of these sudden changes was also meteor impacts. However, we have not identified other widespread ejecta deposits similar to the 'black mat' nor a climatic mechanism that would cause such rapid ***increases*** in global temperatures. Maybe impacts occurred mid Pacific or in Antartica - generating sudden climatic change but with telltale ejecta on the seabed or under the ice.

8.7 Whilst we currently lack evidence of which land masses suffered the full range of consequences from each extinction level episode of the Dryas periods or even certainty that each climate shift was caused by an impact – we do have evidence that the Hiawatha impact ejecta zone extended as far as the Middle East. Excavations at Abu Hureyra, completed before the damming of the Euphrates in north east Syria created Lake Assad, revealed the tell tale ejecta from the Hiawatha impact.

8.8 Having lived through such experiences of aerial pyrotechnics, changing sea levels and sudden changes in normal temperature levels, it is little wonder that memories of such terrifying events were carefully handed down over the generations. Anthropologists have recorded tribal memories of extensive flooding and other calamities from around 500 different cultures around the globe. If these memories have been passed down over 10,000 years then one might expect that 10,000 years ago people would also be very aware of much younger tribal lore which remembered an almost equivalent fall in temperatures only c500 years earlier followed by a subsequent sudden rise in temperatures. Therefore, we might look for evidence that these societies tried to seek shelter from the deadly bombasts raining down from the skies. Cave dwelling and underground food storage would be two obvious precautions humans may have adopted.

8.9 We do have some textual references but no clear physical evidence of such precautions. The author Graham Hancock finds in some Zoroastrian writings what may be echoes of the trauma of the Younger Dryas period. There is no consensus concerning the age of Zoroastrianism or the period in which its founder lived. The Zoroastrian texts comprise the only surviving works in the ancient Avestan language, dated to the 2nd millennium BC (a language related to Vedic Sanskrit) and probably represent the earliest recording of more ancient oral traditions. In Roman times, Greek historians considered Zoroastrianism very old – Plutarch (AD46 to 120) writing that Zoroaster lived 5000 years before the Trojan War which would be c6300BC whilst Diogenes Laertius (AD180 to 240) uses the formula 6000 years before Xerses' Greek campaign, placing Zoroaster around 6480BC. However, more recent historians have suggested much later dates, probably because in the mind set of conventional historians such advanced philosophy should not yet have emerged. One of the most venerated texts is the Vendidad, meaning 'Given against the Demons'. The Vendidad incorporates the Zoroastrian creation story and a dialogue between the Creator (Ahura Mazda) and Zoroaster explaining the forces of evil and how to deal with them. These discussions include warnings of a terrible winter and what preparations should be made in order to survive. The followers are instructed to build an underground retreat, the Vara, with three levels (same as Noah's Ark) and secure seeds of all types of animals and plants together with two of every living thing. There is a Zoroastrian ceremony, also called the Vendidad, in which these discussions are recited – which is only performed at night – maybe in memory of the long period of darkness immediately following the impact. The storage of seeds clearly implies some form of agricultural practise, *prior* to the Younger Dryas event, rather than simple hunter gatherer existence.

8.10 Another enigmatic detail of these accounts, identified by Graham Hancock, is the references to what seems to be the use of artificial light sources. Hancock draws attention to description of underground windows emitting light deep below ground in levels of the Zoroastrian Vara and to references to windows set into each deck within Noah's Ark which shall provide light during the 'year of the Flood' collated from ancient Hebrew traditions by Louis Ginzberg. Egyptologists have often wondered how chambers deep within tombs were decorated with such exquisite reliefs despite a complete absence of natural light and also without any traces being found of soot from lamps or candles. Similarly, the lowest and oldest levels of some Cappadocian cave networks have neither natural light reaching them nor evidence of burning lamps. One might conclude that this points to a pre Hiawatha culture having mastered some form of artificial lighting. The capabilities and purpose of the 'Baghdad Battery', believed to date from the Parthian period (247BC to AD224) is disputed but it seems to be a primitive type of electrical battery. It may be another example of ancient skills being gradually lost over time – implying a significantly more capable culture existing long before.

8.11 We are also familiar with the Sumerian record of Ziusudra and the Biblical record of Noah, which seems to have been derived from it. According to Sumerian king lists, Ziusudra was king when the Flood occurred, meaning he would have been a demi-god and therefore a likely candidate for salvation by the 'gods'. In the Epic of Gilgamesh, Ziusudra is referred to by his Akkadian name, Utnapishtim, which from various records we know was a popular tale at least a millennium prior to Abraham's time. As a side point, it is very surprising that conventionally minded Christians still try to insist that either the stories have a common source or that Ziusudra is derived from the story in Genesis. Given the Biblical understanding that the Israelites were all descended from Abraham, crown prince and heir apparent to the city state of Ur circa 2000BC, capital city of Sumeria – Abraham himself was probably someone who could recite the story of Ziusudra from memory. Where else could the (even then) near 8,000 years old memory have come from? For the Israelites, Abraham is the obvious source. Later, during the Exile in Babylon, when the Levite priests compiled Genesis c550BC, they could compare their orally transmitted version with the original Sumerian text maintained in Nebuchadnezzar's library – which may explain why there are two slightly differing stories of the Flood contained in Genesis.

8.12 A common feature of Vendidad, Ziusudra and Noah is the foreknowledge of the 'gods' and their warnings given to the chosen ones together with instructions to take precautions. This implies that the 'gods' had the skills to view, track and calculate the likely impact of celestial bodies – and to envisage the likely consequences on Earth. Alternatively, perhaps the tribal shaman, custodians of the tribal traditions remembering earlier events, linked the appearance of a fiery comet with the outcomes previously experienced. This evidence also shows that there is little to distinguish between the various gods who warned selected humans. Neither El Elyon (who according to Genesis was the god dealing with Noah) nor his brother Enki (according to Sumerian 'history') would have admitted to their respective followers that a meteor impact was beyond their powers to prevent, so the alternative would have been to 'own' the problem – as in, "this punishment is because of your sinfulness".

Evidence that these cultures built megalithic structures

8.13 The existence of various legends telling us that warning was given, by the 'gods', prior to the devastating impact suggests a degree of sophistication. More attention is now being given to evidence, from many sites around the globe, indicating the existence of cultures, before the Flood, that were far more advanced than conventional history admits. We have remaining evidence of megalithic constructions which would challenge us to repli-

8.14 So far nothing has been found from these pre-Younger Dryas period cultures except their incredible stone masonry – from beautiful decorative work and dressed stone (sometimes finished to a level of smoothness far beyond what is detectible to the naked eye) to an array of megalithic constructions. With the single exception of the Schist Disc (more below) – we have recovered no artefacts, no tools buried near their constructions, no marks revealing their languages or calculations – nothing at all. We have amazing stone masonry – gigantic blocks, in many cases transported surprising distances, hewn to amazing shapes and fitted in many cases with incredibly fine precision - leaving us to puzzle how such constructions could have been built.

8.15 The only evidence presented by these enigmatic constructions are the blocks themselves. Big questions arise when we consider basic issues:

- how were the blocks found? In many cases, specific types of rock appear deliberately chosen irrespective of their proximity to the construction site;

- how were the blocks transported? Distances over land seemed to provide little obstacle; in some Andean sites the transfer of huge blocks to much high elevations was somehow achieved;

- how were massive blocks cut to such incredible precision? These imply knowledge of geometry and mathematical calculations – we have no record of their numbering system nor how such calculations were communicated into cutting instructions – nor what tools were used to cut smooth surfaces with such precision. Where we would use computer controlled machine tools, the ancients seem to have cut complex shapes with incredible precision - yet sites and quarries yield very few examples of discarded mistakes;

- how were giant blocks lifted and fitted into position? We have many examples of stonemasonry requiring delicate handing of enormous weights;

- why were such constructions built anyway? In many cases, it is not really clear why surviving constructions were even built – when in doubt, we tend to assume sites were for religious purposes but with no real evidence to support such assumptions.

8.16 Let us consider some of the enigmatic sites that have been dated back long prior to the Younger Dryas event. All the sites we shall look at are in, or close to, tropical latitudes – this may point to existence back into the last ice age, before 20000BC, at a time when coastlines extended far beyond the current sea level. Remember that before the Dryas events, global sea levels were 120m lower than today – so many pre-flood sites will now be in deep water and hidden by accumulated silt.

9

Atlantis, an ancient story now gaining evidence of a factual origin

9.1 The 'fable' of Atlantis seems linked to the global 'flood' event. We learned of Atlantis from a leading Athenian, Solon (c630BC to c560BC), who was a highly accomplished individual. Solon had taken over a demoralised Athenian army, raised its morale and led it to victories. Solon then became Chief Justice of the city state and introduced many reforms which led to Athens transformation from a tyranny to a democracy. After successfully introducing his reforms, he decided to travel abroad for ten years, apparently in order to prevent Athenians from persuading him to revise the new laws. It was on these travels around the eastern Mediterranean that Solon visited Egypt where he spent time with the Pharaoh Amasis II, learned the history of Atlantis from the priests of Neith's temple at Sais and philosophy from Psenophis of Heliopolis and Sonchis of Sais. Solon also visited Croesus, king of Lydia located in eastern Turkey, and Cyprus. Solon's reforms covered a wide range of issues – constitutional, legal codes, business regulations, weights & measures, parental responsibilities (fathers had to find trades for their sons and sons to care for parents in old age), people could not be pledged as security for loans (abolishing debt slavery), immigration and residency rights for traders and even moral laws. Solon was also famous as a poet. Whilst we have no surviving texts from Solon, as expected of such a polymath, he was widely quoted – by Plato (in two of his dialogues, Timaeus and Critias), Plutarch, Herodotus and many others. Such is the credibility of the source of the Atlantis story that I feel conventional historians have been reckless in dismissing it as merely a myth.

PREQUEL – YOUNGER DRYAS METEOR IMPACTS, THE FLOOD & ATLANTIS

9.2 According to Plato, who quoted extensively from Solon's own writings, which unfortunately are all now lost, we can calculate that Solon visited the Temple of Sais in 600BC. Solon reported that the priests of the Temple of Sais described to him a great civilisation that had been swallowed up by fire and flooding exactly 9000 years previously, indicating a date of 9600BC. This date is amazingly proximate to 9620BC, our best date for the event marking the end of the Younger Dryas period.

9.3 The conventional idea of Atlantis is of a magnificent island nation whose capital city was destroyed in a ferocious storm and was lost in the deep ocean. Solon was told Atlantis was a magnificent capital of a sea trading empire connecting to many islands and other lands. Solon is quoted as saying that Atlantis ruled a wide empire both outside the Pillars of Hercules and inside the Mediterranean along the coast of Libya and as far as Italy. The key clue to the location of Atlantis that became popularised is of being on an island out in the Atlantic beyond the Pillars of Hercules. In fact, Solon's account as transcribed by Plato relates of returning Atlanteans finding their city submerged with only reeds poking through the water level and of extensive mud banks preventing entry to their massive docklands, which had been swept away. The key description of the city is of concentric circles of water with lands between the circular waterways and access to the sea on the southern side. The Greek descriptive term applied to the location of the city is a 'neson', meaning either a peninsula or an area of land within an inland lake. Atlantis is described as having beautiful luxuriant gardens and surrounded on both sides by large fertile plains with distant high mountains on the north side. This description does not point to a location in the mid-Atlantic.

9.4 Atlantis is described as being "in front of the Pillars of Hercules", those that sailed through the Pillars of Hercules, as Phoenicians had done for 2000 years before Plato, hugged the coastline, mainly going north. However, the prevailing current goes southwards – so "in front of" may allude to going before the current, along the west coast of Africa. Therefore, the original description of the location of Atlantis, by the very accomplished statesman whose record Plato preserved for us, was not of an island out in the deep ocean but of three concentric circles of land and water forming an inland area joined by a seaway to the ocean.

9.5 Conventional historians have consistently dismissed Atlantis as a myth, we are told that no such sea faring nation could have existed that long ago. However, a marine research team has found numerous massive stone sea anchors lying on the sea bed off the coast of Doñana, a coastal wetland area just north of Cadiz, on the Atlantic coast of southern Spain. Their size and location are intriguing historians as they indicate the use of large seafaring vessels millennia earlier than conventional history allows. The discovery of numerous stone anchors lying in close proximity, some way offshore, in what is now deep water, raises questions. Why would ships frequently anchor in such an offshore location? It is suggestive that the location used to be a harbour or dockside – in which case, sea levels must have been much lower – either the sea floor has sunk significantly or the seafaring activity originally took place prior to the rise in sea levels caused by the Hiawatha impact. That a stone age seafaring culture existed this early also seems linked to the existence of large numbers of enigmatic but certainly very ancient stone constructions found all over the islands of the Azores – due west of the Cadiz.

9.6 Some have tried to link the events described by Solon with the eruption of Thera around 1550BC which devastated the Minoan civilisation but there are no parallels with Solon's description of Atlantis. Moreover, as with the Edfu texts, it is possible that the priests of Sais held very ancient texts which had been carefully treasured. The history recounted to Solon may have blurred some details and similarly the quotations by Plato and others may have introduced further errors and omissions. But, it seems highly likely that there was more than a grain of truth in these records – and the story fits with what we now understand about the events leading up to the precise time referred to.

9.7 Indeed, the dating given to Solon is highly significant, as we now know that 9600BC marked the end of the Younger Dryas, having witnessed some 1200 years of the fastest rise in sea levels in the last 20,000 years. The Younger Dryas period ended with an astonishing rise of 10C in a very short period. Tales of Atlantis tell of a dramatic end, after which the city collapsed under the sea. We do not yet understand what caused the end of the Younger Dryas period and there is no evidence of a widespread firestorm such as occurred at the start of the period in 10765BC but the cumulative loss of ice cap over the northern hemisphere may well have released enough pressure on the continental plates to trigger local earthquakes and volcanic activity. In addition, persistently rising sea levels may have reached a point where sea defences of an exposed city, built up higher and higher, over a long period were dramatically overwhelmed.

The saga tells of a ship full of returning Atlanteans arriving to find their city collapsed and lost beneath the waves. Re-evaluation of the ancient references to Atlantis is now overdue, particularly as the Edfu Building Texts provide a rich source of corroborative material. These texts not only describe a pre flood culture but how the survivors, benefitting from wise and benevolent visitors, successfully established new settlements in Egypt. These texts go on to describe that they quickly started building megalithic structures – to which we shall revert later, in chapter 11.

9.8   Recently, other evidence has been uncovered which points to the possible location of Atlantis – leading Google to label a site in Mauritania as being the site of Atlantis. An amazing circular structure has been found, known as the Richat Structure, and also as the Eye of Africa. Recent geological examination of this area of western Mauritania has revealed severe water erosion which points to a tsunami coursing over the area. Smack in the midst of the area affected lies the Richat Structure – a huge curiosity, visible from space, which appears to be the remains of a series of concentric circles separated by water which left deep salt deposits. See also the map on pages 112 & 113.

9.9   There is conjecture that the massive tsunami like pattern of water erosion, scouring a wide channel down to the bedrock directly over the Richat Structure may have swept the city away. One is reminded of the Channelled Scablands of Washington State (see 7.24 to 7.27) but could something similar have occurred moving south west across the Sahara? Before we learned of the Kefalonia impacts, I speculated that a meteor might have come in at a low angle, over Athens, bearing about 240° and hit the Mediterranean just south east of Sicily. The resulting tsunami would have been huge, the main force directed south westerly, making landfall in Tunisia. Such a tsunami would have travelled swiftly over the Chott el Djerid, the ancient sea channel of the Trans Sahara Seaway, which today comprises vast salt pans, and funnel through the gap between the Atlas and Ahaggar mountain ranges. These mountain ranges would act to channel the force and potentially carry a destructive force the 2500 kms across the Sahara to Richat. After about 1000km any tsunami would have encountered the main valley of the Tamanrasset river basin, carrying the water downhill, directly south west and close to and almost certainly over the Richat Structure. The Tamanrasset is a paleo-river, originating in the southern slopes of the Atlas Mountains and is believed to have dried up around 5000BC as climatic changes made the Sahara into an arid desert. The course of this river was rediscovered by a Japanese satellite using PULSAR, able to trace the river bed beneath the sand – see article by B Ferreira entitled *'There's a long-lost paleo-river beneath the Sahara Desert nobody knew existed'* published 10 November 2015. Given the huge underwater canyon, the Cap Timiris Canyon 3 km deep and 2.5 km wide, where the Tamanrasset flowed out into the Atlantic, it must have been a very substantial river in its heyday – quite possibly navigable by ship to the Richat Structure. The map on pages 112 &113 shows the possible path of part of a tsunami.

9.10 For comparison, we can look at the modelling data developed for the Ed Nadir impact off the coast of Guinea. This is believed to have occurred quite close in time to the Chicxulub impact, 65 million years ago, maybe it was part of the same meteor shower, or perhaps a fragment detached from the main meteor. Dubbed the Ed Nadir Crater, the impact feature sits more than 300m below the sea, some 400km off the coast of Guinea, west Africa. The crater was identified by Dr Uisdean Nicholson from Heriot-Watt University, Edinburgh. The crater is around 8.5km in diameter pointing to an impact by a meteor a little less than 0.5 km wide. Simulations by Dr Veronica Bray of the University of Arizona estimate the crater was caused by the collision of a 400m-wide asteroid in 500-800m of water, which would have generated a tsunami around one kilometre high. This estimate of 1km seems high when compared with the simulations of other impacts, but if accurate those in the Mediterranean would have caused a hugely greater tsunami.

9.11 As well as the onshore evidence of a massive wave of water moving south westwards over the Richat, offshore marine geologists assessing dangers faced in hydrocarbon extraction have identified evidence of massive land slips and tailings of eroded material (see Sebastian Krastel, *IFM GeoMar Report 2010*). Three massive areas of spoil have been identified directly seaward of the Richat Structure – each almost 100km wide and spreading up to 300km into the Atlantic. The momentum required to create these tailings points to a massive amount of material being suddenly deposited.

9.12 Lets look again at some elements of Solon's description – the concentric circles of land and water (the visual evidence of the Richat Structure is striking and the concentric salt deposits highly suggestive); the extensive plains on both sides of the city (yes, each side of the Richat Structure);

the city of Atlantis enjoyed hot springs (yes, a study of an isolated Cretaceous alkaline hydrothermal complex in the Richat Structure was published in the *Journal of African Earth Sciences*, Volume 94 pps 109-129 in September 2014); and lush public gardens (yes, the climate of North Africa was much wetter with lush vegetation covering much of what today is desert); a seaway channel exiting to the south (yes, indications of); and, a high mountain range visible to the north (yes, the Atlas Mountains). Note the first king of Atlantis was apparently named Atlas, a minor coincidence?

9.13   An authenticated map of the 'habitable' world by Pomponius Mela, a Roman cartographer, dated to AD43, has 'Atlantae' emblazoned across north west Africa. One can only speculate as to the source of his information. We also have a map attributed to Herodotus, dated to 450BC, also showing Atlantis as an inland location in north west Africa. As Herodotus died (425BC) about the time Plato was born (c429BC) he could only have got information on Atlantis directly from Solon's original works. Unfortunately, Herodotus is not known for map making and the authenticity of this map is questioned.

9.14   So what conclusions may be drawn. Certainly, the location of Richat seems to fit many of the details from Solon's description. The records of the Egyptian priests link the reported inundation of Atlantis as coinciding with devastation of the Nile valley. Both events are dated by different Egyptian priesthoods as very close to the end of the Younger Dryas period. If we accept for the moment that we have evidence of extreme water erosion deep into North Africa caused by violent cascades down the Tamanrasset valley and written records of the devastation of the Nile Valley at a similar time – then surely we should find evidence of dramatic sea inundation between these Tunisia and the Nile? Well, yes we do!

9.15   If you take the midway point between Chott el Djerid and the Nile Valley, the wide bay between Misrata and Benghazi in Libya and then look about 1000 km inland in northern Chad, we find evidence of violent water flows and the dried remains of seawater. At Trou au Natron, the crater of an ancient volcano is filled with salt deposits and molluscs which have been radiocarbon dated to between 15500BC and 7700BC – admittedly a wide range but 9620BC sits comfortably in the middle of that range. And, what other events do we know of that might have resulted in a southbound tsunami travelling over 1000km south to Chad?

9.16 And just 200km eastwards lies another volcano, Emi Koussai, the highest in North Africa. The lava flow from its last eruption has been dated to between 12770BC and 10380BC (+/-400). The lava on its lower slopes shows striations indicative of severe water erosion, obviously after the date range given above. Again, what event do we know of after 10380BC that could have resulted in a tsunami driving 1000km south to erode the flanks of Emi Koussai? Both locations are shown on that map, which you may download from the Quintology Publications website.

9.17 And now let us return to look at the Edfu Building texts. By good fortune these provide a second distinctive tradition referring to a pre-Flood culture with details of its destruction which match our understanding of the effects of the twin impacts in the Mediterranean. Whilst the story of Atlantis is widely known and equally widely dismissed as a pure fantasy, the other, telling of the arrival in Egypt of the Shebtiw and their first establishment, could be dismissed as typical ancient pagan religious tracts. But taken together each lends credence to the other and recognised experts are linking the evidence to the Younger Dryas events.

9.18 The record of the Shebtiw, 'the Ancestors', comes from the inscriptions on the walls of the temple of Edfu, located 130km north of the Aswan High Dam. The temple, dedicated to Horus, was constructed relatively recently during the Ptolemaic period, commencing in 237BC and being completed in 57BC. The temple was built to replace a far older temple on the same site which may have dated back before the first dynasty (i.e. before 3100BC). Rather delightfully, whilst being constructed, the builders used the vast store of pre-existing documents to inscribe what they felt were the most important information on its walls and pillars. After the Roman empire converted to Christianity, Edfu was sacked and any remaining documents destroyed but thankfully relatively minor damage was done to the inscriptions and the desert was allowed to gradually cover the site to a depth of 12m. Little remained visible between houses subsequently built on top, when the site was detected by a French expedition in 1798. It was not until 1860 that a French Egyptologist, Auguste Mariette begun digging out the temple.

9.19 The sheer volume of the texts may be appreciated by the efforts of Emile Chassinat who devoted 40 years to the creation of a 14 volume work incorporating 3000 pages of hieroglyphs and six volumes containing photographs and sketches of the inscriptions. Another noted Egyptologist, Eve Reymond (1923 – 1986), also dedicated most of her life to study of these Edfu Building Texts, publishing her conclusions in in a classic work entitled *The Mythical Origin of the Egyptian Temple*.

9.20   Recognising the profound importance of these texts, Professor Dr. Dieter Kurth of Hamburg University started a long term project in 1986 to prepare a complete re-translation and restructuring of the material to overcome the frustrating experience of parallel passages and comparable content being scrambled across the 3000 pages of hieroglyphs, making it extremely difficult to extract a coherent story from the inscriptions. The entire temple site has been resurveyed and many additional inscriptions previously overlooked have been documented. The mass of inscriptions in the Edfu complex are now seen as an attempt to portray a chronological extract of the most important historical documents previously held by the original Edfu temple. Since 2002, the project has been managed by the Academy of Sciences at Gottingen. Whilst a few fully revised volumes have been published it may be decades before the project is fully completed.

9.21   Chronologically, the inscriptions begin with the establishment of a community on an island, referred to as the Island of Trampling by the 'Ancestors of the First Occasion' (typw sep tpy), being the original divine inhabitants. It is not clear where this island community was located. However, this community was wiped out and its buildings were destroyed in a great calamity described as a fire followed by a long period of darkness accompanied by great flooding until the whole island was submerged and covered by a reed bank. This description may be a record of destruction wrought by the massive impact in the Mediterranean. Fires would have resulted from superheated ejecta falling back to Earth and a massive tsunami would have swept far up the Nile valley destroying all the communities settled each side of the river.

9.22   After the destruction, a group of 8 or 10 beings, the Shebtiw (Primeval Ones), arrived in Egypt to establish a new base. These Shebtiw led by one called the Lord of the Wing and prepared for the arrival of one identified as 'the Falcon'. The arrival of the Falcon is followed by the construction of many buildings for which the size, appearance and function are all described. Confusingly, the group as a whole is also referred to as 'the falcons' – some say they might have worn ceremonial headdress resembling a birds head and feathered cloak or it may just be recognition that they could travel by air as well as by sea. There are some references which may be links to Ptah (Enki) and Thoth (one of Enki's sons) – Thoth being widely credited in Egyptian inscriptions as being the original designer and described as the master builder of many large temples. Soon followed the construction of other sacred sites – Memphis (location of the Giza pyramids and the Sphinx) identified as Ptah's abode and Hermopolis for Thoth. Traditionally the Falcon is associated with Horus, to whom the temple was dedicated, but the cult of Horus grew much later, in the early dynastic period, around 3000BC. Horus, born of Isis, being a great grandson of Enki, fathered by Osiris.

9.23   The Edfu Building Texts also provide the sole Egyptian reference to the Seven Sages – the same term as applied by the Sumerians to the Apkallu, the Seven Sages who constructed the first post flood city in Sumer – Uruk. The Edfu inscriptions identify these Sages as those with the knowledge of how to construct temples and of how to create sacred places. The Sages are recorded as 'created by' and certainly junior to, Ptah (Enki), and credited with initiating construction works at the Great Primeval Mound – thought to be the Giza complex – where they are described as teaching Thoth his skills.

9.24   Incredibly, we also find references to Seven Sages in Vedic literature. The Saptarishi are the seven rishis, meaning seven sages, featuring in the Vedas and other Indian works and regarded as the patriarchs of the Vedic religion. In some texts the rishis are described as 'mind born' by Brahma. Brahma being the creator god and head of the Hindu trinity alongside Shiva and Vishnu. It seems extraordinary to find references to Seven Sages across so many cultures – implying a common origin of the record. This is explored further in section 18.

9.25   Of critical importance to our understanding of the ancient 'pagan' gods are Edfu inscriptions which record that after their work was done and these 'gods' died, their bodies were transferred to Henen-nesut (house of the royal child) now known by its Greek name, Heracleopolis, where a cult centre was established to honour their entombed graves, a temple which survived into dynastic times – around 6000 years later. Other inscriptions record how carefully knowledge was passed between the generations, with initiation rites and transfer of knowledge this community became known as the Shemsu Hor, the 'Followers of Horus'. The Edfu texts describe the Followers of Horus maintaining their detailed records and plans at Heliopolis – on the opposite side of the Nile, 8km downstream of the Giza complex. The Edfu texts identify Henen-nesut as the original post flood base of the Shebtiw and record many early links to Memphis (i.e. Giza). According to Reymond, all the earliest Edfu texts have a distinctive Memphis background preserved in them – again implying links to the Giza complex.

9.26 Taken together, the bedrock exposed by the scouring around the Richat Structure, the erosion of the lava flows of Emi Koussai, the evidence of marine life in the crater of Trou au Natron and the records of the Edfu Temple all corroborate a massive tsunami hitting the northern coast of Africa at a date which could plausibly be around 9620BC.

9.27 At the date of writing this there is no known explanation for what occurred at the end of the Younger Dryas period, c 9620BC. Geological and marine analysis indicates that global average temperatures rose quite suddenly, by around 10C, just as they had fallen by a not dissimilar amount at the start of the Younger Dryas period around 1200 years earlier. Strangely, although the two meteor impact events had the opposite effect on global temperatures, both events were accompanied by a surge in sea levels. As discussed in this book, we now have both an explanation of the cause and effects at the onset of the Younger Dryas period and have located the smoking gun - a meteor impact, located in Greenland. It has been suggested that a larger meteor may have fragmented upon entering Earth atmosphere, with a string of lesser impacts across Canada as well as the largest part hitting the Hiawatha Glacier. This impact vapourised a large chunk of the North American ice sheet, disgorging a vast amount of fresh water into the oceans and dust into the atmosphere – which changed salinity and disrupted ocean currents whilst blocking sunlight and causing global temperatures to plunge.

9.28 So what might have caused the end of the Younger Dryas? Something sufficient to raise average global temperatures significantly. The event does not seem to have caused a nuclear winter with a dust filled atmosphere blocking sunlight for some years, there are no signs of continental extinction level events nor any 'black mat' being laid at this time. This would seem to rule out both a mega-volcano and a meteor impact. Instead, the temperature rose? Is it possible that Earth was hit by a meteor with a chemical composition which, when mixed with sea water, released huge volumes of greenhouse gases.

9.29   As the average meteor slams into our planet at 18km per second, any meteor would punch through to the floor of the deepest part of any ocean in a fraction of a second. Therefore, no depth of seawater would provide much protection from deadly ejecta being thrown up into the atmosphere and condemning the planet to a nuclear winter. However, a degree of relief might come from a low angle impact – which would increase the volume of water vapourised (and later rainfall) whilst magnifying the volume of the tsunami sent in one direction. I have already speculated that a meteor on a particular tracking could have caused a tsunami which sent a wall of water across north west Africa to erase a city built on the Richat Structure, the same tsunami would have devastated the coastline of the rest of northern Africa and caused damage some way up the Nile.

9.30   The hypothesis outlined in this chapter may be validated by the Holocene Impact Working Group, an association of scientists looking for impact creators associated with meteor impacts that have occurred since the end of the last major ice age around 20000BC. Their purpose is to understand the relationship between impacts and climate change. Their published activities have focused on three major areas: impacts in North America associated with the onset of the Younger Dryas; an impact south east of Madagascar around 2800BC which might have generated some of the stories linked with Noah; and, impacts in the Gulf of Carpentaria which may be associated with the well documented climate cooling of AD536 to 545.

9.31   In March 2010, a team including D. Abbott, E Bryant, V. Gusiakov and B. Masse, published a paper for the 6th Alexander von Humboldt International Conference on Climate Change held in Merida, Mexico. The paper referred to four craters caused by meteor impacts which have occurred on the last 5000 years. The largest 29km diameter crater, known as the Burckle Crater, dated to between 3000BC and 2800BC, lying at a depth of 3800 metres, some 2.600 km from Mozambique and 5080 km from Western Australia. This impact is estimated to have created a tsunami between 200m and 300m in height – the effects of which would have been felt in the Persian Gulf and the Red Sea. In particular, the residual impact of the tsunami funnelling up the Persian Gulf would have inundated the rich alluvial farmlands along the Tigris and Euphrates. It would be interesting to find Sumerian records making reference to this event.

9.32   As luck would have it, some months after first rewriting this chapter, I came across the work of the Australian geologist who was instrumental in developing techniques of locating undersea impact craters. His research on the Burckle impact is available on OzGeographics on YouTube. The Burckle impact crater lies 3.8km beneath the surface in the middle of the Indian Ocean, so apart from sonar revealing its tell-tale central uplift zone – indicative of an meteor impact, its location renders on site examination challenging. Detailed examination of the chevrons deposited on coasts surrounding the Indian Ocean – in India, Africa and Australia confirm their origin as the site of the Burckle impact. The chevrons are created by the tsunami, resulting from the impact into the ocean, depositing the silt borne by the wave, as it hits obstacles and rising ground, in chevron shaped deposits pointing in the direction of the wave movement. Sample analysis of findings of nano diamonds and micro-spherules, formed only by the heat and pressure of a meteor impact, enable accurate dating of the meteor impact.

9.33   Use of this technique, identifying chevrons and using their directional alignment to track back to likely impact sites has yielded astonishing results in the Mediterranean. Plentiful evidence has been quickly identified in Tunisia and on the Greek and Italian mainland – which has been traced back to impact sites to the east of Sicily. Two typical impact sites with central uplift domes have been located just south west of the Greek island of Kefalonia – one is almost 50km wide and the other around 25km wide. The chevrons indicate the two impacts were simultaneous – two fragments of a single meteor which split apart seconds before impact. The size of the craters points to a tsunami far greater than that created by the Burckle impact. The tsunami is estimated at around 800m high. Painstaking research is now yielding evidence of damage from the tsunami scouring coastal mountains in Greek Peloponnesia, along the Croatian coast and even 300km inland in central Italy – all being directionally aligned with the identified impact sites.

9.34   A tsunami estimated at 800m high would have swept over the low lying parts of North Africa – penetrating furthest into Tunisia, Libya and up the Nile Valley. Little resistance would have been provided by the low lying swampy land of Chott el Djerid in central Tunisia, with the wave sweeping across into northern Algeria where gently sloping lands, rising to a maximum of 340m, would channel the tsunami between the Atlas mountains to its north and the Ahaggar range to its south. The slowing waters would deposit prodigious quantities of sand and silt – creating the vast fields of thousands of crescent shaped chevrons (all directly pointing against the prevailing winds) right across Algeria. Reaching the border with present day Mauritania, the tsunami would have barrelled down the Tamanrasset river system and swept over the area of the Richat Structure. The map overleaf shows the likely course to the Richat Structure.

9.35   When initially developing this book, I had been speculating about a big meteor hit east of Sicily. Imagine my astonishment when learning of the discovery of the two adjacent meteor impacts referred to above, with diameters of 25km and 50km. Neither site has yet been verified by core sampling nor yet named. Hence my tentative labelling of this twin impact event as the Kefalonia Impact for the purposes of this book. This discovery is certain to change conventional history. Samples from the chevrons and the sea bed need to be analysed before having proof that thye were meteor impacts and ascertain tight dating, but the implications are stunning. The resulting mega tsunami would certainly be capable of accounting for the findings in Tunisia, Mauritania, Chad and the historical records of the Temples of Sais and Edfu in Egypt.

9.36   This new technique of searching for chevrons both to track back to the impact site and to enable accurate dating from examination of impact ejaculate contained within the chevrons provides us with a leap forward in establishing where and when impacts occurred. For example, an alternative explanation for the Justinian crisis in which around 1/3rd of the population of the empire died, recently attributed to a possible mega volcanic eruption by Krakatoa might alternatively be attributable to a twin meteor impact off the north coast of Australia. Two impact craters have been identified in the Gulf of Carpentaria, on the north coast of Australia, dated to AD572 (+/-86) which might be linked to the two years without summers (AD536 and 537) recorded in Roman annuals which had a devasting effect on life in Europe. The two craters in the Gulf of Carpentaria lie just off the coast – the 12km wide Kanmare Crater and the 18km wide Tabban Crater.

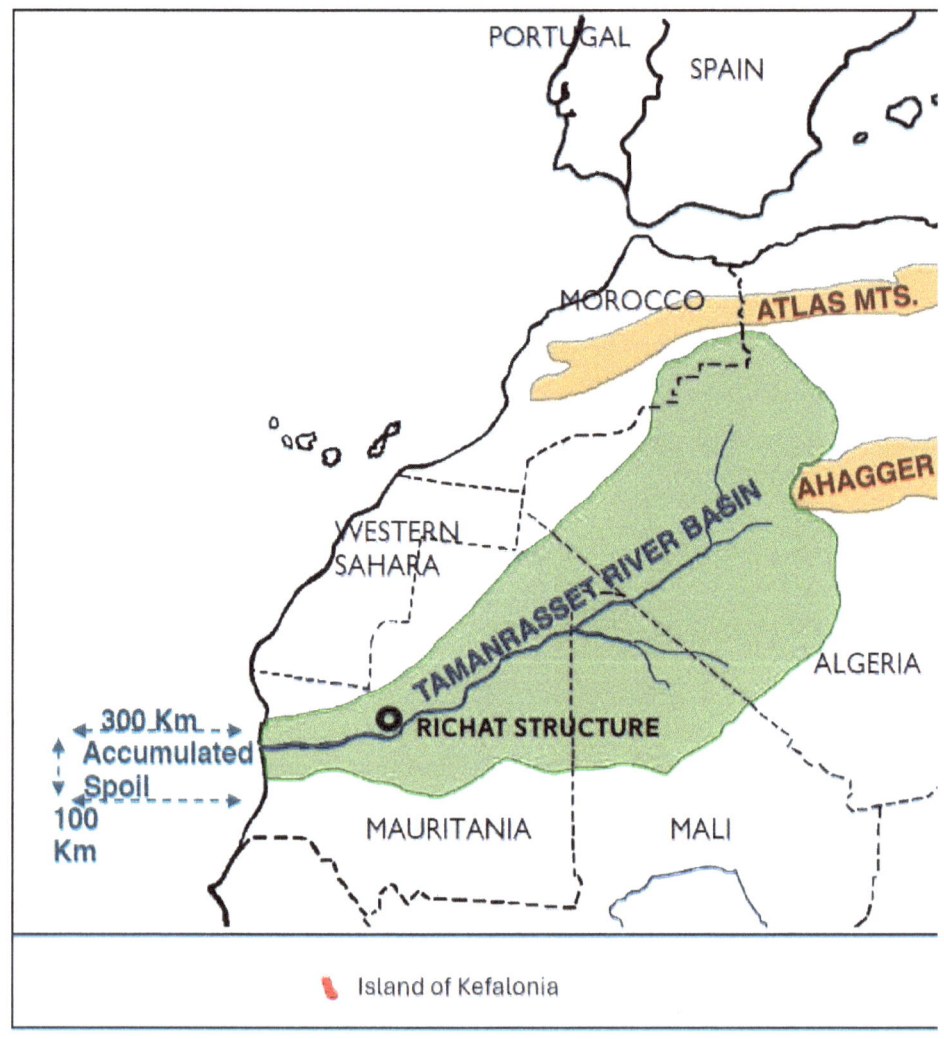

Younger Dryas ended by twin meteor impact off Kefalonia c9620BC

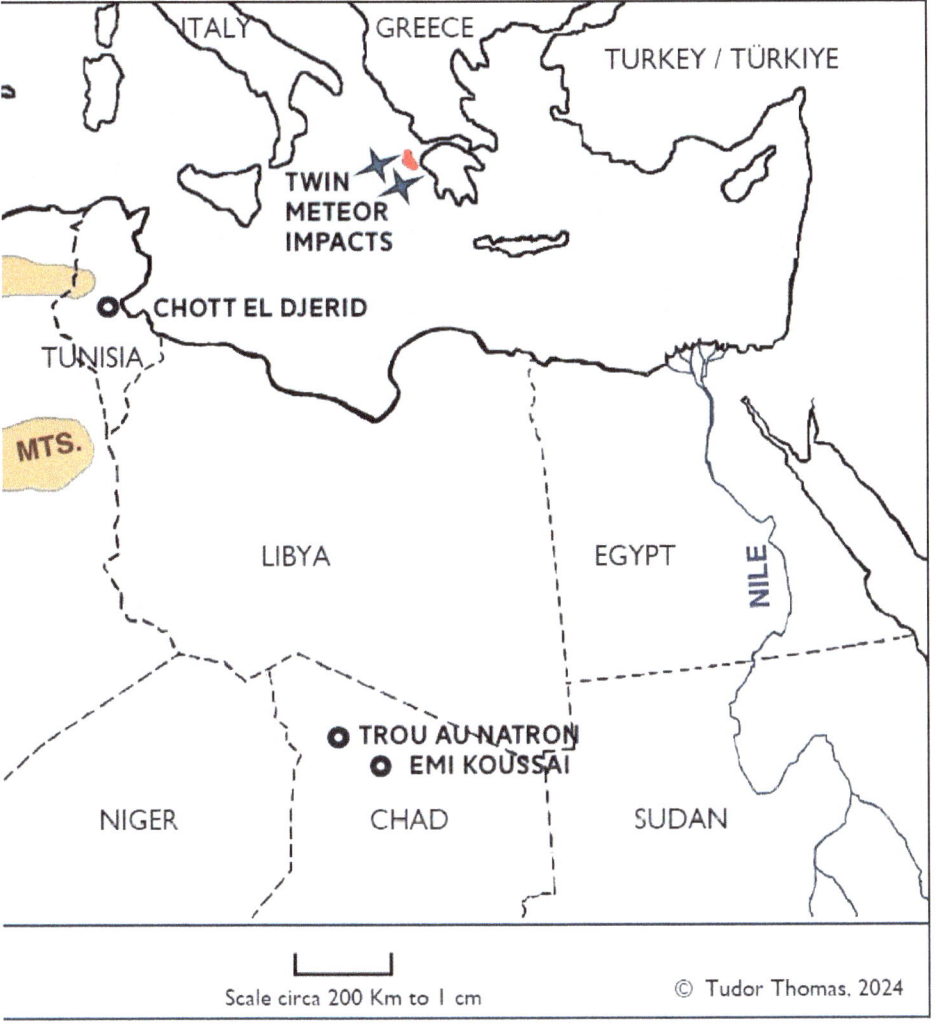

10

Pre Younger Dryas culture at many sites in Turkey

10.1 Discoveries of settlements in Turkey dating to between 11000BC and 8000BC, firstly at Göbelki Tepe, then at Boncuklu Tarla and Karahan Tepe have transformed our knowledge of human development. Recent local surveying has revealed a further 14 buried settlements which are expected to be contemporaneous to Göbelki Tepe. If these do turn out to be contemporaneous, evidence of a major ancient culture has been discovered. Critically, we may have discovered the settlements of a culture that lived through the complete Younger Dryas cycle – through the entire 10765BC to 9620BC climatic whiplash.

10.2 This collection of newly discovered settlements include large urban areas of up to 60,000m2. This implies food production at a scale to provide surpluses to support a wide range of specialised workers – including the highly skilled stonemasons, whose work is much in evidence. Prior to these discoveries, it was understood that the cultivation of crops and domestication of animals, the key to producing surplus food to enable human specialisation and the development of urban centres, only occurred from around 8000BC. Already, this understanding was challenged by findings that cities such as Harran, Damascus and Jericho appear to have already been founded by that date.

10.3 The astonishing dimension to the discoveries is the number and scale of settlements being unearthed. So far only a tiny portion of each site has been uncovered but the findings point to a substantial settled culture that predates the onset of the Younger Dryas event and endured throughout the dramatic climatic changes and impact events. Beware of articles making claims that these were purely ceremonial sites, and that the people remained hunter gatherers because no evidence of farming or domesticated animals have been found. Such claims have been made in respect of Karahan Tepe but appear to be rearguard action to preserve the conventional view of history. One fact stands out – despite the claims made it is also admitted in the same articles that the settlement of Karahan Tepe covers 60,000 square metres and that less than 1% has been excavated so far.

10.4   This chapter focuses on just two sites, Boncuklu Tarla and Göbelki Tepe. Ground penetrating radar has proved invaluable in revealing the scale and general layout of these ancient sites but at both sites only a tiny fraction has so far been excavated – about 5% for Boncuklu Tarla and about 10% for Göbelki Tepe. So, whilst the findings are extraordinary they only represent the tip of the iceberg in terms of what we might learn. In coming years much more may be learned which revolutionises our understanding of the development of human civilisation. So, as well as tracking developments at these two sites, you might also look out for discoveries at the following sites: Karahan Tepe, Tasli Tepe, Hamzan Tepe, Sefer Tepe, Urfa, Nevalt Çori, Kilisik Tepe and Körtik Tepe.

10.5   When did this culture emerge? The early findings at Göbelki Tepe indicated settlement from soon after the end of the Younger Dryas, around 9600BC – but so far only six constructions of the 55 or so revealed by ground radar have been excavated – and already the pattern points to the pit like constructions being built successively over a long period to track the path of the helical solstice as it migrates over time. So, we may find indications of older construction dates in other pits yet to be excavated. Early work at Boncuklu Tarla has already revealed evidence of a surprisingly advanced culture which dates back earlier than any dates so far from Göbelki Tepe. The initial dating by Ergül Kodaş, an archaeologist at Artuklu University, estimates Boncuklu Tarla to date from 10000BC, whilst subsequent estimates have pushed this to 11000BC. Critically, occupation of this settlement has been pushed back before the Hiawatha impact in 10765BC and the onset of the Younger Dryas.

10.6   To maintain some suspense let's examine the findings at Göbelki Tepe first, which some have argued do not represent a settled culture of a permanent population supported by farming but a seasonal gathering place for rituals and worship. This seems an attempt to maintain the conventional view of when food cultivation started and permanent settlements were established. It does not however explain how a hunter gatherer culture could develop exquisite stonemasonry skills nor astrological knowledge. Then we will look at the initial findings at Boncuklu Tarla – be prepared to be blown away!!

10.7 Göbekli Tepe (meaning "Hill of the Navel") is currently accepted as the oldest monumental architecture found anywhere in the world – at least until Gunung Padang is excavated. It is located in south east Turkey – most significantly only 50km from Harran – a very ancient city dating back to c8000BC, that formed the northern capital of the Sumerian Empire - where Abraham's father, Terah, relocated his family from Ur, c2000BC.

10.8 The first phase of excavation of the complex was undertaken by the German Archaeological Institute led by Klaus Schmidt, who unfortunately died in 2014. The architecture comprises dozens of intricately carved megalithic T shaped pillars – around 5.5m tall and weighing up to 20 tons. The first four enclosures that were excavated each contained 14 massive T shaped pillars and all the enclosures appear to have been deliberately filled in – with earth and cobbles. The in-fill is definitely not from accumulated sediment but deliberately filled in – effectively sealing them in and preventing contamination by later organic material which enables accurate dating to be determined. The total area is huge, maybe 30 times the area of Stonehenge. Each pillar is polished limestone given a golden hue by the sun, each stands on a polished plinth, resting on grooves only 10cm deep. Enclosures are elliptic 20m at widest and 14m at narrowest. Carvings are predominantly in bas relief, with carved features standing proud of the polished limestone pillar. It is difficult to believe such skilled stonemasonry was achieved by nomadic hunter gatherers! It will be interesting to see if any discarded or broken tools are found in any of the enclosures yet to be excavated. The carvings denote a variety of birds, animals, insects and humans – noteworthy amongst the human accessories are 'handbags' resembling rectangular boxes with curved handles. Another curiosity is the carving of humans invariably with arms resting on the stomach and outstretched fingers narrowly failing to meet. It is noteworthy that both of these design features appear in carvings of humans at other ancient megalithic sites - found on other continents!

10.9   Most pillars heavily adorned with bas relief figures of animals and symbols – most relate to recognisable zodiacal signs. It is stunning to realise that the zodiac signs we know were already used 12,000 years ago!!

10.10   The concept of a 12-member Zodiac dates so far back in time that it also points to an earlier civilization on Earth, or, knowledge shared from a common source. The zodiac we use today, we attribute to the Sumerians:- we still use the twelve periods and the same signs for each period of the Zodiac as the ancient Sumerians did 6000 years ago. Astonishingly, we have found the same use of a zodiac of 12 periods in use in the Mesoamerican civilizations. The use of 12 is entirely artificial, if we all used a zodiac of 10 segments we might attribute it to humans having ten fingers. Even more intriguing, the names and symbols used show a common source: The sign of the Bull, Taurus, in Mesopotamia was the Tupa Taruca (Pasturing stag) in the Andes; the sign of the Maiden, Virgo, was called Sara Mama (Mother Maize) – in Mesopotamia represented by a maiden holding a stalk of wheat or barley, whilst in the Andes she holds maize. Thus the 12 wards of Cuzco, represent the signs of the zodiac, with the first being the Ram (Aries) denoting the city plan was laid out after precession had moved from the Age of Taurus to the Age of Ares – i.e. after 2160BC.

10.11   The use of a common, partly locally adapted, zodiac in both the Middle East and South America dating back to the period prior to 'kingship being lowered from heaven' in the 4th millennia BC, indicates the common source must have been even older. Maybe the zodiac was a system devised by a pre-Hiawatha impact megalithic culture – whose transportation devises enabled them to disperse globally.

10.12   Returning to Göbekli Tepe, the four pits excavated so far indicate that the site was occupied for at least 1500 years. The oldest of these four pits appears to have been filled in around 9600BC and the site appears to have been completely abandoned in 8200BC. Göbekli Tepe must have been an institution supported by a significant team of skilled stonemasons. Strangely, the local area has no previous indication of any organised farming, the indigent population were hunter gatherers. Such people roamed in small bands and were incapable of tasks involving long term planning, complex division of labour and management skills required to plan, measure plots, the undertaking of exquisite stone masonry and carving – and on such an immense scale.

10.13 Researchers with the University of Edinburgh have interpreted the famous Vulture T Stone, Pillar 43 in enclosure D at Göbekli Tepe as being created as a commemoration of a devastating event – namely the Hiawatha meteor impact which caused an immediate environmental disaster globally and large scale loss of life. The team scanned the images carved onto the pillar into an astronomical program to determine if they might be linked with constellations. This showed calibration between the characters on the pillar and astronomical symbols in the sky for the year 10950BC. The fact that the people took the time and considerable effort to create the characters on the pillar suggests something very important must have happened during the same time period that the Greenland ice core suggests a comet struck, approximately 10,890BC. One carved image is of a headless human. [NB, for this book, I have stuck with the midpoint date of the most detailed analysis yet published – the 354 black mat samples from right across the strewnfield analysed by UC Santa Barbara in 2015, which gives a midpoint of 10765BC. See paragraph 7.16]

10.14 Interestingly the circles at Göbekli Tepe are aligned with the star Sirius – as are 30 or so very ancient remnants of temples on Malta.

10.15 A key emerging issue is that, as in Egypt, the oldest megalithic architecture, art, sculpture, etc., appear to be the finest quality and, over time, the quality degrades – it is as though these cultures sprang into life fully formed without a series of gradual evolutionary improvements but over time deteriorated in quality. It is as though the culture arrived at the location fully developed and gradually lost its skills and craftsmanship over succeeding generations. Such an advanced culture could not emerge overnight. This surely suggests that the builders of Göbekli Tepe arrived from somewhere else, bringing skills and knowledge but without the full range of support to be able to sustain their culture – indicating they were effectively cut off from their origins, maybe having fled from disaster.

10.16 The Göbekli Tepe megaliths are close to twice the conventional age ascribed to the next oldest megaliths – the first Pyramids and first phase of Stonehenge both being dated to around 3000BC. However, new disciplines have challenged the dating of the Sphinx and the Giza Pyramids – see the next chapter.

10.17 Indeed the intricacy and beauty of the Göbekli Tepe monuments look so advanced that when originally discovered they were deemed to be very modern and were ignored. A joint team from University of Chicago and Turkey had visited the site in 1964 looking for stone age remains and finding the tops of T shaped pillars poking out the ground, they inspected the bas reliefs and determined they were much too advanced to be very old, concluding it was the remains of a medieval cemetery and ignored them !!

10.18   Noting that each pit appears to have been deliberately filled with earth and rubble, Klaus Schmidt explained that this infilling has prevented intrusion by younger organic material and enables very reliable carbon dating to be established. The dates determined are from organic material recovered at the base of the pits – thus dates are when each pit was filled, sometime after the megaliths in each pit were erected. This observation also suggests that dates applied to some other, more exposed, megalithic sites may be underestimated due to the infiltration of much later organic material which then affects the dating.

10.19   Why were enclosures filled in? It has been suggested that the pits were burial chambers – but no skeletons have been found. Graham Hancock postulates that the pits are a time capsule, containing a message for the future. The oldest calibrated carbon dating is 9600BC – calibrated means adjusted for differences in oxygen isotopes in different epochs.

10.20   The site at Boncuklu Tarla covers 2.5 hectares of which 5% had been excavated by the start of 2023. Already this initial excavation has revealed 30 domestic habitations and 7 buildings without any trace of habitation which are classified as being for communal purposes. If 5% of the site contains 37 buildings, the total site may contain 700 buildings – that constitutes a large permanently settled community – which is already being dated as existing before the Hiawatha impact and of having been continuously settled for 4,000 to 5,000 years until around 8000BC.

10.21   A settled community of this size would need to be supported by extensive cultivation and animal husbandry. This has been strengthened by the discovery of a grain store. Specialisation would then support development of skills unrelated to food production – a sewage system has been detected and an abundance of adornments. Over 100,000 beads have been recovered, giving the site its name - Boncuklu Tarla means Field of Beads in Turkish. Not only have vast quantities of beads been recovered but many are intricately carved and polished – the scorpion is a popular symbol. Also over 2000 copper beads have been found. The production of jewellery of such a scale points to a sophisticated culture, a thriving luxury segment and lots of free time. Such a culture would not have emerged overnight but over many centuries – we have a lot to discover.

10.22 The evidence now emerging from excavation points to a human culture which had already developed from wandering bands of hunter gatherers maybe comprising a few dozen people into settled urban centres of a few thousand people. These urban centres had to be supported by crop cultivation and have lots of surplus labour for the construction of hundreds of stone buildings, sewage systems and tons of jewellery. How would the Hiawatha impact have affected Boncuklu Tarla?

10.23 Firstly, the terrifying sight in the sky of the approaching meteor, particularly at night. Whilst the Earth's curvature would have likely prevented the impact explosion being seen, although given how high the ejecta would have risen, maybe not if it had occurred at night. Then the sound and probably the vibration of the impact would have terrified people. The 10 megaton Tunguska event in Russia in 1908 was reported as being heard as far away as London. The Hiawatha impact was hugely bigger, at around 700 megatons, so the sound of the explosive impact may have been quite loud given Turkey is much closer to Greenland than London is to Siberia. As shown in chapter 7, the whole of modern Turkey lies within the Hiawatha ejecta impact field – whilst ejecta might have cooled to solid rather than have still been liquid metal when raining down upon the people of Boncuklu Tarla, it will probably have caused a number of fatalities. Then the skies went dark as dust clouds filled the skies for a long time, probably some years, maybe a decade. This would have caused growth in vegetation to be severely stunted – leading to starvation and a collapse in population levels. Skills would become difficult to pass on and the culture would regress.

10.24 With the emerging knowledge of an even bigger meteor impact, possibly 1200 years later and much closer, one can look again at how the peoples who constructed all these ancient sites might have reacted. Certainly, they would retain tribal memories of the earlier destruction, when faced by an significantly greater and closer impact. The Hiawatha impact occurred almost 6000km from Göbelki Tepe whilst the impact off Kefalonia was around 1500km; the Hiawatha crater is 31km wide whilst the much nearer twin craters off the Greek coast are 25km and 50km. The approach, even in daylight, would have been highly visible and the sound of the impact explosion deafening. If Hiawatha led to a nuclear winter without any growth in vegetation for a couple of years, the subsequent larger impact would caused even more prolonged damage to vegetation.

10.25 Frightened survivors would certainly think of moving to live in caves, soft rock offered the opportunity for more organised and larger refuges. Could these impact catastrophes have triggered the start of development and occupation of what can only be described as the underground cities of Cappadocia?

10.26 The next few paragraphs are factually accurate but the tentative conclusions are purely speculative on my part. Later we shall refer to the Longyou caves of Zhejiang Province in China. If you then check out available images of the Longyou caves you may well conclude that they could be linked to an ancient megalithic culture. However, the Cappadocia caves simply do not give that impression. One might speculate that, whilst responsible for the amazing stone obelisks found at the various sites referred to in paragraph 10.4 above, this culture did not leave megalithic structures on the scale seen in Egypt or Bolivia. Maybe the frightened population just wanted to quickly dig out a secure shelter – so adornment and precision were not a priority.

10.27 Cappadocia, a region in central Turkey, enjoys a spectacular landscape – a contrast of deep valleys and soaring rock formations dotted with homes, chapels, tombs, temples and entire subterranean cities harmoniously carved into the natural landforms. Spread beneath 250 square kilometres lie more than 200 underground villages and tunnel towns complete with hidden passages, secret rooms and ancient temples. One finds a remarkably storied history of each new civilisation building on the work of the last. This makes Cappadocia one of the world's most striking and largest cave-dwelling regions. Cappadocia lies on a plateau 1000 metres above current sea level. This is sounds good if you have heard about an 800 metre high tsunami.

10.28 The city of Derinkuyu is eleven levels deep, has 600 entrances, miles of tunnels connecting it to other underground cities and can accommodate thousands of people. It is truly an underground city, with areas for sleeping, stables for livestock, wells, water tanks, pits for cooking, ventilation shafts, communal rooms, bathrooms, and tombs. And Derinkuyu is not alone. More than forty complete underground cities and 200 underground structures have been discovered in the Cappadocia, many of them connecting to each other via tunnels.

10.29 How long ago the construction of these underground living spaces started is unknown. Some cite Hittite occupation, which would date from c2000BC to 1177BC, others date to remains excavated from the modern town of Kültepe dating from the 3rd millennium BC. At Kanesh, tens of thousands of cuneiform clay tablets have been recovered from an ancient Assyrian merchant colony, constituting the oldest written records found in Turkey. It has been noted that the oldest parts appear to have been excavated by stone implements rather than metal – indicating considerable age.

10.30 Following the defeat of the Hittites by the Greek Sea Peoples in 1177BC, every subsequent culture utilised and extended the underground facilities – many were seeking protection from enemies. Extensive use was made by Christian groups in the first millennium, seeking refuge from persecution by Romans and later from Muslim armies.

10.31 But it occurs to me that, if local people had witnessed the effects of the Hiawatha impact, the ejecta raining down and the broiling black clouds created by the firestorms blocking out the sun for months – underground cave systems would seem very inviting. The horrific climatic changes would remind people of a similar sharp drop in temperatures that had occurred only a few hundred years earlier – the end of the Older Dryas also saw a 6C drop in average temperatures in a very short period of time. Perhaps that sudden change was also associated with meteor impacts. Perhaps a group of asteroids, travelling in convoy, were repeatedly crossing Earth's orbit.

10.32 Furthermore, the site of Göbekli Tepe lies only 500km east of Cappadocia – so skilled artisans were definitely in the area at the end of the Younger Dryas period.

10.33 With details emerging from Boncuklu Tarla in particular, we now find large urban centres supported by extensive farming of cultivated crops dating back to a time before the Hiawatha Impact. This dramatically lengthens the time humans have lived in urban civilisations, at 13000BC this is twice as old as the c3500BC which conventional history still contends.

11

Egyptian engineering points to an earlier advanced culture

11.1 Despite dogged rear-guard defence by traditional Egyptologists, there is a growing groundswell of opinion, based upon assessments by engineers and professional stonemasons, that the traditional attribution of all ancient Egyptian artifacts to the historical period of the dynastic pharaohs starting from around 3200BC is patently wrong. It defies logic that the most sophisticated remains are held to be from the oldest dynasties, as if Egyptian technology went backwards throughout the dynastic period (c3200BC to 50BC) instead of progressing?

11.2 Even Flinders Petrie (1853 – 1942), the renowned British Egyptologist, writing 150 years ago, found artifacts which he said were challenging to attribute to the pharonic period. Despite bearing inscriptions linking artifacts to Old Kingdom pharaohs, he noted that some stonemasonry was inexplicably better than anything from later periods or even by his contemporaries. The conventional description of ancient Egypt has been drawn from translation of inscriptions and writings, of which vast quantities have been found. Traditional Egyptologists and archaeologists insist all ancient artifacts were manufactured by the simple copper and stone tools displayed in museums and refute well-argued objections by trained engineers and stonemasons who try to explain the impossibility. The first use of iron historically recorded by Egyptians dates from 1200BC, arising from interaction with those the Egyptians referred to as the Sea Peoples, warrior tribes of Greek origin who developed the first iron weapons. The first evidence of iron smelting in Egypt only dates to the sixth century BC.

11.3 Egyptian traditionalists are so protective of the conventional explanations that they often prevent non-invasive measurements and evaluation, and sometimes block access to potentially important discoveries to everyone. For example, clear evidence suggests more passages and chambers have been identified within the Great Pyramid, lengthy subterranean passageways have been seen entering under the Sphinx and the fabled Egyptian Labyrinth at Hawara has been found – but access, even by Egyptian archaeologists has been blocked. Similarly, whilst a few artifacts have been analysed, most requests have been refused. The only stone vase that has been subject to scientific investigation is the one brought to the UK by Flinders Petrie over a century ago – more on the stunning stone vases below.

11.4 I shall explore this huge and technical subject at a summary level and try to highlight key issues which those interested in digging much deeper may take up to spearhead their own research. There is a great deal of technical analysis now available complete with lavish photographs and drawings. Although a personal visit is also highly instructive. I shall try to focus on five key aspects:

- The Giza pyramids and the Sphinx

- Vast underground structures

- Planning, logistics and construction

- Stonework achievements far beyond tools claimed to have been available

- Wider implications – tool making and energy sources

The Giza pyramids and the Sphinx

11.5 As we have examined in 2.3 to 2.7 above, there are now serious doubts about the conventional dating of the Giza pyramids and the Sphinx. Analysis of the weathering of the surface of the Sphinx, revealing vertical erosion channels, is widely agreed by geologists as caused by rainwater – not flooding as water levels rose but of sustained rainfall over a very long period. Throughout the dynastic period the Sphinx has sat in permanent dry desert conditions but traditional archaeologists ascribe surface weathering to wind borne erosion by particles of sand – which would obviously cause horizontal sculpting. Climatic analysis shows the current desert climate was established around Gaza thousands of years before the start of the dynastic period, and at least since 6000BC. Before 6000BC the rainfall would have been light and failing – for really torrential rainfall one would need to look at the impact events which vented vast quantities of water vapour into the atmosphere. Such events could well have produced biblical downpours lasting 40 days or more. The Hiawatha impact c10765BC and the as yet unnamed twin impacts off the Greek mainland (named as the Kefalonia impacts in this book) which may have occurred around 9620BC, would both have caused torrential downpours. The twin impacts of c9620BC would have first caused a massive tsunami which should have washed over the Sphinx. Evidence of that tsunami may have been eroded by the torrential rain that followed and by the remaining 3 millennia or so of tropical climate rainfall before the weather turned arid.

11.6 The construction of the Sphinx, cut from solid strata of limestone, shows the extraction of limestone blocks measuring up to 10m by 5m by 3m and weighing up to 200 tons. These blocks were used in the foundations of a nearby temple – examination of the blocks reveals layers matching the exposed bedrock of the flanks of the Sphinx. Whilst the surviving temple seems to date from the dynastic period, it may well have reused foundations dating from a much earlier period.

11.7 Traditional Egyptologists attribute the Sphinx to Pharaoh Khafre, c2500BC but the age of the Sphinx has been long disputed, as depictions have been found of a Sphinx in ancient Sumerian and Egyptian art dating back prior to the dynastic pharaonic period – i.e. pre 3200BC. Some have linked Khafre to repair work performed on the outer limestone casing of the Sphinx – suggesting it was already old during Khafre's reign. The Inventory Stela (believed to date only from 670BC but whose age is disputed), includes an intriguing statement that the plans of the image of Hor-em-Akhet were brought to the site of the Sphinx by Khufu – which implies restoration rather than construction work. Oddly, no references to the Sphinx have been found in Egyptian records from Khafre's reign through to Amenhotep II (ruled 1426BC to 1400BC), who also refered to the Sphinx as Hor-em-Akhet (Horus of the Horizon) and similarly refered to the nearby Giza pyramids as the 'Pyramids of Hor-em-Akhet' – note this is only 1000 years after the reigns of Khafre and Khufu, suggesting contemporary records did not associate these pyramids with the pharaohs that conventional historians do today. The references to

Horus chime with the Edfu temple inscriptions speaking of Horus and the establishment of the first grand sacred buildings near Memphis in the aftermath of floods which devasted Egypt around 9620BC.

11.8   Amenhotep II was succeeded by his son, Thutmose IV, who left us the stele recording his dream. The stela describes Thutmose resting under the head of the Sphinx whilst out hunting and in a dream learning that he would take the throne in place of his elder brother if he cleared away the sand almost burying the Sphinx – as they say 'the rest is history'! Once fully revealed, the Sphinx, in conjunction with the three Giza pyramids forms the most impressive sight – so perhaps the absence of any references to the Sphinx throughout the dynastic period prior to Thutmose IV was simply because it had remained buried up to its neck in sand.

11.9   A quick review of the sheer scale and stunning accuracy of the construction of certainly the two largest pyramids, conventionally attributed to Khufu and his son Khafre, strongly point to technology being available which there is no evidence existed in that era (see sections 2.3 to 2.6). These are megalithic structures of the scale and precision only associated with pre flood cultures.

11.10   Two much earlier dates than the conventional dating for the Sphinx have been determined which broadly corroborate each other. Dr Robert Schoch, a geologist, reported to the Geological Society of America in 1991 that meteorological studies of the Sphinx, its weathering, watermarks and its layering, indicated a date for its carving out of solid bedrock must have been earlier than 5000BC and possibly as early as 10000BC. Dr. Thomas L Dobecki, a geophysicist from Houston, and Anthony West, and an Egyptologist from NY also concluded a construction date in the range 5000BC to 7000BC based on the amount of weathering evident in the carved rock making up the body of the Sphinx and the quarry excavated around it. This research has been well reviewed but for years it was rejected as impossible because native Egyptians in this period were believed to be simple hunter gatherers without knowledge, skills or organisation to undertake such a huge project.

11.11   The development of the science of astro-archaeology is slowly changing this view. Astro-archaeology provides a clear date, presumably the completion date or the commemoration cum dedication date – of 9023BC, being star-rise for Regulus, the brightest star in the constellation of Leo, on the vernal equinox. What important past date does Regulus mark in the zodiac's polar precession chronometer and what was its significance? We find that the vernal equinox would have been conjunct the Regulus ecliptic marker in 9023BC. To derive this date properly we must find the exact position of Regulus in this past era. According to the FK5 star catalogue, Regulus has a low proper motion of about 25 seconds of arc per century. Based on its current position and stated proper motion, we find its ancient position in celestial coordinates and then convert this into ecliptic coordinates. This yields an ecliptic longitude and latitude for Regulus of $l = 150.546°$, $b = +0.711°$. To find the past date when the vernal equinox would have had this same ecliptic longitude position, one may use an accurate precession calculator which takes into account changes in the rate of polar precession due to the 40,000 year polar nutation cycle. Applying the precession calculator, one arrives at a date of 9023BC.

11.12 In his book *The Orion Mystery* (1995), Robert Bauval presents the hypothesis that the Sphinx and the three Giza pyramids are a representation of Leo at the vernal equinox and the three stars comprising Orion's Belt. This caused great controversy, as conventional historians could not accept megalithic building skills being practised that far back in antiquity. However, in fact, the argument has more credibility than ascribing the Sphinx to Khafre and is consistent with far earlier dating for megalithic structures elsewhere. Using the exact alignments of the Sphinx and the three Giza pyramids to reflect the relative positions of the three main stars of Orion's belt provides a celestial date lock – Orion's Belt viewed as due north and the Head of Leo being due east at the vernal equinox – only occurs at the start of the Age of Leo. If one allocates exactly 30° of arc to each 'house' of the zodiac, precession gives the Age of Leo as running from 10970BC until 8810BC. Bauval dates the time when the vernal equinox was conjunct with the boundary between the constellations of Leo and Virgo at 10500BC using the assumption of a constant polar precession rate. Using a more accurate assessment of polar precession which takes into account of the nutation cycle, moves the date back to 10700BC. This it might mean construction was partly motivated to commemorate survival of the Hiawatha impact around 10765BC. On this date the eastward facing Sphinx would have been gazing at the constellation of Leo - which at dawn would have been fully positioned above the horizon, its body reclining in a horizontal orientation.

11.13   Regulus is the brightest star in the Leo constellation. Was the Regulus symbology intended to mark the date of the creation of the Giza Sphinx and of the Temple of the Sphinx which was built from megalithic stones excavated from around the Sphinx? If so, for what purpose was it carved? Could the purpose of this construction have been to memorialize this 9023BC date, one that was very significant to our paleo ancestors? What event occurred around this time that was so important that it should be so memorialized with the construction of such a prominent monument?

11.14   One possibility is that this nine millennium BC date was intended to mark the definitive end of the mini ice age and the Younger Dryas period of glacial cold that had gripped the Earth. For 4,000 years prior to that date, Earth had experienced many periods of rapid warming and freezing (the Dryas periods) after the previous glacial ice age, now by around 9000BC perhaps some leaders could see Earth was set fair for a long period of warmer weather, with large new land areas becoming accessible. Based on climatic data from the accurately dated Carico Basin varve record retrieved from the coastal waters of Venezuela, we know that the Younger Dryas mini ice age ended abruptly around 9615BC with a 100 year-long period of unusual warmth which caused rapid melting of the ice sheet, continental flooding, and a rapid rise in the sea level. This flood period spans the date 9600BC which the priests of Sais gave to the ancient Greek ruler Solon as the year of the fabled sinking of Atlantis. This seems an amazingly accurate link between ancient legend and modern geological data.

11.15   For almost 1700 years prior to the 9023BC date, during its passage through Leo with the precession of the equinox, the 'sunrise' vernal equinox pointer had resided beneath Leo. Upon transiting Regulus, this precessional clock pointer metaphorically passed through the breast of Leo and emerged into the day world as it followed a trajectory that took it above the extended paws of the Leo constellation. This is a prosaic way of depicting the Earth's rise out of the ice age.

11.16   In *Earth under Fire*, LaViolette, attributes the onset of the Younger Dryas to a phenomenon he terms 'galactic superwaves', volleys of cosmic rays originating from the centre of our galaxy. A period of hardship, described as occurring 'at the end of the ice age' climaxed with a series of extinction level solar storms, that brought about the mass extinction of the Pleistocene mammals. The largest of these he dates to 10887BC and 10689BC. Whilst I find these descriptions less convincing, for example the mass extinction was limited to areas where the black mat was deposited rather than being global as would have resulted from Earth continuing to spin whilst bathed in ultra violet radiation – the dates mentioned are reasonably accurate for the Hiawatha impact. Also an impact of the scale of Hiawatha would have significantly damaged the ozone layer, at least in the northern hemisphere, thereby increasing radiation levels recorded at ground level.

11.17 The Sphinx date may also mark the approximate time of construction of the Great Pyramid of Giza located to its south. Researcher Roger Cunningham found that the builders of the Great Pyramid left a star constellation map in the ceiling of the air shaft that leads upward from the Queen's chamber toward the pyramid's outer surface. The map appears to be engraved into the rock just above Gantenbrinck's door, a name given to the stone plug that blocks the upper end of the air shaft and which has the remains of two copper 'handles' embedded into the rock plug. The available photo of the shaft ceiling is a bit fuzzy since high resolution photos have not yet been released by the National Geographic Society. However, according to Cunningham the ceiling displays a map of the ancient sky as it would have been seen in 9200BC ± 400 years. Cunningham concluded that the builders of the pyramid had left this map intentionally as a time capsule message marking the date of the pyramid's construction. As we see, within the stated error range, this date matches that of the Regulus time marker.

11.18 To conclude, the weight of evidence that may be drawn from the scale and precision of the construction strongly links the Giza complex to the megalithic building culture, whilst the layout portraying a time stamp of Leo rising at 90° to the three main stars of Orion's Belt seems to verify its age as just after the end of the Younger Dryas period.

Vast underground structures

11.19 Dynastic Egypt developed subterranean vaults beneath many temples, including the majority of the vaults at the Serapeum in Saqqara, but the scale of four examples reviewed below seems very different. I refer to the Egyptian Labyrinth at Hawara, the subterranean spaces beneath the Sphinx, the oldest vaults at the Serapeum and the Osirion at Abidos.

(i) the Egyptian Labyrinth, Hawara

11.20 The Egyptian Labyrinth, beneath the south side of the pyramid of Amenemhet III at Hawara, some 80km south of modern Cairo, was one of the wonders of the ancient world. It was documented by famous Roman and Greek historians – Herodotus, Strabo and Pythagoras. They reported a huge underground complex comprising 3000 rooms laid out within 12 palaces and courtyards on two subterranean levels. Originally rediscovered by Petrie, it was extensively mapped by the Mataha expedition in 2008 using ground penetrating radar. Data from the discovery was published in the scientific journal *MRIAG* and Columbia University sponsored a YouTube, but soon afterwards the Secretary of Egypt's Supreme Council of Antiquities, Dr Zahi Hawass, suspended all disclosure. After some time, the Mataha Expedition researchers decided to share their incredible discoveries with the world by creating a thematic website. But Egyptian officials continue to block all further exploration – something very bizarre as, quite apart from the benefit to mankind of understanding early civilisations, one might think the benefits to tourism and the image of Egypt would trigger exactly the opposite reaction.

(ii) Hall of Records beneath the Sphinx

11.21 Herodotus (c484BC to c425BC) also referred to there being access between the paws of the Sphinx to huge chambers including a Hall of Records containing details of ancient history and of construction plans for major projects. Herodotus description of the subterranean galleries beneath the Sphinx were corroborated by the writings of Iamblichus (245AD to 325AD), a widely travelled Syrian philosopher. Iamblichus wrote of an entry between the paws of the Sphinx, leading to underground passageways entering into vast chambers beneath the Sphinx and also into the Great Pyramid.

11.22 Nothing more was heard about subterranean spaces under the Sphinx until last century. An Egyptian archaeologist, Salim Hassan (1886-1961), excavated areas on the Giza plateau for a decade from 1929 to 1939 by which time he had been appointed deputy of the Egyptian Antiquities Service responsible for the care of all monuments in the Nile Valley. Hamilton Wright, an American working with Hassan, wrote articles published in the US and UK reporting he had discovered a huge subway system, with shafts and chambers descending 40m. Rivalries probably explain why the Egyptian authorities put a gagging order on any further announcements and unfortunately further work soon finished due to the outbreak of war. Rather weirdly, Edgar Cayce, the famous American clairvoyant (1877 to 1945), had predicted the discovery of a large underground network of tunnels a few years previously, in 1932. Cayce went on to predict the discovery of a Hall of Records beneath the paws of the Sphinx, claiming it would be rediscovered in the 1990's and found to hold information on the origin of mankind and the history of Atlantis – red meat to conspiracy theorists who have made lots of YouTube videos claiming discoveries made by ground penetrating radar!

11.23 In actions almost designed to fuel the conspiracy theories, Dr Zahi Hawass, previously in charge of access to all historical sites, seemed to respond to the breathless YouTubes by commencing excavations himself, right next to the Sphinx. Soon after he announced discovery of shafts and released a short video teasing about what might lie below. Equally suddenly he then announced the work was terminated and gave no explanation – but four access points on the top and around the sides of the Sphinx were then cemented over. These actions by the authorities, defy rational understanding – what is the perceived risk? Either, nothing is found that changes conventional explanations of Egyptian history – and Dr Hawass is vindicated. Or, he could have been celebrated for all time as the hero who discovered Egypt's history is far greater than currently believed – the evidence collated in my humble book points to a technically more advanced culture than the Greeks or Romans existing along the Nile 12,000 years ago. Arguably, this would be the most important historical discovery ever made!! It is widely recognised that professional archaeologists tend to date artifacts by reference to what they are found with and what may be written about them but it seems perverse that opinions from other disciplines are routinely dismissed if they challenge the conventional interpretation. It is particularly surprising that many controlling Egyptian museums and archaeological sites routinely block access to promising new excavations and even non-invasive scientific investigation of artifacts. One might assume that Egyptians controlling access to sites and treasures would leap at the prospect of Egypt's civilisation being reset to date more than twice as old as currently claimed. Perhaps they worry about having to re-catalogue some items!! Understandably, the web is hot with rumours.

11.24 Moreover, it is worth noting that the Edfu Temple texts also refer to a Hall of Records as being used by the followers of Horus – as a depository for the construction plans of the Sphinx and the Giza pyramids as well as other major construction projects. This also ties in with a reference found describing Pharaoh Khufu utilising drawings found in the Hall of Records to carry out repair work following a lightning strike damaging the Sphinx, circa 2570BC.

(iii) the Serapeum, Saqqara

11.25 The Serapeum temple complex at Saqqara, some 25km south of Cairo, sits above a vast subterranean network of what are generally believed to be burial chambers – for sacred bulls, cats and ibis. The oldest part of the complex contains enormous granite coffins of exquisite manufacture which barely fit the presumed burial chambers in which they are positioned. I describe these as presumed burial chambers because no evidence at all has been found that these special granite coffins have ever been used – although conventional history describes their use as being for internment of mummified sacred bulls.

11.26 Well known to classical scholars from the Renaissance period onwards as being famous in Greek and Roman times, even Napoleon sought to locate the Serapeum at Saqqara but he failed. It was not rediscovered until 1850 by Auguste Mariette and has been progressively excavated ever since. The underground burial vaults are vast. Tunnels mined out of solid rock link hundreds of burial chambers.

11.27 The Serapeum was the main site of the Apis cult which worshipped bulls especially selected for their black and while colouring with particular white patches. At death, the bulls were ceremonially mummified and buried on stone plinths or in wooden coffins. Some 67 Apis bulls have been identified, with dating stretching over a period of 1400 years. The cows from which the selected bulls were born were also revered and buried in underground vaults. There are also sections of the vaults where large numbers of mummified cats and ibis have been found. Temple records indicate which pharaoh initiated the various extensions to the underground vaults for cows, cats etc.

11.28 One section of the vaults is different and raises many questions. This section contains 24 huge granite stone boxes with closely fitting lids, some barely fitting into the underground chambers. The stone boxes vary in dimensions but the granite stone is outstandingly finished. The boxes measure between 3m and 4m in length and around 2.5m in width. Heights vary between 3m and 4m. These colossal stone boxes weigh around 75 tons each, with lids weighing around 30 tons each, and yet were quarried from Aswan, over 500 km distant. The internal and external surfaces are incredibly flat – measured by a precision straight edge as being accurate to 0.005mm. All the corners are filleted, surfaces are square and parallel to each other, and surfaces are flat vertically and horizontally – both internally and externally. Removal of the internal stone to finish with perfectly smooth, polished, rectangular internal surfaces reveals astonishing manufacturing skills.

11.29 The weight of the stones quarried must have been between 600 and 800 tonnes each prior to their being hollowed out. The 'machining' of the boxes must have been close to their resting place in the Serapeum, but could not have been carried out in the cramped and dark underground resting places. The clearance for some boxes within their chambers is only around 30cm – raising questions of how the boxes could even have been inserted into the spaces. What were these boxes for ? They appear to be coffins, and it is claimed they were also for sacred bulls – but no mummies or anything else were found in any of these monster coffins. What kind of tomb robbers would raid the tombs of mummified bulls – even if the mummies were covered with gold cloth, who would bother to cart away all the bones of a mummified bull? Plenty of less grand coffins and plinths accommodating mummified bulls remained largely undisturbed – so why are the special granite boxes found completely empty? The resource that must have committed to manufacturing and placing these 24 huge and exquisitely produced coffins in the underground chambers seems totally out of proportion.

11.30 The conventional explanation is that all the coffins were used for burial of sacred bulls of the Apis cult at Memphis. These bulls were believed to be reincarnations of the god Ptah, which upon the bull dying then became immortal as 'Osiris-Apis'. The adoption of bulls as representing the reincarnated god must reflect the cult being prominent during the age of Taurus – c4300BC to c2150BC. This seems strange as Osiris was held to be a great, great grandson of Ptah – why would a very senior god, Ptah no less (aka Enki) reincarnate as a bull? Surely, Ptah, who passed over long, long ago would already be immortal – why the need to live as a bull and only afterwards gain immortality and as his great,

great grandson Osiris – what happens to the existing Osiris – also long dead and also immortal in 'heaven'? The conventional explanation smells of poor translation. Furthermore, the whole idea is undermined by the complete absence of any mummified bulls in the special coffins. Finally, why would the bulls get such grand coffins, far larger than they need, when even some of the greatest pharaohs got tightly fitting wooden coffins?

11.31 Considered rationally, these huge granite boxes could not have been produced during the dynastic age of Egypt but far earlier when advanced pre Hiawatha technology was available. The perfection, the size and the underground positioning in vaults does strongly suggest they were intended as burial chambers but for larger beings – perhaps the 'renown men of old'!

11.32 The question raised in my mind is why the ancient Egyptians would put so much effort into constructing underground facilities. One might assume reasons of durability and safety but whereas early man liked to use caves for shelter from the weather, safety from wild animals and maybe from other local groups competing for resources – the Egyptian state would not share these concerns. The experience of living through the Dryas periods, between c14000BC and c9600BC, when the probable explanation for the multiple cycles of abrupt climate change are a series of cataclysmic meteor impacts – would have led to fear of destruction from the skies. The best protection would clearly be to go underground. So, perhaps this points to the oldest parts of the Serapeum dating back to during or shortly after the Dryas Periods?

(iv) Osirion, Abidos

11.33 This temple like construction was first rediscovered in 1912 but serious excavation work only proceeded during the 1920's. The intriguing design includes massive granite blocks weighing around 80 tons which must have been moved circa 8km uphill from the Nile. The most surprising aspect is the inner core of the site, which comprises a rectangular 'island' measuring 22m by 15m. This has been found to extend down 15m below the surface of the surrounding water – so the visible area is, in effect, on top of a five storey construction. Repeated attempts have been made to pump out the water surrounding the island – the most recent using powerful modern pumps extracting 500 gallons an hour – yet the water level barely changed. The construction seems to be sitting atop a spring – how could such a tower have been constructed on top of such a strong natural spring?

Planning, documentation and logistics

11.34 Firstly, let's consider planning. The stupendous scale of the Giza pyramids, and also the excavation of extensive underground facilities, would have required planning, computational and logistical skills which we would find impossible without the use of computers. The largest Giza pyramid required an estimated 2.3 million blocks averaging 1 cubic metre after finishing - estimate by Sir Flinders Petrie. Each block had to be hewn from bedrock, transported hundreds of kilometres and at some point finished to a large variety of precise dimensions before being hauled up into positions where they all fitted with extreme precision. Finishing must presumably have been done at the construction site so that the correct flow of individual blocks ascended in the right sequence. Working back, hewing blocks from the bedrock must have been planned to ensure a steady supply of different sizes for finishing whilst cut to rough sizing to minimise the time required for finishing and to reduce the weight transported. Loading and unloading the dhows used to sail the blocks downstream would have been very skilled work.

11.35 Most of the blocks used in pyramid construction are relatively small, 'only' 2.3 metric tons and quarried from a distance of around 500km. However, many statutes at Tanis, identified as quarried at Aswan must have weighed up to 1000 metric tons and have been transported over 1000km – and there are hundreds of huge granite columns at Tanis.

11.36 Documentation and communications. Drawing up the detailed plans using lead and papyrus, calculating stress and loadbearing, checking the details fit together and then producing the minimum number of copies for the various key construction leaders would have required an army of scribes.

11.37 Measurements and alignments. We are told the Egyptians used wooden rods, string and celestial measurements to align their buildings – yet the alignments of the pyramids are perfected to an incredible degree. A few years ago it was discovered that the four faces of the Giza pyramids are each slightly concave presenting two equal faces to catch the light at a precise moment in the day. This would have greatly complicated the construction of each course of blocks.

11.38 Today we use modern sophisticated measurement devices to capture the amazing accuracy of alignments, the smoothness of stone surfaces, etc. Aside from achieving amazing accuracy, alignment and smoothness - how did the ancient Egyptians determine that they had achieved their target precision? The degree of accuracy achieved is far higher than can be detected by the naked eye. So, not only did they have precision tools far more advanced than conventionally admitted but also very precise measuring devices.

11.39 Nowadays extreme levels of accuracy in dimensions and smoothness are largely dictated by function. What functional applications did the Egyptians intend for some of the extremely precise surfaces and shapes – some have suggested they had mastered the use of sound waves in way we have not yet fathomed? Pride in workmanship and reverence for the designated prospective entity (god, pharaoh or other) seem to have been sky high!

11.40 Artificial lighting. Having noted the scale and importance attached to underground facilities noted above and also the hundreds of tombs – how were these excavated, finished and in most cases given extensive fine graphics, hieroglyphs and painted walls and ceilings which must have been worked on for weeks – yet, in many of these installations, no trace of soot from oil or other fuels used to light the pitch dark interiors has been found.

Stonework achievements far beyond tools available

11.41 Stonemasons and engineers have highlighted numerous inconsistencies in the traditional explanations of Egyptologists. Conventional history attempts explanations based on use of copper tools, laborious grinding and polishing plus the use of logs and ropes to achieve construction of huge but exquisite monuments. A demonstration trying to use copper tools for working granite showed the copper tools wore away as fast or faster than the granite being worked on!! If using only copper tools, the Egyptians would have consumed more copper than the entire world does today – clearly they did not use copper tools.

11.42 Three aspects standout as impossible with the tools conventionally taught as being used by ancient Egyptians and where the evidence presented in stone strongly points to the use of power tools – cutting, drilling and polishing.

11.43 **Cutting of stone.** Perfect straight cuts abound, both external and even more astoundingly, internal, with smooth right angle surfaces – cutting will often cause chipping which cannot be filed or polished away, it creates gaps – yet these cuts are not only precisely straight but also crisp and clean. The perfect internal right angled corners defy explanation.

11.44 **Circular saws.** Evidence for the use of massive circular or swing saws has been found in quarries at Aswan. This makes much more sense than the traditional explanation that copper chisels and pounders were used to cut out rough obelisks weighing up to 1000 tons. One amazing example clearly shows a circular saw cut with a diameter of 30 metres (!), yet the ridge at the outer edge points to a blade thickness of just a few millimetres! When water is poured over the smooth cut surface it reveals the striations which clearly indicate use of a saw blade. Cutting stone by the use of copper chisels and grinding surfaces with copper bars and sand leaves completely different striation marks.

11.45 **Symmetry.** Monuments and statutes of pharaohs from all dynasties abound. Measurements have shown that the two sides of the faces of many of the oldest statutes have amazing levels of symmetry. On some statutes, the polished finish achieved to all parts of the face is not only astonishing but the two sides when separately measured, reversed and placed one over the other show startling symmetry. Achieving the finish and the symmetry with the tools claimed to have been used beggars belief.

11.46 Normally, a pharaonic attribution is emblazoned on such statutes, but often the quality of the stone working of the royal cartouche is markedly cruder than the statute upon which the name has been chiselled out. It is visually obvious that the technology used to apply the dedication fails to match the technology employed in making the statute itself. One can readily understand pharaohs trying to recapture past glories by repurposing legacy artifacts.

11.47 **Machining of stone vases.** Tens of thousands of exquisite stone vases have been unearthed, astonishingly some 40,000 from under the step pyramid of Djoser, a 3rd dynasty pharaoh ruling c2670BC to 2650BC. Whilst some other discoveries are attributed to later pharaohs, it is conventionally thought that production of stone vases ceased until the 10th century BC when alabaster vases started to be produced from gypsum and calcite – a much softer stone, far easier to work than those found in Djoser's pyramid. What stands out in the conventional explanation is that after 2000 years of further development of Egyptian culture and the adoption of a far softer stone – the finished product in alabaster is clearly inferior in finish than the much older vases, crafted in much harder stone, from Djoser's pyramid collection.

11.48 The vases found at Djoser are made of granite, diorite, conundrum and even lapis lazuli. Not only are these extremely hard materials – conundrum is rated second only to diamond, but the vases were in many cases produced to extremely fine thickness – Petrie famously described a stone vase he found as being the thickness of a playing card. How were these made? Conventionally, the answer is using the type of hand turned wheel illustrating the production of alabaster vases from far softer material at least 2000 years later! Crafting the perfectly smooth curved surface both outside and inside these stone vases, certainly to the finished thickness stated by Petrie would require a computer numerical control machine. The vast cache found under the Djoser pyramid was clearly not made during his reign.

11.49 One claim relating to a stone vase warrants verification. Excavations at Toshka yielded a stone vase containing some organic material which when radio carbon dated is claimed to be 17,000 years old. Upon reading this, I looked for evidence of carbon dating of anything found in the 40000 vases under Djoser pyramid – but only found comments that no permission for scientific analysis of any vases from there has been approved.

11.50 **Machining of stone columns.** The vast Egyptian temple complexes contain thousands of stone columns varying in length from 8m up to 24m. These columns tend to fall into two distinct types – columns made from sandstone blocks stacked up on top of each other (clearly within capability of the dynastic period) and columns of solid granite and basalt. Tanis is littered with granite columns, mostly fallen and broken into pieces, which appear to have been manufactured as single columns, the majority being around 15m tall. The top of these columns have beautiful palm leaf motives which increase the diameter of the column to some 2.5m. This suggests the original hewn slabs must have had dimensions approaching 3m square and 15m long – a stone of this dimension would weigh about 340 tons. Apart from the precision of the finished product the top and foot of the columns clearly show central circular insets – pointing to having been turned on a massive lathe to be worked. The mind boggles at the idea of a lathe capable of holding and turning a stone weighing 340 tons!!

11.51   I could not find data on how many single piece granite columns have been found in Egypt but clearly, from what we see today, there is evidence that many thousands were made. If these were crafted using hand tools the work would have left little resource to grow wheat! Therefore some mechanised process must have been available.

11.52   **Tube drilling.** Many examples of what appear to be drill holes have been found in ancient quarries and on the oldest artifacts. A number of factors stand out as extraordinary:

- The drill holes found in various solid stone boxes are often flush with inside corners – something technically challenging as the chuck holding the drill has, by definition, to be wider than the drill itself;

- The diameter of holes drilled ranges up to 20cm into granite, basalt and diorite – again challenging even today;

- The speed of drilling into granite has been calculated at up to 500 times what we achieve today with diamond tipped drills.

11.53   **Drilling** – there are numerous examples of perfectly round holes drilled into extremely hard stone objects, flush with recessed internal corners. This is an extremely challenging task as the drill bit clamping the drill core cannot proceed beyond the outer lip of the article. This suggests both the object being drilled and the drilling device were firmly held in the vice of a single machine of substantial dimensions.

11.54   One of the artifacts brought to the British Museum by Flinders Petrie is labelled as 'Core No 7'. It is the broken off core of a drilled hole. What caught Petrie's eye was the spiral groove around the core. He rightly recognized this attribute as extraordinary. Unlike modern drills which rotate at high speed and grind down the middle core of the hole being drilled, it appeared that Egyptian technology drilled a circular ring in just a few rotations – leaving a single spiral groove. That Egyptian technology could drill into granite and diorite at such a rate is astounding – and has been calculated as 500 times faster than modern drills. Frustratingly, the new breed of engineers and researchers trying to study ancient Egyptian technology have not been granted permission to even take plaster casts of the inside surfaces of other drill holes in artifacts in Egyptian possession. We are lucky that, in the 19th Century, Petrie was not bound by such regulations.

11.55 I too was dubious of the 500 times faster claim. I deduced the claim is based upon the rate the drill chews through the material. The Petrie core shows the groove cut by the drill cutting about two revolutions per centimetre. Modern diamond tipped high speed drills used on hard stone, after initially penetrating the surface slowly, are run at a huge range of speeds – I have found quotes from 3,000rpm to 20,000rpm. For ease of comparison, let's assume a modest 6,000rpm – which equates to 100 revolutions per second. Personally, I do not regularly drill into granite, let alone basalt or diorite, but I can readily accept it could take 10 seconds to drill to a depth of 1cm. Thus, even with a relatively modest modern drill speed, it would take 1000 revolutions of the drill to chew 1cm versus 2 revolutions indicated by Petrie's core.

11.56 To penetrate these extremely hard stones as though cutting through butter, makes one wonder if the technology was quite different – maybe laser, high pressure water or sound waves. But the physical mark of the spiral groove would point to use of a solid hard material – a type of drill, maybe tipped with an alloy we have not discovered yet.

11.57 I must also note that a truly astonishing hollow tube of lapis lazuli has been recovered, partially wrapped with filigree gold leaf – illustrating the ability to undertake extremely delicate and precise drilling.

Polishing of stone

11.58 Ancient Egyptian stonemasons seemed to favour extremely hard stone – granite, basalt and corundum. To appreciate the relative hardness, these materials are rated 7, 8 and 9 on the Mohs Hardness scale – where steel is 6 and diamond is 10. And yet, many ancient Egyptian artifacts, produced from single pieces of such hard stone, are finished to a level of smoothness that when measured today are astonishing. Some polished surfaces have maximum imperfections limited to 30 microns – given there are 1 million microns in a metre, that is within 3% of a millimetre. This is far less than can be detected with the naked eye. According to conventional Egyptologists, these ancient stonemasons had no way of measuring to anything near the accuracy they achieved.

11.59　The conventional explanation that surfaces were smoothed by grinding sand over the stone surfaces fails to explain the smoothness of the surfaces, the incredible perfection of flat surfaces or the incredible polish achieved to the surfaces.

11.60　Hard volcanic stone is very difficult to polish yet the high polish brightly reflecting light was achieved not just on flat surfaces but on variably curved surfaces and delicate features such as eyelids and finger nails. Moreover, the finish achieved on ancient statues, which are claimed to date back as far as 3000BC, do still in many cases brightly reflect light. In fact, from the research we are now reviewing it seems likely the polished surfaces have survived their reflectivity over more than twice that length of time – dating back to at least 11000BC.

11.61　By comparison, modern specialist granite polishing falls far short of these measures. In 1958, sections of a new Cairo monument, named Egypt Rising, were sent to a specialist Italian stone company for polishing. However, only 50 years later the reflective finish is reported to have completely faded away.

11.62　The only plausible explanation is that the numerous statues, stone boxes and stone vases present evidence that is impossible to attribute to the simple soft metal tools, stone pounders and grinding and polishing by use of grains of sand. Clearly a technically more advanced culture must have been responsible for these artifacts. And yet, we find no remains of any sophisticated tools and equipment. This points to the evidence having been swept away with the culture – quite likely by the tsunami estimated at 800m high, created by the twin impacts now identified off the Greek coast which are likely to have swept up the Nile valley and far beyond the modern border with Sudan. Such a scenario seems to be corroborated by the Edfu Building texts and the history related to Solon by the priests of the Temple of Sais. The quotes attributed to what Solon learned from the priests at Sais, do not refer to destruction along the Nile but this does not preclude whether this was discussed. The location of the Temple of Sais lies midway between the Mediterranean coast and Cairo - so any tsunami making landfall there would have completely obliterated any pre-existing temple.

11.63 A very erudite source of further information and visual evidence of these types of tool working is Ben van Kerkwyk who has published a number of videos about this on YouTube.

Wider implications – tool making and energy sources

11.64 We have identified hard evidence that tooling used in the manufacture of some artifacts was far more advanced than traditionally ascribed to any stage of the dynastic period. However, not only do we lack any examples of advanced tooling being recovered but we see no representations of advanced tooling or manufacturing in the copious records and drawings remaining from the dynastic period. This points to the very existence of these advanced tools ***predating*** the dynastic period. Only catastrophic devastation could have removed all traces of advanced tooling and manufacturing facilities from the entire Nile valley – so that no trace remained in the dynastic period.

11.65 However, there is one extraordinary artifact, which looks like a skilful copy of an ancient spare part from an advanced machine, the Schist Disc - more on this below.

11.66 The absence of any advanced tools raises two further fundamental issues. How were such tools themselves manufactured? Where were the machine shops and toolmaking facilities? It is difficult not to think in terms of a metallurgical basis for the production of the tools required for the artifacts we have inherited. Why, apart from these artifacts, are there no remains of any advanced culture? Given the extent of archaeological excavations in various parts of Egypt, something should have emerged. Maybe the Hall of Records, when eventually opened up, will provide compelling evidence or at least an explanation?

11.67 As we have seen, there also seems to have been use of an energy source – to power tools and to provide lighting   as well as for metallurgy and for toolmaking. Again, so far we have identified no technical remains, no visual representations and no written references. The answer must be that all traces were swept away and now lie buried under sand and silt.

11.68 Magical theories abound – anti gravity devices, geo-polymerisation of stone so that it becomes pliable. Yet a moments thought should cause such ideas to be dismissed – it is difficult to think of anti-gravity devices which would not comprise metals and need metal smelting and toolmaking. Granite and diorite, widely used in the extraordinary artifacts are composite stones comprising different materials compressed together – the partial liquification envisioned by geo-polymerisation would cause visible changes of the appearance of the veins typical of these types of stone which are just not seen.

11.69 How could the evidence of an advanced civilisation be completely wiped away? As we have explored in this book, the Hiawatha impact would have caused a global nuclear winter with no sunlight for a few years. If vegetation stopped growing, the absence of crops would cause mass starvation and societal collapse. Many manufacturing facilities would have been abandoned. Then around 1200 years later, a huge tsunami swept up the Nile sweeping away any remaining traces.

Schist Disc

11.70 The Schist Disc was found by British Egyptologist Brian Emery in 1936 while excavating the tomb of Prince Sabu – who died c3000BC. It was found among typical funerary objects - canopic jars, knives, arrows, copper tools. Emery listed the item as 'a container in the form of a schist bowl'.

11.71 The Schist Disc looks like the steering wheel of a truck, it is perfectly circular with a diameter of 61cm. It has a thicker outer rim and a thin solid interior 1cm thick from which it looks as though three curved sections have been cut and bent back to provide hand holds. The centre of the disc has an opening with a collar that would appear to function as the receptacle for the axis of a wheel or perhaps a central hub designed to fit onto a driveshaft. Your first impression is that this must be an engineered machine part – so far it is unique and it seems completely out of place in an ancient Egyptian tomb.

11.72 The Schist Disc would not appear to serve any purpose on its own, neither functional nor ceremonial – its utility must have been as part of a machine. And yet, it has been exquisitely produced out of a delicate stone material!!

11.73 The name of the material, schist, reflects from the ease with which it can easily be split along the lateral plane. Derived from clay and mud being transformed by heat and pressure into shale then slate and into phyllite, most schists are made of mica, graphite and chlorite.

11.74 Logic suggests this amazingly carved artifact was a replication of an older metallic object. Furthermore, the material of the object itself rules out it being made with crude copper or bronze tools. Cutting this shape out of a brittle stone such as schist is itself an incredible achievement but clearly far too brittle and delicate to have been intended for use as part of a machine. With mechanical equipment the disc would be easy to produce and replicate – in steel.

11.75 And perhaps most importantly, why would the Egyptians invest the time, tools and skills needed to create this object if it didn't serve a specific and very significant purpose? The current label of 'incense container' given to the Schist Disc in the Egyptian Museum of Cairo is clearly risible - it clearly not a designed as a container of anything.

11.76 Since discovery in 1936, nearly a century of conjecture has naturally concluded that it is proof of alien visitation or that there must have been a technically advanced civilisation in Egypt in the past.

The Schist Disc rediscovered in 1936

EGYPTIAN ENGINEERING POINTS TO AN EARLIER ADVANCED CULTURE

Conclusion on engineering

11.77   To conclude, all the articles referred to above which seem impossible to ascribe to Egyptian workmanship from the dynastic period must have survived from an earlier, more technologically advanced culture. These artifacts represent a legacy from that civilisation.

Construction in Egypt's Asian territories – Baalbek and Jerusalem

11.78   Records show Baalbek was regarded by the Romans as an ancient and holy place. Local Arab legends regard Baalbek as so ancient that they link it with Cain and Abel. Its name derives from 3000 years ago, when the Phoenicians worshipped Baal at Baalbek. Later the Ptolemy's, who ruled Egypt from 305BC until Cleopatra, renamed Baalbek "Heliopolis", City of the Sun, with clear religious overtones. The Israelites referred to Baalbek as 'Beth-Shemesh', the abode of Shamash – Shamash being associated with the Sun and, in one Psalm, clearly identified as being one and the same as Yahweh – at least during the Monarchical period (c1000BC to 596BC).

11.79   In 27BC, Emperor Augustus decided to build the largest and grandest temple of the Empire at Baalbek, a fairly remote location within the Roman Empire. Using the huge Baalbek platform gave the Temple of Jupiter an imposing appearance – the temple and courtyard being atop a huge retaining wall containing 27 giant limestone blocks. All the blocks in the retaining wall weigh over 300 tons and the three largest weigh more than 800 tons each – world renown as the "Trilithon". Augustus choice of Baalbek, a small town on the trading route to Damascus, on its way through the Bekaa Valley was very unusual. It has been noted that such lavish architecture for a remote location was unusual - as all the grandest projects were normally reserved for Rome.

11.80   Some have suggested that the large foundation platform was built by the Romans but this is unlikely. The massive blocks forming what now appears to be a huge U shaped retaining wall effectively provide a curtain around the temple platform. Although the Temple of Jupiter is the largest temple ever erected by the Romans, it does not stretch far enough to use the curtain wall as a foundation – which begs the question of why the Romans would have even bothered to build such a massive curtain wall and then not use it to support anything – it would be completely pointless.

11.81 Records show that the Romans had great difficulty moving weights of more than 300 tons. More than three centuries after Augustus, Constantine ordered an Egyptian obelisk be transported to his newly built city of Constantinople but he died before it arrived. His son diverted the 323 ton Lateran obelisk to Rome but also died before it could be delivered – finally after 50 years it was erected in the Circus Maximus in AD357. Roman engineers had tried to move the 455 ton Thutmose obelisk but could not even budge it from its plinth. Secondly, the appearance of the larger foundation stones clearly shows far greater erosion than the indisputably Roman construction – which indicates a far earlier construction date. There must have been an earlier culture of megalithic builders with some technology we no longer understand – but who were they and what happened to them?

11.82 The final nail in the theory of Roman construction (or anyone else we know of) of the curtain wall, are the unused blocks from the nearby quarry from which the Trilithons came. One largely separated block, long visible, known as the Stone of the Pregnant Woman is estimated at 970 tons – why would the Romans have devoted so much labour to quarrying something nearly 3 times heavier than they could move? Recent excavations at the quarry site have now revealed even larger, partly quarried, blocks – one unearthed in 1990 is estimated at 1242 tons and another unearthed in 2015 is estimated at 1650 tons.

11.83 Also, one might ask, how could the ancient Egyptians transport and erect such huge obelisks that Roman engineering skills could not budge?

11.84 Whilst we have no documentary evidence indicating the age of Baalbek, there are a number of possible associations with the megalithic structures at Giza. The Canaanite tablets recovered from Ugarit refer to the Sphinx as either Huaron or Hurna, denoting a falcon (Horus). Two noted Egyptologists, Selim Hassan (who led excavations at Giza from 1929 to 1939) and Christiane Zivie-Coche of UCLA, both refer to inscriptions at Giza where the term Hurna is added as part of the name of Horus. Alex Whitaker, ancient-wisdom.com, has identified an intriguing coincidence – Baalbek is exactly 4 degrees north and 5 degrees east of Giza, which creates an angle of 51°51' from true north, the exact angle of the exterior faces of the Giza pyramids. That the construction and purpose of Baalbek and Giza may in some way be linked fits the general feel of both sets of enigmatic remains - but provides no answers.

11.85 Another intriguing factoid links with Baalbek. From our earliest records, the local people have always been pioneering navigators – as early as 3000BC, the Canaanites helped the Egyptians develop seaborne trade from what we now call Lebanon. During the second millennium BC, the Canaanites were trading all over the Mediterranean. The Ugarit cuneiform tablets tell of navigation skills based upon the use of special magnetic stones, which were stored for safe keeping at Baalbek. The Canaanites in Lebanon seem to have survived the 1177BC invasion by the Greek Sea Peoples and swiftly re-emerged as a trading power known as the Phoenicians, inventing the world's first alphabet c1050BC. Soon the Phoenicians broke out of the Mediterranean and founded settlements along the Atlantic coast of Portugal, venturing as far as Britain where they purchased ropes, tin and lead from what today is Cornwall and Dorset. They founded Carthage at the surprisingly early date of 814BC. Even today, communities of Lebanese are to be found worldwide and they remain recognised as expert traders.

11.86 Apart from the seemingly ancient but still undated Baalbek Terrace, the only other possible structure qualifying as megalithic anywhere in the Fertile Crescent is the foundation structure used today by the Al Aqsa mosque and the Wailing Wall. This is attributed, without any evidence, to Solomon. The Old City part of Jerusalem was built over three hills – Mounts Moriah, Zophim and Zion. According to the biblical record, Mount Moriah has always been regarded as sacred, it was the site of the First and Second Temple and currently, the Al Aqsa Mosque. Recent excavations have revealed that the natural bedrock of Mount Moriah slopes considerably from north to south. It has been estimated that the original c90,000 square metre platform was supported by infill averaging a depth of about 20 metres. This would have required an estimated 1.7 million cubic metres of infill beneath the original platform. Such an effort would have been a gigantic task – yet the Bible is completely silent about this. By comparison, the biblical record describes in enormous detail every dimension, material and size shape of the Temple building and the material. weight and design of every utensil in the Temple. In stark contrast, 2 Samuel and 1 Kings describe in great detail the infilling undertaken to make the small extension of the base of the City of David, built on Mount Zion, to extend it towards the sacred platform on Mount Moriah. Yet, while the much smaller extension to Mount Zion is portrayed as a huge project, the biblical record is silent about the project to build the platform beneath the Temple. One can only conclude that the platform on which the Temple was built was already pre-existing – and its construction clearly required logistics more suited to the builders of Baalbek than the Israelites in David's time.

11.87   After Israel captured the whole city in the Six Day War of 1967, Israeli archaeologists have gradually cleared away millennia of building and constructions obscuring the Wailing Wall remnant of the original Temple. What is today an underground tunnel but in Roman times was an open air street, has been excavated revealing yet another example of the ancient stonework being the best dressed and most monumental. The beautifully dressed ashlars revealed in the lowest courses of stonework along the Western Wall comprise stone blocks of huge size – the largest blocks with estimated weights of 355, 570 and 600 tons. Given that even the Romans (see section 11.81 above) could barely move 300 ton blocks, it is clearly impossible for David's new kingdom to have constructed the temple platform.

Mummification – perfected long before the dynastic era

11.88   Recent examination of mummification ingredients and their sourcing has produced results which seriously undermine conventional history which claims Egyptian culture originated under the 1st Dynasty, around 3300BC.

11.89   Researchers compared the chemical composition of a mummy which is radiocarbon dated to 3600BC, i.e. before the 1st Dynasty, with another dating from the 26th Dynasty (664BC to 525BC) and were amazed to find the forensic test results showed the two used near identical ingredients and in neaar identical proportions. This strongly suggests that the embalming recipe was developed and finessed to the stage where it was judged to be perfect - a few centuries prior to the first pharaoh!!

11.90   In article published in the *Journal of Archaeological Science* in 2018, a team led by Dr Stephen Buckley, an archaeologist from the University of York, reported on analysis of a pre-dynastic mummy held in The Egyptian Museum in Turin, Italy. They identified the chemical fingerprint of every ingredient whilst stating that each element could have come from a number of sources.

11.91   Meanwhile another team of researchers were trying to identify the source of these ingredients – what they found was astonishing. In 2016, an Egyptian scientist, Ramadan Hussein, discovered an underground embalming workshop at Saqqara. The workshop, now 12 metres below ground, dates to Egypt's 26th Dynasty (664-525 BC), a time of Babylonian and Persian regional influence when Egyptian power was waning. In early 2023, researchers published results of biochemical analysis of the composition of embalming compounds found in 31 ceramic vessels at the workshop. These vessels were labelled with names common to even more ancient texts and included instructions as to the use of each compound.

11.92 The effectiveness of the embalming technology in preserving skin and preventing decomposition reveals a surprisingly deep knowledge of microbial biology. Philipp Stockhammer of the Ludwig Maximilian University, Munich, published an analysis of the source of the ingredients in *Nature*. Most of the substances were not native to Egypt. Many came from the eastern Mediterranean region – such as cedar oil, juniper and cypress oil and tar, bitumen and olive oil. But surprisingly some substances were sourced from much further away – gum from the dammar tree from forests in the Western Ghats (India), Malaysia and Indonesia; and, resin of the elemi tree native to The Philippines.

11.93 A co-author of the study, Maxime Rageot of the University of Tübingen, noted that whilst there have been numerous studies of Egyptian embalming, our lack of knowledge of which names were given to which substances and the lack of practical process descriptions have limited our understanding. She gives an example, a substance referred to as 'antiu' in ancient texts had long had been translated as either frankincense or myrrh resin. This study revealed it to be a mixture of cedar oil, juniper, cypress oil and animal fats. Three recipes, with ingredients such as elemi resin, pistachio resin, by-products of juniper or cypress and beeswax, were identified for embalming the head. Other recipes were used for skin softening or body cleaning. Ancient Egyptians knew how to select and mix antimicrobial substances which enabled perfect skin preservation.

11.94 Embalming was carried out in a well-organized, institutional way, supported by an effective international trading organisation to source the multitude of materials utilised. Moreover this well organised sourcing supported the application of a standardised recipe established before 3600BC. For the embalming recipe and processes to have become standardised, presupposes a lengthy period of experimentation over a period of literally centuries for the results to be confirmed.

11.95　Whilst the Harappan Indus Valley culture in what is now Pakistan and northwest India has been connected to the Sumerians, the rise of this culture is only dated from 3300BC. Yet it seems the Egyptians were trading with peoples in The Philippines long before that? How did the Egyptians stumble upon the useful properties of resin from the elemi tree growing in The Philippines? Nowadays research operations of big pharma routinely test the properties of natural flora from exotic corners of the world – but the pre dynastic Egyptians supposedly lacked physical access, analytical tools and computerised testing? Neither could they contract DeepMind to forecast the protein shapes required to establish critical functions of their formula.

11.96　Supposedly primitive stone age hunter gatherers are unlikely to have been able to sample and test myriad combinations of leaves, roots, flowers, resin, bark, etc from thousands of species from across half the world. The origins of Egyptian embalming recipes must lie in an earlier culture equipped with some scientific resources and a far flung trading empire.

EGYPTIAN ENGINEERING POINTS TO AN EARLIER ADVANCED CULTURE

12

Sumerians – legacy knowledge & links to Stonehenge

12.1 The conventional view is that humans evolved slowly from wandering hunter gatherers who may have followed migratory patterns of big game, and slowly started settlements as they begun to domesticate animals and cultivate crops. The development of farming around a fixed settlement is seen as encouraging specialization and the growth of knowledge. Eventually a form of recording knowledge emerged which hugely extended the accurate sharing of knowledge leading to a virtuous cycle progressing to civilization.

12.2 That all seems very logical but when examining evidence to support this logical path of development, the experts agree such development happened almost overnight. Whilst it took hundreds of thousands of years for humans to slowly fashion improved flint stones – it appears that the development of improved grains and crop cultivation occurred across Mesopotamia in just a few thousand years. There is evidence that dozens of large well laid out cities emerged across Mesopotamia and Egypt during a period of just a few hundred years. Excavations of these cities reveal careful planning, with large carefully aligned ceremonial buildings whilst the written records we have recovered (baked clay tablets covered with cuneiform writing) show the extensive knowledge of the inhabitants – legal codes, medical knowledge, history, astronomy, trading ledgers, school text books, etc.

12.3 In particular, the astronomical knowledge of the ancient Sumerians is astonishing. The Sumerians used a twelve-fold division of the sky, using zodiac names we still use today to describe constellations, based upon a 360 degree circle. They not only knew all the planets of our solar system but even the colours of each planet – that Uranus is pale blue and Neptune is mid blue - this is almost unbelievable. Contemporary knowledge says Herschel 'discovered' Uranus in 1781 and an astronomer named Adams 'discovered' Neptune in 1843. We could only confirm the colour of Uranus is pale blue in 1985 and Neptune is mid blue in 1989 when Voyager 2 reached these planets. And, the book in which I read of this Sumerian knowledge was published in 1976!

12.4   I can only think of four possible explanations:

(i)   the Sumerians developed telescopes far superior to ours – extremely unlikely as there is neither written or physical evidence remaining of any such advanced metallurgical and optical engineering – and we have hundreds of thousands of their cuneiform tablets which make no reference to such engineering;

(ii)   the Sumerians also launched space probes - surely even more implausible than telescopes and again without any written evidence in the extensive records we have so far translated; or,

(iii)   the more likely explanation – somebody told them. But, that somebody similarly requires one of these other three explanations! The most likely explanation must surely be records of a legacy civilisation that achieved such skills and knowledge prior to the meteor impacts of 10765BC and 9620BC.

(iv)   the fourth possibility is drawn from the Sumerians own records, which relate that their knowledge came from space faring humanoids, which conventional historians have labelled 'gods'. Perhaps, as an alternative because (i) and (ii) seem impossible, and (iii) also raises eyebrows - this must be considered as a possible explanation. Accepting the Sumerian explanation seems a big ask – so let us keep exploring!

As we have seen, this is not an isolated enigma. However, I am very sceptical and seek irrefutable evidence before accepting the possibility of something as extraordinary as option (iv) above.

12.5   The problem with our current knowledge of early Sumerian history is the gap – the earliest records we have recovered can only be positioned back to 5000BC at the very earliest. This leaves a huge gap after the Younger Dryas events – what happened after the survivors landed in their boat somewhere in Armenia and then set about recreating the wonders of the first Sumerian city states?

12.6   It is also interesting that unlike all the other peoples of the Fertile Crescent, those nowadays collectively known as Arabs, the Sumerians were not a Semitic people. Nor is it known from where the Sumerians originated, although during the last 500 years or so of their Empire, the Sumerians formed a close almost symbiotic relationship with the Semite Akkadians. Part One of this series of books explores Sumerian knowledge in greater detail.

12.7   The legendary conveyors of wisdom, Oannes and the Seven Apkallu, are confusingly recorded historically. Arguments can be made that these wise sages dispensing wisdom to promote civilised values had travelled to Sumeria prior to the Flood, or had arrived after the Flood to assist the devastated survivors. Berossus, a priest of Marduk (Ra) in Babylon wrote a History of Babylon (Babyloniaca), in Greek around 285BC under the Persian Seleucid court, in which he described pre flood kings of Sumeria and identified the names of their sages/wise men. Berossus' work, now lost, was abridged and widely copied by later historians including Josephus and Eusebius – thereby gaining great credibility. The crucial point for me is whether the 'wise men', or sages of Apkallu, were trying to spread the finer points of civilised life prior to the Flood or afterwards and indeed which devastation the references are linked to. Whilst both the Hiawatha impact and the Kefalonia impacts would have resulted in grossly swollen rivers from torrential rains, Hiawatha resulted in a greater rise in sea levels which would have affected the confluence of rivers into the Persian Gulf – the most likely location of the biblical Eden. In contrast, the tsunami created by the Kefalonia impacts would have been partly rebuffed by the high lands both sides of the Jordan valley but probably sufficient force would still have devasted cities built of mudbricks along the Euphrates and Tigris.

Sumerian references to antediluvian history

12.8   The fertile alluvial soils deeply overlaying the bedrock of Mesopotamia meant no stone was available for construction. This forced the use of baked bricks for all building works but has also resulted in a wonderful store of ancient clay tablets from which we can gain great insight. Most translators agree that the Sumerian record of their history makes reference to five cities pre-dating the flood – Eridu, Bad Tibira, Larak, Sippar and Shuruppak – strung out along the lower Euphrates and Tigris rivers, between modern day Baghdad and Basra. These cities are described as being swept away by severe flooding, maybe from the tsunami following the Kefalonia impact or maybe from the persistent rainfall, particularly collected from the Caucasus, Taurus and Zagros ranges, grossly swelling the Tigris and Euphrates rivers and sweeping away the low level riverside mud brick cities. If correct, the implication that a number of sizeable urban centres already existed raises many questions, including how farming had developed to generate the surplus crops to feed the urban dwellers and what specialised activities and trades had the urban dwellers developed?

12.9 The story of Zisudra, conventionally referred to as a myth, might more accurately be regarded as a story of survival from the effects of one of the impacts. One clay tablet, known as the Schøyen fragment, records Zisudra as 'king' and as a priest to Enki. This reveals several points: (i) as king at the time of the either the Hiawatha impact, c10765BC, or the Kefalonia impacts c9620BC means that according to the Sumerian king lists, Zisudra must have been a demi-god (product of a union between a human 'god' and a native); (ii) the warnings given by the god, Enki, were based upon prediction and assessment of the effects of an impact; (iii) why was a decision made to help only a chosen few survive the impact events? Particularly as the danger must have been identified well in advance if it allowed time for the construction of a special boat; and, (iv) pre flood technology was sufficiently advanced to enable the construction of a fairly large vessel.

12.10 Conventional historians recognise that ancient Middle Eastern cultures were familiar with the story of a massive flood in the distant past which had devastated a pre-existing civilisation. A famous inscription (British Museum, inscription L) attributed to the Assyrian king Ashurbanipal (ruling 668BC to 627BC), boasts of his intellectual skills, his knowledge derived from the descendants of the Apkallu sages and his joy from studying cuneiform tablets which dated from before the Flood.

12.11 In 2003, Jeanette Fincke published details of her study of the British

Museum's collection of tablets recovered from Ashurbanipal's library at Nineveh. The Museum houses almost the entire collection of tablets recovered during Layard's excavation of a huge 72 room palace at Koujunjik between 1849 and 1851. Study of correspondence amongst the tablets reveals fascinating details. Ashurbanipal originally appointed one of his brothers to rule Babylon but later they fell out and Ashurbanipal undertook direct rule, removing from the local temples many old records which he took to his palace in Nineveh. The correspondence recovered indicates that various governors of other Babylonian cities had tried to protect their temple records, which they clearly regarded as precious stores of old and secret knowledge. It is from these, already ancient, looted Babylonian records that Ashurbanipal based his boasting of intellectual prowess: "I learned the craft of Adapa (understood to be a descendant of an Apkulla sage), the secret knowledge…..I am well acquainted with the signs of heaven and earth, I can deliberate with the experts…I have solved complex mathematical problems….I can understand obscure Sumerian texts (already at least 1500 years old) and Akkadian explanations of difficult passages….I enjoy the texts of tablets dating back before the Flood."

12.12 Jeanette Fincke's work points to some tantalizing possibilities. Ashurbanipal wrote of being taught how to read the secret knowledge and ancient texts – if some of these texts taken from then ancient temples originated pre-flood they would already have been 9000 years old. How did these texts survive and who could interpret what must have been an alien language after such a long period? Whilst the southern heartland of Sumeria, containing the truly ancient cities of Eridu (now dated to 5400BC), Ur, Uruk, Nippar, etc, was devastated around 1960BC – many records tell of skilled craftsmen, physicians and astronomer priests fleeing north – some would have resettled in Babylon and others probably in Harran (founded c8000BC, now in southern Turkey). These refugees would obviously have tried to carry their most revered records with them and once re-established, no doubt continued to maintain these records and their 'secret' knowledge of language and interpretation. So, it is perhaps possible that some truly ancient pre-flood records and interpretative knowledge was passed down over the millennia.

Links between Stonehenge & Lagash?

12.13 Stonehenge is a famous site in Wiltshire, southern England, comprising the remains of concentric stone circles with megalithic uprights and connecting lintels forming trilithons. The history of the discovery of the purpose of Stonehenge is itself fascinating. The site has long attracted great attention – an eighteenth century manuscript lists more than 600 works about Stonehenge in a catalogue of ancient monuments in Western Europe.

12.14 The perceived dating of Stonehenge has moved progressively backwards. The earliest recorded attribution was by Geoffrey of Monmouth, in his *Historia regum Britanniae*, written cAD1136, who stated the stones were originally built in Ireland by giants from Africa and then moved to Wiltshire on the advice of Merlin in Arthurian times – cAD750. Writers in the 17th and 18th centuries ascribed Stonehenge variously to the Romans, Greeks, Phoenicians and Druids. The Druids became the favourite - mainly due to William Stukeley's work entitled *Stonehenge: a Temple Restored to the British Druids* published in 1740 which referred to Julius Caesar's descriptions of an annual Druid festival at a sacred place involving secret ceremonies including human sacrifice.

12.15 Writing in the first century BC, Diodorus Siculus, *History of the World* quotes from a now lost book by Hecataeus of Abdera, dating to c300BC, stating that on an island inhabited by Hyperboreans (generally identified as Britain) there is a magnificent temple to Apollo which is spherical in shape. One of the most significant features of Stonehenge is its circular shape in contrast to almost all other ancient temples – which are built to a common 'three rectangles' standard layout. Quite how Druids might have constructed Stonehenge was never explained.

12.16 No Roman or Greek connection has ever been established and attempts to find links to Phoenicians were similarly seeking to identify a more advanced people who might have had skills which Neolithic Britons clearly lacked. The Phoenicians were known to have traded with the south coast of England to buy supplies of tin, lead and ropes – from as far back as 1500BC. But each of these proposed builders not only lacked the engineering skills but also would have left some written evidence on site such as inscriptions or some links to images of their gods – but nothing of this kind has ever been found.

12.17 Jacquetta Hawkes, a historian who married the assistant keeper of the British Museum in 1933, wrote extensively on the Minoan civilization and in her 1968 work, *Dawn of the Gods*, speculated on similarities with the creators of Stonehenge – potentially moving the date back to the period of the Minoan civilization - between 2600BC and 1600BC.

12.18 The common underlying theme of all the supposed foreign races proposed as the builders of Stonehenge is that the indigenous people clearly had none of necessary skills, organization or knowledge to do so. Moreover, the unanswered question was why would any of these peoples come and commit so much effort and resources to build, in remote Britain, something far larger than they had in their own lands?

12.19 Finally, radiocarbon dating and astro-archaeology (dating of monuments by reference to their astronomical alignment) have provided collaborative evidence of the stages in the construction of Stonehenge that are now universally agreed. Evidence collected indicates that the area was very sparsely populated by small groups of herders with minor farming activity before 2500BC. After 2500BC, small groups arrived from Europe bringing knowledge of metals (gold and copper) who used clay utensils and who buried their dead in round mounds. These are known as the Beaker People after the shape of their drinking cups. Around 2000BC, bronze appeared and the population grew more prosperous – this culture referred to as the Wessex People, and there is evidence that they traded metal goods with Western Europe and the Mediterranean.

12.20 The first stage of Stonehenge was constructed around 2900BC, comprising a wide circular ditch (4m wide and 2m deep) with a circumference of 380m. The excavated soil was used to make two banks on each side of the ditch. A section to the northeast was left undug to provide an entrance to the enclosed site, marked with two 'Gateway Stones'. A massive Heel Stone, 6.8m long with 1.5m buried in the ground and angled at 24°, is aligned to view sunrise at the summer solstice moving back and forth between the Gateway Stones. Just inside the Ditch, 56 post holes have been found, named the Aubrey Holes after the person who identified them. These have been carefully excavated and refilled with cement caps – which shows they form a perfect circle. Finally, the four Station Stones date from this initial construction. The precise positioning of these Station Stones may indicate the true purpose of Stonehenge and why its location was chosen.

12.21 There is no evidence of any further works or alterations until c2100BC when a burst of activity took place. Eighty massive dolerite and rhyolite blocks weighing up to 4 tons each, known as the Bluestones, were hauled from Pembroke, some 250km away, to create two concentric circles of 38 stones (using holes known as Q and R holes) and an inner horseshoe shape comprising 19 stones. In 2015, the actual quarry from which the bluestones were hewn was identified in the Preseli Hills. Geologists and archaeologists identified the outcrop of Carn Goedog as the main source of Stonehenge's 'spotted dolerite' bluestones and the outcrop of Craig Rhos-y-felin as a source of the 'rhyolite' bluestones. Quarrying, dressing and transporting these massive blocks, weighing up to 5 tons, must have been a huge challenge – these outcrops lie c10km from the Welsh coast and even if the River Avon was navigable for such craft nearing Stonehenge there was another 3km or so of haulage required to deliver to site. However, no evidence has been found that early man, 5000 years ago, had ships capable of carrying such stone blocks from Pembroke around the Welsh coast and up the Severn Estuary to navigate the River Avon. Even 500 years ago, the cargo capacity of the largest European merchantmen was still only 50 tons.

12.22 But the most significant change made c2100BC was the repositioning of the Heel Stone – to give revised sight lines out through the gateway stones. The change made to the position of the Heel Stone correlates with known changes caused by a combination of precession (every 2160 years the Earth moves from one house of the zodiac to the preceding house) and in the earth's tilt to the solar plane – the obliquity of the earth oscillates between current extremes of $22.1°$ and $24.5°$. This oscillation is very slowly declining under the moderating gravitational force of our Moon. The oscillation in the axial tilt of our planet to the solar plane represents the residual wobble from the severe impact of Earth colliding with a large celestial body (referred to as a large part of Tiamat or another body referred to as Theia) resulting in the separation of what became our Moon. Tiamat was the planet originally orbiting between Jupiter and Mars. As reviewed in chapter 4 (4.5 to 4.12), Sumerian history tells of Tiamat being smashed into pieces by collision with another planet sized body and, later, the largest part then impacted Earth. The remaining debris from what had once been Tiamat, remained in its old orbit and was known as the 'rakia', meaning Hammered Bracelet. Rakia is translated as 'heaven' in the Bible. Nowadays this planetary debris is known as the Asteroid Belt.

12.23 We digress a bit, but knowledge of the changing obliquity of our planet provides proof of dating for the two positions of the Heel Stone, which corroborates with radiocarbon dating of bone fragments found in the post holes.

12.24 Less than 100 years later, the final addition to Stonehenge was the incorporation of the massive sarcen stones. These weigh 40 to 50 tons each and 77 of them were brought from Marlborough Downs, some 30kms away. These stones were erected as a circle and an inner half oval (originally described as a horseshoe but more recently found to describe a perfect oval shape) – with carefully cut curved lintels, complete with protruding pegs, to form Trilithons. The task of transporting these, erecting them and placing the lintels on top required a massive effort. In addition, the erection of the sarcens involved removal of the bluestones and their re-erection as a single outer circle of 59 stones.

12.25 One enigma, which astronomers were the first to understand, is why there were so many uses of 19 and multiples of 19? This is also linked to the original Station Stones. A solar observatory is relatively simple to construct and use to track solar events. Such an observatory can easily be used to predict solar movements – the position of sunrise moves progressively north and then returns south in an annual cycle. The turning points being midsummer and midwinter days, the solstices, literally when the sun stands still before retracing its daily movement. But tracking and predicting lunar movements is much more complicated, the Moon has four major 'solstices' and four minor 'solstices'.

12.26 Gerald Hawkins of Boston University was the first to announce far reaching conclusions concerning the capabilities of Stonehenge. In a series of articles published between 1963 and 1965, entitled *Stonehenge Decoded*, *Stonehenge a Neolithic Computer*, etc., Hawkins described how the sight lines between the Station Stones identified all the major and minor solstices of the Moon. As the Moon's orbit around Earth is not in exactly the same plane as Earth's orbit around the Sun, the Moon's orbit crosses the Earth's orbit around the Sun twice every year (creating an eclipse) – the Standing Stones could be used to predict when these events would occur. However, these nodal intersections do not appear at the same point every year but describe a cycle of 18.61 years. Hawkins postulated that the adjustment each 19th year could be identified by using the 56 Aubrey Holes, moving 3 markers at a time – $18 2/3 \times 3 = 56$. Hawkins papers generated a great deal of opposition – but the doubts focused on the impossibility of people contemporary with the construction having the knowledge and skills to build such a stone computer.

12.27 Alexander Thom, an engineering professor at Oxford University, undertook extremely accurate measurements at Stonehenge and showed that the "horseshoe" of sarcens was in fact half of an oval – an amazing construction feat but one well suited to tracking planetary orbits more accurately than a circle. Thom also calculated that the Station Stones, erected forming a perfect 90° angled rectangle, provided sight lines to every lunar solstice. Thom concluded Stonehenge was primarily a lunar, and not just a solar observatory.

12.28 But it was a relative layman, Cecil Newham, whose calculations showed the 56 Aubrey Holes could be linked to the eight alignments of the rising and setting Moon. He also calculated that the perfect rectangle formed by the Station Stones only applied at the precise latitude of Stonehenge – and therefore might have been a reason behind the choice of location. This becomes even more relevant when trying to determine who built Stonehenge.

12.29 The case was brought to general acceptance by the involvement of Sir Fred Hoyle, mathematician and astronomer, a leading proponent of the Big Bang theory and developer of theories on stellar formation, during the 1970's. Hoyle's conclusion was also that Stonehenge was a lunar observatory and agreed the role of the Station Stones and the Aubrey Holes. Having achieved a consensus of the purpose of Stonehenge, Hoyle raised an obvious question – to have constructed the Station Stones and Aubrey Holes in their precise positions, the builder must have already known in advance the precise length of the solar year, the Moon's orbital period and the lunar cycle of 18.61 years. Hoyle described Stonehenge as a Predictor of celestial events, but certainly not constructed by the Neolithic stone age hunter gatherers inhabiting Britain during the third millennium BC. Hoyle concluded that the builders of Stonehenge came from afar, looking for a suitable site on the right latitude, much as modern astronomers look for suitable sites for modern observatories. Hoyle mused that if a veritable Einstein had computed that Stonehenge was the spot to build, where was the university he had learned mathematics and astronomy? Moreover, many more than a single genius was required to plan, execute, supervise and develop the operating proce-

SUMERIANS - LEGACY KNOWLEDGE & LINKS TO STONEHENGE

dures required – given that Stonehenge was built in two phases, the second of which required over a century to complete?

12.30 So, we now have a consensus of when and why Stonehenge was built and for what purposes. But the big enigma is who built Stonehenge? Foreknowledge of the astronomical information used in the layout of Stonehenge at the time the Station Stones were erected, 2900BC, was very limited – essentially such knowledge was only known to Sumerians and Egyptians. This period predates even the Akkadians and conventionally the Sabians in Harran – although both could be candidates for the Phase 2 and Phase 3 building. It goes without saying that any people with such knowledge must derive it from being able to write out their observations, calculations and conclusions. But there is no evidence of any form of writing anywhere in Europe prior to c1000BC (long after Stonehenge appears to have been abandoned) when Phoenician traders started to spread their newly invented alphabetic script. The candidates nominated in earlier studies of Stonehenge:- Greeks, Romans, Minoans – all fail the knowledge test and all these civilizations only arose after Stonehenge was fully completed.

Who else could have built Stonehenge?

12.31 Therefore, one is left with only two possible candidates – Egypt and Sumeria. But major difficulties quickly rule these two out as well, except for puzzling similarities with Lagash.

12.32 Is there any record of either Egyptians or Sumerians travelling as far as Britain or even having the capability to do so? No. As covered in Part Two of this series, the earliest evidence of Egyptian seafaring up the Levant coast to trade with what is now Lebanon dates from around 4000BC (from analysis of cedar ash in Egyptian kitchens). The craft were fragile reed boats quite unsuited to venturing far from the coast and certainly crossing the Mediterranean would have proved fatal, therefore venturing out into the Atlantic surely impossible. The Sumerians had ships but the first record of them venturing out into the Indian Ocean was during the reign of Gudea, 2144BC to 2124BC – when a Sumerian colony was established in what later became Goa. An interesting remnant from that early colony is that the width of tilling used in planting crops in Goa remains the standard used in Sumer – and different from the rest of India. However, there is no record of any Sumerian ships venturing southwards down the east coast of Africa, round the Horn and all the way back northwards to Britain. Indeed, there is negative evidence supporting this – as it was always believed that Africa was joined to Asia, if one travelled south in Africa one would find part of Asia. Pharaoh Necho II ruled Egypt from 610BC to 594BC. Between 608BC and 606BC, Necho built a new canal through the Wadi Tumilat. He then commissioned triremes built by Greek shipwrights to operate in the Red Sea – potentially opening up a new route to attack the Babylonians. At some point between 606 and before 594 BC, Necho commissioned an expedition by Phoenicians, of who it is said in three years sailed from the Red Sea, around Africa and back to the mouth of the Nile. An account by the historian Herodotus, which he attributes to oral tradition is believed credible primarily because he stated his disbelief that the Phoenicians had accomplished such a voyage because "as they sailed on a westerly course round the southern end of Libya (Africa), they had the sun on their right" - to northward of them (*The Histories* 4.42). In Herodotus time it was not known that Africa was surrounded by ocean – thus the tradition of Phoenician circumnavigation of Africa was also dismissed by Strabo, Ptolemy and Polybius.

12.33 Is there any evidence at Stonehenge of Egyptian or Sumerian presence? None whatsoever, indeed no carvings, markings or symbols of any kind have ever been found that could be connected with any ancient civilisation. Note: no inscriptions of any kind have been found in the Giza pyramids on the Sphinx or the original stones of Baalbek – an odd feature seemingly common to these ancient megaliths. Furthermore, the stones used to construct Stonehenge remain basically unshaped from when hewn from the bedrock, definitely not indicating Egyptian workmanship.

12.34 In these ancient civilisations, what we consider as separate subjects - religion, astronomy and kingship - were all very closely intertwined. Kings sought permission from gods to build temples, the written records show that often permission was refused (e.g. Yahweh refused David). What we describe as temples appear to have actually been dual purpose 'homes for a god' and frequently also astronomical observatories – served by astronomer-priests. All temples in Mesopotamia and Egypt were precisely aligned east-west – as equinoxal observatories aligned with the spring equinox. Interestingly, one exception is Solomon's temple which, whilst also precisely on an east-west axis, upon Yahweh's instructions was aligned with the autumnal equinox. Therefore, if there had been a project to build what we call Stonehenge, we would surely have found some references to it. Fundamentally, with a single partial exception (see section from 12.39 below on Lagash, Sumer), Stonehenge is completely alien in design to all other temples – being circular and aligned to the sunrise of the summer solstice.

12.35 Whilst the Egyptians did quarry stone to build monuments and temples and could easily have manipulated 40 ton sarcens, in Egypt there were huge armies of labourers involved in the major construction projects – extensive workers' villages have been excavated indicating a labour force of up to 100,000 might have been deployed on building a pyramid. By comparison, estimates of the population of the entire British Isles around 1500BC (long after Stonehenge was completed) are of only 10,000 – so recruiting even 500 able bodied adult males in one location would have been very difficult. The Sumerians were very active builders but almost exclusively used baked clay bricks – so Stonehenge would seem to be far removed from their experience and expertise.

12.36 If the key criteria for the location of Stonehenge is the magic of basing the Station Stones at that precise latitude – why build in southern England? An Egyptian or Sumerian project would more naturally travel north to find that latitude – a much shorter sail north through the Dardanelles and across the Black Sea – they could have then travelled to reach the required latitude in what is now northern Ukraine or in Poland.

12.37 It is also puzzling that having identified Stonehenge, the builders then searched around as far as western Pembroke to quarry the bluestones – 250km away. Human exploration would have been on foot – the earliest attribution of horse riding is 800BC in what is now Kazakhstan, from where it spread rapidly. The earliest recorded horse riding in the Middle East was by Assyrian cavalry around 650BC. One can hardly imagine that the intellectually gifted astronomer priests would send out search parties on foot to scour the whole of the southern Britain to identify the right stones – an effort which could have taken decades. And how would the results be brought back? Those returning would have to provide samples of various hard stones they had found and remember how to locate each of the sample rocks that they had brought back – without any writing and without any maps to identify locations nor determine the easiest direct route given they may have wandered around searching for some years. Such a random approach seems very unlikely.

12.38   It is difficult to avoid the conclusion that the source of the bluestones was discovered by aerial survey. And, who exactly is widely recorded as having aerial craft, usually with temples designed to securely house such craft – the very 'gods' written about as contemporary with the millennia in which Stonehenge was built. There are a number of references in the Bible as well which speak of making a place for the name of the Lord and to worship the name of the Lord. But if you look into the Hebrew text, it is the word 'shem' that is translated as 'name'. There is debate over what 'shem' meant, for want of any other explanation it is argued that the context indicates 'shem' means 'name'. However, the word 'shem' is not from a Hebrew root but what is termed a 'loan word' – loaned from Sumerian where it means 'vessel' or 'ship'. The Sumerians used 'shem' to describe vessels sailing through the air or water. What could be more obvious than the Israelites wanting to build a house for Yahweh, where Yahweh could station his personal shem machine, thereby 'tethering' their god to their city for their protection.

The temple of Lagash

12.39   One set of cuneiform tablets provides a helpful guide to the Sumerian temples of their gods. Written c2300BC by a high priestess, a daughter of Sargon (an Akkadian king), it lists all the temples of her time. Translated by Sjoberg and Bergmann, in vol.3 of *Texts from Cuneiform Sources*, the text details the name of each temple, its location, the god for whom it was built, a description of the building, its functions and history. 42 temples are listed, starting with Enki's temple, E.duku (House of the Holy Mound), the list includes Enlil's ziggurat E.kur (House like a Mountain), Ninharsag's E.ninharsag (House of the lady of the mountain). Enlil's first born son by his official spouse (Ninlil) was Nannar (more widely known by his Akkadian name:- Sin), who was associated with the Moon, his celestial counterpart. Nannar was greatly praised by his father for producing successful offspring – hence his temple was named E.kish.nu.gal, meaning "House of Thirty, the great seed". Nannar/Sin's foremost son, Utu/Shamash (who may also have been known as Yahweh) had his temple in Sippar named E.babbar (House of the Bright One) as his celestial counterpart was the Sun. The names of the 'temples' clearly indicate each was the home of a god, where he kept his shem (flying machine) as well as being where offerings and gifts were brought, no doubt often such offerings were associated with pleas for favourable rulings when disbursing justice in relation to human disputes!

12.40 The design of Ninurta's second temple at Lagash offers a link to Stonehenge. Gudea, who ruled 2144BC to 2124BC, secured the great honour of building a new temple for Ninurta. Gudea was so proud of his task that we have very extensive writings describing every aspect of the construction, the materials used, their sourcing and the dedication of the new temple – the E.ninnu (House of Fifty). Fifty being Ninurta's numerical rank as inherited from his father Enlil. His writings relate how Gudea was very worried by the challenge of building something incorporating all the requirements of Ninurta – and his relief when Ninurta called for the assistance of Kothar-Hasis, the "skilled and knowledgeable craftsman of the gods" who lived in Egypt, generally believed to be Thoth (a son of Enki) who determined the detailed design. This new temple was to be very grand, Gudea's record claims he recruited a workforce of 216,000 – the new temple was to be built of cut stone, hauled from the Zagros mountains, cedar from Lebanon and much precious stones and metals. The descriptions explain in detail the specific designs of the mud bricks made for the ziggurat but, uniquely in Mesopotamia, the brick structure was encased with a stone facing. This is reminiscent of the Egyptian method of facing pyramids with bright limestone casings. According to Gudea, a dozen or so gods were involved in the planning and design of different aspects of the temple. Once the construction was completed, great effort was expended on the adornments – interiors were dressed with cedarwood panels, gardens planted with flowering bushes, ornamental pools stocked with fish – features we might associate more with a home than a temple. Special enclosures are described for Ninurta's 'war bird' his Divine Black Bird, as well as armouries for his special weapons, granaries and cattle pens. The consecration, on New Year's Day, was extremely elaborate – requiring a similar length record to that of the design and construction phase!

12.41 The most interesting details are the astronomical-calendrical design of the observation platform on the temple terrace. Seven upright stones, stellae, took a full year to carve but were erected feverishly over a seven day period – suggesting they were positioned exactly to fix sight lines of specific lunar or solar alignments. Clearly, these stellae were not to align the building itself – this had been ceremonially accomplished when the foundations were marked out. The haste with which erection of the stellae was carried out, during the seven days prior to the inauguration on the 10th day of the first month of the new year - which indicates that the positioning of the stellae was linked to an auspicious astronomical

PREQUEL – YOUNGER DRYAS METEOR IMPACTS, THE FLOOD & ATLANTIS

event. There are numerous references of planned dates of inauguration of other temples being set to mark significant astronomical events – even Solomon had to wait for nine months after completing Yahweh's temple before he was allowed to consecrate it. Gudea describes the positioning of six of the stellae as forming a circle (unique in the Middle East temple design) and an avenue or pathway to provide an unimpeded sightline towards the rising sun.

12.42   Stonehenge 1, c500 year earlier, had also started with 6 pillars (4 Station and 2 Gateway Stones) plus the Heel Stone forming a circle – could this just be a coincidence? Gudea then describes how, after the consecration, a second set of 13 uprights were erected in an outer circle – connected by lintels – akin to the Trilithons at Stonehenge. The numbers of pillars also point to two possible uses – 12 lunar months plus a 13th for intercalation to keep solar and lunar calendars aligned – and the use of 19 again – to accommodate the 18.61 year lunar cycle. In yet another echo of Stonehenge, Gudea explains the two types of stones used for the pillars were brought from a great distance – one type from Nubia, south of Egypt (from mountains which he notes that no Sumerian had visited before) and the other from Egypt. Sourcing stone blocks from such a far distance seems incredible – apart from getting the stone blocks from the quarry in Nubia down to the Red Sea, the builders faced a 4000km sea journey around the Arabian peninsula before reaching the mouth of the Euphrates. It seems that the design of the observatory at Ninurta's 'house' included features of both Stonehenge stage 1, built c500 years before, and a simplified version of what was then being constructed concurrently as Stonehenge stage 2. This seems a remarkable coincidence.

12.43   There seem to be remarkable similarities between Stonehenge and Lagash – both in design and in timing. However, it does not seem credible to suggest that the Sumerians built Stonehenge – and it is out of the question to think the sparse numbers of ancient Britons could have recruited to build anything in Sumeria. But, could both have shared the same designer?

12.44   I also found an interesting echo of Lagash in the Book of Joshua. Consider, Abraham's father, Terah, who was oracle priest to the Lord Most High (Enlil) based at Nippur. Born, it is estimated in 2193BC, Terah would have been priest when Enlil granted Ninurta the right to have the new E.ninnu temple complex constructed by Gudea around 2144BC.

Abraham could have been around 10 years old when Terah moved the family to take up governorship of Ur and would have been well versed in religious and astronomical knowledge – hence familiar with the trendy new circular temple at Lagash. Perhaps this became part of Israelite oral tradition. A few centuries later, after Joshua crosses the Jordan with divine help, Joshua chapter 4 relates that Yahweh instructed the Israelites to erect 12 stone pillars in a circle and commemorate their miraculous crossing – on the 10th day of the first month of the new year – i.e. the exact anniversary of the consecration of Lagash!! Remembering the exact day of the consecration was obviously as highly important. So is it a mere coincidence; was it reuse of an auspicious date in tribal memory; or, was the author of Joshua (probably writing in Babylon c 550BC) simply importing noteworthy historical references?

12.45   The only other ancient monument incorporating a circular design is the Rujum el-Hiri, located on the Golan Heights. Like Stonehenge, there is no evidence of any grand building nearby, no temple or multi-function palace. Like both Stonehenge and Lagash the design is devoted to near perfect circles – but, unlike both, Rujum el-Hiri has no evidence of having had columns or lintels. The site is huge, enclosing more than 20,000 square metres with five concentric circles of basalt boulders, each raised to between 2m and 2.5m with an aggregate weight estimated at more than 40,000 metric tonnes. On Syrian Army maps the site was named as Rujum el-Hiri – Arabic for "stone of the wildcat".

12.46   Over the years, excavation works at the site have revealed pottery fragments and flint tools, which in turn have aided in determining the date of construction of the monument, corresponding to the Early Bronze Age II period (3000BC to 2700BC) – contemporary with the construction of Stonehenge I and prior to Lagash. But who constructed this monument, and for what purpose, remains a mystery. In 2010, a study published in the *Biblical Archaeology Review* concluded that Rujum el-Hiri was a calendrical devise to determine the summer and winter solstices. But quite why the simple nomadic farmers whom conventional historians claim inhabited the area would need to know dates of the solstices or devote so much energy to the construction in order to know, is a mystery.

13

Cuzco & Tiahuanaco, Peru/Bolivia – ancient technology

13.1 Various Nahuatl and Inca legends record peoples arriving in South America by boat rather than the conventional belief that people had trekked south from Alaska.

13.2 In Peru, according to legends and data recorded by the Spanish priest and explorer, Fernando Montesinos, in his *Memorias Historiales* of 1644 (better known as the Quito Manuscript), the Inca did not found their capital of Cuzco but took over an ancient city founded by Manco Capac at the direction of Viracocha, estimated by Montesinos as being around 2400BC.

13.3 When the Spanish arrived in Cuzco four thousand years later in 1533, they found a city with more than 100,000 dwellings surrounding a large governing and religious centre. The Spanish learned that the city was arranged in an oval, divided into 12 zones with boundaries running along sightlines delineated from observation towers built on surrounding peaks. The use of 12 zones would seem to imply a reference to the zodiac – which as elsewhere noted, uses signs uncannily similar to the Eurasian zodiac. But their main attention was transfixed by the principal temple, the Coricancha (meaning golden enclosure) – a temple complex built with perfectly dressed ashlars covered with gold plates and surrounded by artificial gardens of corn and flowers made entirely of gold and silver. One trophy snatched by the Spanish was an immense gold disc – which they assumed meant the Incas worshipped the sun. Later, Montesinos learned that the disc was designed to reflect light illuminating the whole temple at sunrise on the winter solstice. Rolf Müller, who headed an astronomical observatory at La Paz in 1928 and 1929, used the obliquity of the ecliptic (the earth's axial tilt relative to the equator) to calculate the date of construction of Coricancha – whose sightline equated to obliquity of 24° – indicating it was built c2500BC, corroborating the estimate recorded by Montesinos in 1644 referring to the establishment of the Ancient Empire.

13.4   Andean myths also knew of the Flood and refer to post-diluvial migrations to repopulate the area led by gods and using boats. The leader of the first expedition is remembered as Naymlap, who landed at Cape Santa Helena now in Ecuador. They had a pantheon of 12 gods and built a temple with twelve pillars arranged in a circle. The legends of the Aymara people refer to earlier arrivals by sea, describing them as *Uru*, 'olden people', a people apart whose remnants still exist in the 'Sacred Valley' (the valley of river Urubamba) – could these people and their river be named after Ur, people who maybe originated from Ur, founded around 3800BC and acting as capital of Sumer circa 2200BC to 1960BC.

Megalithic structures

13.5   A series of megalithic structures across the high Andes in Peru present many questions. Each appears to use huge blocks of carefully hewn stone, invariably not native to the site but hauled over high mountains and steep valleys. Moreover, the huge blocks, some weighing hundreds of tons, are precisely cut into incredible polygonal shapes, an extreme example at Machu Picchu has 32 faces, which fit tightly together without any mortar:

13.6   Sacsahuaman, overlooking Cuzco, towers up as a promontory, with massive polygonal boulders fitting perfectly together, rising as successively higher walls, zigzagging in unison up to some 300m in height. The rocks are covered in twisting channels, tunnels, grooves and niches. Inspired by a local legend that a boy had fallen into a tunnel atop the structure and later emerged down in Cuzco city, local archaeologists begun limited excavations and discovered the area behind the parallel walls was honeycombed with subterranean tunnels and chambers.

13.7   Machu Picchu was rediscovered by Hiram Bingham in 1911. Rolf Müller dates the Intihuatana at between 2300BC and 2100BC. In their book, *Archaeoastronomy at Machu Picchu*, D.S. Dearborn and R.E. White of the University of Arizona, also arrive at dates of between 4000BC and 2000BC. Legend tells that the three Ayar brothers set out from Machu Picchu at the direction of Viracocha to form three Andean kingdoms (which seems to echo the biblical Ham, Shem and Japhet?). The site at Machu Picchu contains evidence of three successive and distinct cultures – original megalithic builders using exquisite polygonal boulders; walls of beautifully shaped ashlars of more manageable dimensions dating from the Ancient Empire period and most recently use of undressed field stones attributed to additions made by Incas having fled to their last redoubt from the Spanish. Once again, we see graphic evidence of megalithic construction skills fading over time to relative mediocrity. For readers who haven't been there or have forgotten the detail, please review pictures of Machu Picchu on Google Images.

13.8 Tiahuanaco (aka Tiwanaku) presents another enigma. The structures indicate a city for around 20,000 people built at an altitude of 3850m bordering a saltwater lake – with neither fresh water nor any supply of food nearby. The ancient complex covers a huge area with megalithic structures, a temple observatory and what appears to be a huge port facility with capacity for dozens of ships. The temple is known by the name of the remaining gigantic gateway – the Puerta del Sol (Gate of the Sun) together with what was initially thought to be a temple, with a series of large pillars known as the Kalasasaya; and a raised platform area called Akapana (aka Puma Punko) and linking the two are extensive areas of walls, tunnels, underground chambers, sunken pipelines and what appear to be quays revealed by Lidar scans – which have yet to be excavated. Whilst humans can adapt, not many would be capable of hard labour at such an altitude, whilst being a desolate location lacking any resources – a very strange choice of venue at which to build a city?

13.9 The first detailed exploration of the area was undertaken by Professor Posnanski, a Bolivian archaeologist, born in Austria, he was by turn, an engineer, ships navigator, entrepreneur and city counsellor of La Paz. Posnansky undertook decades of excavations at Tiahuanaco, uncovering chaotic remains of human and animal bones, jewellery and shards indicating a natural disaster that he dated to between 11,000BC and 10,000BC. Whilst many have challenged his dating, the scale of the destruction at the site is indicative of seismic shocks rather than warfare, whilst his estimated dating strongly suggests a link to the destruction wrought by the Younger Dryas event. If the analysis for the impact event set out in section 7 is correct, then the sudden vast redistribution of mass from the north American continent across the rest of the globe would have been sufficient to affect the tectonic plates. Substantially relieving the land mass of Canada of a few kilometres thickness of ice cap would slowly result in that plate rising up, whilst the meltwater which raised global sea levels by an estimated 130m would exert downward pressure on parts of other tectonic plates. An area high in the Andes might well have suffered multiple earthquakes as a result.

13.10   Climbing the Akapana, an artificial hill which is believed to have originally had the shape of a step pyramid, one can look out at what seems like a transplanted *Arc de Triomphe*. It is indeed a gate but intricately carved from a single massive block of stone. The stone reliefs include a giant image of Viracocha, flanked by three rows of winged attendants (looking like direct copies of Mesopotamian reliefs) and a multitude of symbols representing calendrical features. There is evidence that a similar gate stood at the other end of a quadrangle opposite the Puerta del Sol. Aligned on a perfect east – west axis stand 13 marble pillars (known as the Kalasasaya), which using sightlines from the Gates provide for calculation of solstices and equinoxes – the complex being a combined lunar and solar calendrical observatory. The obliquity of 23.09° indicated by the observational sightlines noted by Posnansky created disbelief in the scientific community. Based upon the obliquity formulas determined by astronomers at the International Conference of Ephemerides in Paris in 1911, which also adjusts for the longitude and elevation of a site, Posnansky announced that the Kalasasaya was constructed c15,000BC. This date means that Tiahuanaco would be the oldest known city in the world – dating back long before the Flood.

13.11   Posnansky's announcement created a storm of interest. The German Astronomical Commission sent an expedition which included Professor Hans Ludendorff (Director of the Astronomical Observatory, Potsdam), Professor Arnold Kohlscütter (Director of the Astronomical Observatory, Bonn and honorary astronomer of the Vatican) and Dr Rolf Müller (an astronomer from the Potsdam observatory). This team made measurements and observations at Tiahuanaco from November 1926 to June 1928. They confirmed Kalasasaya was indeed an astronomical-calendrical observatory, with the width and positioning of the pillars designed to enable very precise measurements of solstices. The team evaluated the formulae and an alternative curve for calculating ancient obliquity – they concluded that the date of construction could be c15,000BC as calculated by Posnansky, or a later date of c9,300BC – which is still far earlier than any conventionally accepted date for civilisation in South America.

13.12 The scientific community remained incredulous and yielding to criticism, Rolf Müller returned to Bolivia and teamed up with Posnansky for further fieldwork. They found additional sightlines which might have been employed and whether ancient astronomers calculations were based on the time the sun touched the horizon, was half obscured or completely obscured – which indicated different degrees of obliquity. Müller published his definitive report in a leading journal, volume 14 of the Baessler Archiv, concluding that the most likely angle of obliquity was 24°6'52" – which, due to the oscillation in the Earth's tilt then indicated two possible dates of construction – either 10150BC or 4050BC. Posnansky then presented these findings to the 23rd International Congress of Americanists in 1928. When confronted by incredulity, Posnansky agreed it needed further study. One possibility that we can now consider is whether construction was led by the remnants of the ancient megalithic culture that survived the Hiawatha impact – in which case all the dates dismissed by conventional historians become plausible.

13.13 The conventional explanation of Tiwanaku is barely more credible than the more radical ideas that it was an ancient space port. The original explanation for the huge collection of monumental buildings was that it comprised a vacant ceremonial site visited only by pilgrims to observe festivals. However, from the 1920's local Bolivian archaeologists, led by Ponce Sanguines, developed explanations of large scale local indigenous populations, who developed the Tiwanaku structures between AD500 and AD1100. Construction on this scale obviously required a huge local population – to bring the large stone blocks from remote quarries, to fashion the intricate stone masonry and undertake erection. Accordingly, it is postulated that the population in this period numbered c400,000, heavily dependant upon intensive agriculture before later succumbing to a series of harvest failures and then scattering to the surrounding hills before disappearing. This conventional explanation seems fraught with problems. Sustaining such a huge population in such a forbidding location seems perverse. Even today, the population of La Paz, 70km to the east and a few hundred meters lower than Lake Titicaca is less than 800,000.

13.14 However, other evidence seems to corroborate the date of 4050BC:

- The Inca calendar adopted its 'beginning', drawing on traditions inherited from the Ancient Empire long predating the Inca, as the age of Taurus. The Age of Taurus was from c4300BC to c2000BC – (the sign of the bull is significantly wider than 30° – 1/12th of the arc of the sky)

- Independently, Müller had determined at a date of c4000BC for the megalithic structures at Machu Picchu.

- Maria Schulten de D'Ebneth studying the Grid of Viracocha had measured obliquity of 24°8' and thus a date of c3170BC.

- Ponce Sanguines, a renown Bolivian archaeologist, reported in *Tiwanaku: Space, Time and Culture* that newly developed hydration dating techniques applied to some obsidian objects indicated dates most recently worked of c2134BC.

13.15 So, whilst conventionally accepted explanations place Tiwanaku's construction only 1500 years ago, other evidence suggests points to a date between 4000 and 6000 years ago. I recommend viewing some of the many 'YouTube' videos available. You will quickly find Tiwanaku has attracted numerous excited conspiracy theorists – but setting aside the wilder explanations, just view the amazingly elaborate stone work. From visual exploration of many of the stone blocks, one is struck by what looks very much like the results of machine tooling – and many features clearly indicate technical functionality rather than any decorative purpose. The production methods that must have been used for some of the detailed profiling indicate a far more advanced culture produced the structures – and for functional purposes we cannot yet fathom out. Some try to explain how such intricate designs could be formed with copper tools and the use of sand grains to polish surfaces. My own conclusion is that the local Aymara Indians may well have occupied this complex during the periods conventionally stated, and added some of their own symbology – but the relative crudity of the recognisable symbols compared with say the winged attendants of Viracocha strongly suggest the originals were far older and carved by far more skilled stonemasons. Readers may wish to view Google Images of Tiwanaku and Puma Punku – the precision stone carving and circular hole boring raise many questions.

13.16 The twin complexes of Puma Punku and Kalasasaya lie at the southern end of Lake Titicaca. The largest of the stone blocks at Puma Punku is 7.8m long, 5.2m wide, averages 1.1 meters thick, and is estimated to weigh about 131 metric tons. The second largest stone block is 7.9m long, 2.5m wide, and averages 1.8m thick. Its weight has been estimated to be 85 metric tons. Both of these stone blocks are part of the *Plataforma Lítica* and composed of red sandstone. Based upon detailed petrographic and chemical analyses of samples from both individual stones and known quarry sites, archaeologists concluded that these and other red sandstone blocks were transported up a steep incline from a quarry near Lake Titicaca 10 kilometres away. Smaller andesite blocks that were used for stone facing and carvings came from quarries within the Copacabana Peninsula about 90 kilometres away from and across Lake Titicaca from the Puma Punku and the rest of the Tiwanaku site.

13.17 Archaeologists argue that the transport of these stones was accomplished by the large labour force of ancient Tiwanaku. However, the area is barren, far above the tree line, with Lake Titicaca itself at 3810m. A large labour force would require importation of foodstuffs from far lower altitudes. Several theories have been proposed as to how this labour force transported the stones, although these theories remain speculative. Two of the more common proposals involve the use of llama skin ropes and the use of ramps and inclined planes requiring timber logs to also be transported uphill over significant distances.

13.18 In assembling the walls of Puma Punku, each stone was finely cut to interlock with the surrounding stones. The blocks fit together like a puzzle, forming load-bearing joints without the use of mortar. One common engineering technique involves cutting the top of the lower stone at a certain angle, and placing another stone on top of it which was cut at the same angle. The precision with which these angles have been used to create flush joints is indicative of a highly sophisticated knowledge of stone-cutting and a thorough understanding of descriptive geometry. Many of the joints are so precise that not even a razor blade will fit between the stones. Much of the masonry is characterized by accurately cut rectilinear blocks of such uniformity that they could be interchanged for one another while maintaining a level surface and even joints. However, the blocks do not have the same dimensions, although they are close. Indeed, the blocks are so precisely cut as to suggest the possibility of prefabrication and mass production, technologies far in advance of the

Tiwanaku's Inca successors hundreds of years later.

13.19 Tiwanaku engineers were also adept at developing a civic infrastructure at this complex, constructing functional irrigation systems, hydraulic mechanisms, and waterproof sewage lines.

13.20 A notable feature at Puma Punku are I-shaped architectural cramps, which are composed of a unique copper-arsenic-nickel bronze alloy. These I-shaped cramps were analysed by Lechtman in a report issued in 1998 *Architectural cramps at Tiwanaku: copper-arsenic-nickel bronze* and were also used on a section of canal found at the base of the Akapana pyramid at Tiwanaku. These cramps were used to hold the blocks comprising the walls and bottom of stone-lined canals that drain sunken courts. I-cramps of unknown composition were used to hold together most of the massive slabs that formed Puma Punku's four large platforms. In the south canal of the Puma Punku, the I-shaped cramps were cast in place. In sharp contrast, the cramps used at the Akapana canal were fashioned by the cold hammering of copper-arsenic-nickel bronze ingots.

13.21 Very similar 'I clamps' were also used in the construction of the E.ninnu temple at Lagash, Sumeria, completed by King Gudea in 2130BC.

13.22 In *Subsurface Imaging in Tiwanaku's Monumental Core* (2007), Ernenweini and Konns published the results of their surveying of the largely undisturbed area covering the kilometre separating the Puma Punku and Kalasasaya complexes. Using ground penetrating radar, magnetometry and electrical conduction, tests revealed the presence of numerous man-made structures. These structures include the wall foundations of buildings and compounds, water conduits, pool-like features, revetments, terraces, residential compounds and widespread gravel pavements, all of which now lie buried and hidden beneath the modern ground's surface.

13.23 Conventional history dates the Tiwanaku civilization and the use of these temples to the period from AD700 to AD1000, by which point the temples and surrounding area may have been home to some 400,000 people. An extensive civil and agricultural infrastructure had been developed, including a complex irrigation system that extended over more than 80 km^2 to support cultivation of potatoes, quinoa, corn and other various crops. At its peak, the Tiwanaku culture dominated the entire Lake Titicaca basin as well as portions of Bolivia and Chile. This culture seems to have dissolved rather abruptly, some time around AD1000, and researchers are still seeking answers as to why. A likely scenario involves rapid climate change, probably involving an extended drought. Unable to produce the massive crop yields necessary for their large population, the Tiwanaku are belived to have scattered into the local mountains only to disappear shortly thereafter. It seems possible that conventional historians hugely overestimated the likely Tiwanaku population based on the assumption that they were responsible for the extensive megalithic constructions and then found this huge population simply 'disappeared' soon afterwards. Given that we now have evidence pointing to even more extensive buried structures, the population estimates for the conventional explanation would have to be revised upwards to far greater numbers.

13.24 Others link the construction of Puma Punku to the Aymara Indians, dating construction to around AD300. However, the theory that such natives could produce such a stunning range of carefully carved blocks using simple copper tools sounds fanciful and ignores the obliquity calculations by several highly regarded astronomers. It is true a few hieroglyphs in the Aymara script appear cut into the blocks – but, even from simple pictorial evidence, these carved images are far cruder than the precision carving on the other blocks.

13.25 I conclude that the culture identified in conventional history may well have occupied the Tiwanaku site as written in the section above – but I do not think they had the technology to construct the temples, etc, themselves, which they inherited from a far older and long disappeared culture.

13.26 Sadly, as noted by several explorers over the past four centuries, the local people have treated Tiahuanaco as a source of dressed stone for their buildings – blocks from Tiahuanaco have been recognised in numerous colonial era structures – including La Paz cathedral. However, the largest blocks, proving too heavy to move, remain in situ – as well as the suspected extensive subterranean works. To Posnansky's credit, his efforts resulted in the Bolivian government declaring the site a national monument and stopping the looting of the stone blocks.

13.27 The principal records we have of Inca culture and beliefs are those of the early Spanish narrators, particularly those narratives recorded by:

- Padre Blas Valera – born 1545, the son of one of Pizarro's force and an Inca mother, Valera was fluent in Quechua and became a Jesuit;

- Father Cristóbal de Molina – a respected priest regarded as an outstanding Quechua scholar who travelled widely in Peru and between 1570 and 1585 wrote numerous works widely quoted by later writers; and,

- Garcilaso de la Vega – born in Cuzco in 1539 of a Spanish conqueror and an Inca noblewoman, he is recognized primarily for his chronicles of Inca history, culture, and society. Vega sailed to Spain at 21 where he lived and worked for the rest of his life. His works were widely read in Europe where, known as El Inca, he was influential and well received.

13.28 The various recorded Inca beliefs of their origin are consistent in telling of the god Viracocha arriving at Tiahuanaco with 200 followers to establish the first city. Some recount Viracocha being so angry with the behaviour of the descendants of the first man and woman that he ordered the Flood as a punishment. From these legends one can recognize why the Spanish believed the Inca were one of the Israelite lost tribes. Again, the legends tell of a winged god bringing people to Peru (by air or by sea), their descendants being described as the sons of the Sun.

Conclusions on South American megalithic cultures

13.29 One might expect human settlements to develop in areas rich in food resources and fresh water. A navigable river providing fresh water, ample fish and access to the sea, adjacent to verdant habitations rich with fruit, nuts and wild game – offering land with productive soil for growing crops. The availability of such resources should attract people to settle in the area. And yet, the first major settlements, based on the available archaeological evidence appear in very remote, inaccessible and harsh environments far above the tree line. Why exert such stupendous effort to build Tiahuanaco at an altitude of almost 4000 metres and Machu Picchu at 3400m – heights which even make Cuzco, at 2430m, look reasonable?

13.30 Recently evidence of very early crop cultivation has been identified in Northern Bolivia. An article published in the journal *Nature* on 8th April 2020, reported on evidence of human crop cultivation in the Llanos de Moxos area of Bolivia dating back as far as 8830BC. A team led by Umberto Lombardo had researched the 'forest islands' in the south western Amazon, so named because slightly raised land is now covered with forest separated by areas of flood plain savannah. 82 of these forest islands were surveyed and archaeological excavations were carried out at 4 islands. These islands were found to enjoy enriched soils containing evidence of early human habitation and darker sediment rich in organic matter, charcoal and burned earth together with shell and bone fragments. Early plant domestication has been detected by comparison of genetic markers in domesticated and wild strains of different crops giving earliest cultivation dates of 8230BC for squash and 8330BC for manioc – far earlier than had been expected. Given that the 4 sites sampled represented a tiny proportion of the 6643 forest islands identified in the Llanos de Moxos, it is entirely possible that those excavated were not the earliest where humans had settled. As in the ancient myths of Egypt and Sumer, tales of wise men arriving and teaching about planting crops have survived in places along the Andean coast. If more forest islands were to be excavated it might well identify settlements dating closer to 9600BC and the dramatic climatic end to the Younger Dryas period. The Llanos de Moxos lies 600 km from Tiahuanaco.

14

Indonesian anomalies

14.1   Throughout the last maximum glacial period, from 26,000 to 20,000 years ago, the entire Sunda Shelf was dry land. The present islands of Sumatra, Java and Borneo were conjoined with south east Asia. It was not until the rapid rise in sea levels caused by the Hiawatha impact around 10765BC that these three large areas became separate islands cut off by rising sea levels. This short chapter will look at two anomalies which point to a more sophisticated culture existing a long time before the sea came in over the Sunda Shelf.

Gunung Padang, Java, Indonesia.

14.2   Gunung Padang, rediscovered in 1914, is located on a hilltop at an altitude of 900m, in the local Sundanese language means Mountain of Light or Mountain of Enlightenment. It covers an area of 150m by 40m comprising a pyramid and five terraces. The locals say it has been a site for meditation since time immemorial. In 2011, Danny Hilman Natawidjaja, a senior geologist at the Geo-technology Research Centre of the Indonesian Institute of Sciences, undertook a geophysical survey. Radiocarbon dating under the surface of the ground around the megaliths gave readings of 1500BC to 500BC, but when cores were drilled it was found that man made megalithic structures extended far below the surface. Core samples continued to bring up samples of worked basalt as well as organic material – as the cores went deeper, radiocarbon dates went back far further than expected – with successive readings of 9600BC, 15000BC and finally at a depth of 27.5m dates of 20000BC to

22000BC – back into the period of the last ice age maxima. Further surveying using a range of equipment, ground penetrating radar, seismic tomography and electrical resistivity, revealed stunning outlines of massive constructions using basalt beams down to 30m below the surface – from whence the radiocarbon dating had yielded results back to 22000BC.

14.3   Whilst electrifying in its implications, we have to be circumspect as it appears that various Indonesian researchers, including Natawidjaja, are competing to present Gunung Padang as the origin of the Atlantis legend. Disputes and fanciful claims have led to government authorities stepping in to try to control developments. If the survey data are reliable then there are huge implications for Indonesia, its self-image and its tourism industry. Unfortunately, the result has been to effectively halt archaeological works for the past few years. It does seem highly fanciful to try to link Gunung Padang with Atlantis, almost nothing about the site matches Solon's description. Even after the sudden rise in sea level during the Younger Dryas period and further rises since, today Gunung Padang remains 900m above sea level – so it was never anywhere near serving as a flourishing port. If excavation works do reveal ancient structures and corroborate the sample dating, then it will provide clear evidence of a sophisticated pre-flood culture.

14.4   Apart from testing conventional credulity, these earliest dates take the development of Gunung Padang back before the Younger Dryas interlude into the depths of the last Ice Age – when sea levels were 120m lower than today and the Indonesian archipelago was a massive continuous land area, referred to as Sundaland and contiguous with the Mekong peninsula of Asia.

Ancient medical procedures

14.5   Another recent discovery was made 1000km north east of Gadung Palung and points to a surprising level of sophistication far earlier than conventional history teaches. An article in the September 2022 edition of *Nature* magazine, described an amazing find in Liang Tebo, a cave on the Sangkulirang–Mangkalihat Peninsula of eastern Borneo. A team from Griffith University in Australia, excavating the oldest grave ever found in South-East Asia, found a 31,000-year-old skeleton missing its left foot and part of the left leg. Timothy Maloney, a lead author of the latest study, described the recovered parts of the left tibia and fibula presenting with a very unusual bony growth which closely matches clinical instances of deliberate amputation. The surface of the bone suggests that the young man underwent amputation as a child and survived for six to nine years after the fact, recovering well and apparently thriving as an amputee. To pull off such a sophisticated medical procedure would have required detailed knowledge of human anatomy and the ability to negotiate exposed tissue, veins, arteries and nerves, never mind the risk of infections. If correct, this pushes back the earliest evidence of surgical procedures by around 24,000 years.

15

Longyou Caves, Zhejiang Province – an anomaly

15.1 In the village of Shiyan Beicun, deep in the Zhejiang province of China sits the Longyou caves. These caves remained undiscovered for millennia until one local man decided to test the validity of the local legend.

15.2 Myths about the local ponds being "bottomless" were the talk of local lore for as long as anyone could remember. One man decided that this myth finally had to be put to the test, so he rallied others in the community and they bought a large hydraulic pump. After pumping for 17 days, the man and thus the world discovered numerous extensive hand-dug caves beneath the surface of the town's ponds.

15.3 After first discovery in 1992, a total of 36 grottoes have been discovered equating to about 30,000 square meters of hand dug caverns. While these caverns represent one of the largest ancient excavation projects in history, their origin has absolutely no documentation – leading to great mystery. The caverns were carved into solid siltstone descending about 30 meters in each grotto. These caverns contain separate rooms, bridges, pools, and gutters, even intricate carvings on the walls. Pillars carved throughout the caves allow for the ceiling to be uniformly supported. Chisel marks on the walls in a series of parallel lines indicate that the expansive caves were hand carved by a now unknown culture. Today, one of the caves is open for tourism, chosen because it was the most extensively ornate cave of all of the Longyou caves. Even with current archaeological research and engineering examination, the origin of the caves still remains a mystery.

15.4 Of all of the mysteries around the caves, perhaps the biggest is figuring out just how they were constructed. The quantity of rock that would have been removed is equivalent to around 1 million cubic meters. When experts consider the average digging rate of humans tasked with the tools of the time, they estimate that simply excavating the dirt would have taken 12 years using 1,000 people working 12 hours a day. These calculations only consider the amount of time that it would have taken to remove that volume of dirt, it doesn't take into account the precise engineering and artistry displayed in the caves' construction.

15.5 What perplexes experts is this project of extensive magnitude was never documented and no tools were ever found on-site. Construction on this scale would have involved the Emperor and the direction of considerable resources. Hence the absence of any references is particularly puzzling considering how good the ancient Chinese were at documenting their activities.

15.6 Another befuddling mystery of the caves' construction lies in the markings on the walls. Every wall is covered in uniform parallel chisel marks. This particular form of excavation would have been much more labour intensive than raw excavation. Experts cannot explain why the people of the time would have laboriously chiselled away the caves instead of using more effective tools like picks or haphazard blunt objects.

15.7 Whilst many of the 36 grottos are virtually identical, there are no interconnections, many are excavated back to back with parallel walls dug extremely accurately leaving supporting walls only 50 centimetres thick between two grottos. Measurements reveal surprising uniformity of thickness – despite having being dug by two separate teams. No theory has been developed to explain how this feat could have been achieved without modern technology. The grotto entrances are uniformly small and the further recesses pitch black and yet the marked patterns on the walls remain of a uniform design throughout – and no evidence of how the grottos were illuminated has been found.

15.8 Apart from the unknown and confusing means of construction, other weirder mysteries surround the Longyou caves. The local area is known for having deep naturally occurring caverns that are filled with water. When these caverns are explored, they teem with life and fish. When the Longyou caverns were first pumped dry, no evidence of life and absolutely no fish were found inside their walls. This mystery could be purely coincidence, but it still raises questions as to what might have made the man-made caverns different.

15.9 The intriguing properties of the caves are not limited to weird natural phenomena either, engineering experts question how the caves were able to endure practically unharmed for so long. The caves show no signs of damage, no piles of rubble, and no signs of seismic movement. And this is despite many of the walls being as thin as 50 centimetres and the region prone to natural disasters. The insides of the caves are so well preserved that it is as though they were built very recently.

15.10 The Longyou caves remain shrouded in mystery. With no evidence of what they were used for, who constructed them, or even how they have survived for so long, they may continue to be at the centre of future speculation. Conventional history will tend to date such enigmas solely by reference to the already known cultures and related technology.

15.11 The reason I have included this discovery in this book as possibly linked to very ancient evidence rather than just pre-history is a common thread with a few other works. The careful hollowing out of large subterranean spaces not connected with the mining of special ores is not a normal human activity. These spaces are so huge that they must have been used or intended for use as living space. The survivors of the Hiawatha impact would have good reason to take precautionary action to enable better survival in the event of a repeat occurrence.

15.12 Having read the above, please check out 'Longyou caves' on Google Images.

16

Antikythera Mechanism – an anomaly

16.1　This devise is generally regarded as around 2200 years old, and so is difficult to link to any pre-Hiawatha culture but it is exactly the kind of missing link that would greatly help to prise open the issue of whether an advanced civilisation existed prior to the meteor impacts of the Younger Dryas period.

16.2　Now understood to be of Greek origin, it was found in AD1902 within the cargo of a Roman shipwreck, dated to around 65BC, off the island of Antikythera. The exact date of its construction is unknown but it is possibly the most astounding piece of ancient technology ever discovered. The Antikythera Mechanism has baffled historians with its incredible intricacy and design. It is now understood to have originally contained thirty-seven gears, thirty having been identified from the remaining fragments. It was not until the 17th century that so many gears were again incorporated into a single machine. The mechanism is very complex, able to predict the movements of the sun, moon, some major stars, the 12 Zodiac signs, and the five planets the Greeks knew of. Amazingly, the mechanism tracked the Saros cycle (periods of solar and lunar eclipses), the Metonic cycle (the basis for the Greek calendar, an 18.61 year cycle corresponding to 235 lunar months), and Callippic cycle (a lunar cycle which included four Metonic cycles).

16.3　As noted above, the Metonic cycle was the basis of the Greek calendar, a construction that worked with the Earth centric view of the cosmos, an understanding also inherited by the Romans. This theory of the flat

Earth with a hemispherical dome above it, represented a major degradation of human knowledge compared with the earlier knowledge of the civilisations of the Fertile Crescent. I'm not an astronomical engineer but I do not think a mechanical computer could predict planetary movements of a heliocentric solar system by assuming they orbited the Earth? Could this point to construction of the Mechanism by a far earlier culture with a true heliocentric knowledge, far more advanced than the Greeks of the 2nd century BC?

16.4 The Mechanism is the size of a shoebox – 33cm tall and 18 cm wide but only 8cm deep to accommodate the 37 astonishingly complex gears and cogs. Quite how these intricate cogs and gears were manufactured presents another enigma. The components of the mechanism are made of bronze, easy to cast but very difficult to use to make intricate gear wheels and gradient cogs. By comparison, medieval astrolabes built around AD1500 were made of malleable brass or iron and look like clumsy toys compared with the Antikythera Mechanism.

16.5 A study, published in November 2014 in the journal *Archive for History of Exact Science*, focused on the Saros dial (the eclipse predictor) of the Antikythera Mechanism. It concluded that the prediction calendar includes a solar eclipse occurring on 12 May 205BC. This has been used to suggest the device was assembled around this date. Previously, research based on radiocarbon dating and the style of the Greek letters used had concluded it was constructed between 150BC and 100BC. Maybe, its creator was Archimedes – he died in 212BC but may have devised the mechanism predicting the later eclipse.

16.6 Is it possible that the Antikythera Mechanism was a treasured artifact carefully preserved by astronomers and handed down over millennia? Could the Greek text engraved on the device have been added around 200BC to help preserve the detailed instructions on how to operate the Mechanism? If this level of advanced mechanical engineering was available to the Greeks – why did clock making not flourish? Given the extraordinary accuracy of the Mechanism (e.g. 16.8 below), is it possible that the Saros dial remained accurate for say 10,000 years – possibly being manufactured before the devastation of the Kefalonia impacts?

16.7 In March 2021, UCL (University College London) published an article in *Scientific Reports* that they had used computer modelling to reconstruct the complete Antikythera Mechanism. Professor Tony Freeth explained that, using 3D X-rays and surface imaging undertaken in 2005, the team managed to work out how the Mechanism predicted eclipses and calculated the variable motion of the Moon. The breakthrough came from gaining a full understanding of the gearing system at the front of the device. Only about a third of the Mechanism has survived, split into 82 fragments. The largest fragment, known as Fragment A, displays features of bearings, pillars and a block. Another, known as Fragment D, features an unexplained disk with an intricate 63-tooth gear and plate.

16.8 The X-ray data from 2005 revealed thousands of text characters hidden inside the fragments. Two numbers were startling – 462 and 442. These numbers represent the number of years for special cycles of Venus and Saturn respectively – which from an Earthly perspective include periods when retrograde motion would have been observed. Accurate knowledge of these values would depend upon very extensive observation over a number of centuries – something unlikely for the Greeks alone to have accomplished. If the Mechanism was constructed by Greeks around 200BC, the designer almost certainly relied on data from other sources. Greek astronomical knowledge would not seem capable of calculating such values, maybe the knowledge came from the Sabian community at Harran – who were still going strong in 200BC.

16.9 Evaggelos Vallianatos, author of many books on the Antikythera Mechanism, writing in the *Greek Reporter*, described the machine "as much more than a mechanism, it is a sophisticated, mind-bogglingly complex astronomical computer." Employing advanced astronomy, mathematics, metallurgy, and engineering to construct the astronomical device 2,200 years ago, the age of the computer and its flawless high-tech nature profoundly disturbed some of the scientists who studied it. A few Western scientists of the twentieth century were shocked by the Antikythera Mechanism, Vallianatos said: "They called it an astrolabe for several decades and refused to call it a computer. The astrolabe, a Greek invention of the 16th century, is a useful instrument for calculating the position of the Sun and other prominent stars. Yet, its technology is rudimentary compared to that of the Antikythera device."

17

Egyptian colonies in Central America?

17.1   A number of cultures arose in Central America broadly coincident with the conventional dating of Egyptian culture and with some remarkable similarities – particularly a shared fondness for constructing pyramids.

17.2   The earliest post Younger Dryas advanced central American culture appears to be the Olmecs. The Olmecs have been traced to early farming cultures in the Tabasco province of Mexico between 5100BC and 4600BC which established the food crops and technologies used as the Olmec civilisation flourished. The Olmecs, based on their facial characteristics and knowledge of Egyptian building techniques, were most likely immigrants from north east Africa. The Olmec are conventionally dated from 1600BC to 400BC – when they appear to have abandoned their cities. The Olmec appear to have known of an impending disaster, maybe a plague, as they took care to dismantle the statutes of their gods at the La Venta pyramid and bury them in a deep trench cut into the side of the pyramid. A huge quantity of valuables was also buried in the same trench – over 1000 tons of smooth serpentine blocks; 48 piles of polished jade stones; pottery, figurines and polished hermatite mirrors – treausre representing millions of man-hours of stone working. The primary deity of the Olmec appears to have been Quetzalcoatl, which translates as 'feathered serpent', with a famous carving on La Venta monument 19. The name immediately brings to mind the Middle Eastern gods – 'feathered' implying the ability to fly and 'serpent' usuallly denoting wisdom. Quetzalcoatl, regarded as a great benefactor and teacher was credited, amongst other things, with giving the people a calendar.

17.3   The people of Mesoamerica used three calendars – two were cyclical, measuring the cycles of the Sun and the Moon, the third was chronological – the Long Count calendar. The zero point of the Long Count was our equivalent of 3113BC. To intercalate between solar and lunar calendars, all Mesoamerican cultures used a cycle of 52 years – when 13 lunar cycles, 365 solar days and 20 solar 'months' coincide every 18,980 days. Intriguingly, the great god of Mesoamerica, Quetzalcoatl was represented in iconography in remarkably similar ways to the Egyptian god Thoth – known as skilled in astronomy, calendars and temple building. In Egypt, 52 was the magical number of Thoth, the Game of 52 was also known as the Game of Thoth. When Quetzalcoatl departed from Mesoamerica, he vowed to return in the year known as "1 reed" of the 'sacred cycle' – which seems to have been carefully measured through the millennia – as Cortes, the tall, fair skinned and bearded god, duly reappeared in the promised '1 reed' year of 1519. The centrality of 52 in Mesoamerican beliefs is a strong pointer to ancient links with Egypt – and 3113BC could have witnessed the arrival of a party from Egypt.

17.4   It is interesting to speculate that the date when a party from Egypt may have arrived in Central America to establish the Mesoamerican civilisations is very proximate to the date the first dynasty in Egypt was established. Perhaps, the trigger for the founding of the first dynasty of purely native human pharaohs in Egypt was a decision by the ruling 'gods' to depart on a new civilizing mission. Could advanced astronomical knowledge have identified the high probability of an pending impact – for example the meteor impact we have recently located and named as the Burkle Impact, mid Indian Ocean, estimated at between 3000BC and 2800BC?

17.5   Some traces of Maya settlements have been dated back to 2600BC, but the zenith of the Mayan civilization is dated between AD250 and AD900 during which many Mayan cities are estimated to have contained over 100,000 citizens. The most recent date of a monument dedication found so far, shows a Long Count date equivalent to AD909. After this, over a period of about 50 years, it seems most of the Mayan cities were simply abandoned – explanations put forward include overpopulation leading to famine, or a plague – leaving a rich legacy of architectural remains for archaeologists to explore.

17.6   In February 2018, the first phase of the PACUNAM Lidar satellite mapping initiative revealed 60,000 newly identified Mayan structures in an interconnected series of cities. Estimates of the Mayan population at its peak have now been raised to 15 million. After the severe contraction of urban centres during the 9th Century AD, it seems some population centres endured but new defensive walls and ramparts were added and the next few centuries seem to have witnessed constant warfare. From first contact with the Spanish in 1511, Mayan cities were methodically defeated, with the Itza capital being the last in 1697.

17.7 Based in central Mexico, the Toltecs (AD510 – AD1063) were another Nahuatl people famed for building cities with substantial ceremonial centres. The Toltec capital Tollen, aka Teotihuacan, built on the edge of Tenochtitlan, is renowned for its two pyramids, dedicated to the Sun and the Moon. The two pyramids are connected by a broad avenue which extends 5 km on a perfect north south alignment. The pyramids share one amazing similarity with the two largest pyramids of Giza. One looks modestly bigger than the other, but whilst the Pyramid of the Moon looks smaller – it is built on ground that is 30m higher – and, as in Egypt, the cap stones of both are at identical elevations above sea level. Quite how the Toltecs could calculate and plan the construction to achieve this result is unknown – Teotihuacan is 270km from the sea.

17.8 This design feature of two pyramids with top capstones at identical altitudes points very strongly to common architects – the ancients would have attributed both Teotihuacan and Giza to Thoth.

17.9 The Aztecs (AD1325 – AD1519) were the last native group to flourish in Mesoamerica, also taking over Tenochtitlan as their capital in AD1325. Between 1517 and 1519 Tenochtitlan suffered a series of major earthquakes resulting in severe flooding – which the people saw as an omen of worse disaster to come. So, when Cortes arrived at Tenochtitlan in AD1519, despite finding a city with a population five times that of contemporary London, he managed to subdue it with a minor force. After an initial warm welcome, Cortes found resentment at his attempt to replace the ruler and a battle ensued. Finding it easier to pronounce, Cortes renamed Tenochtitlan as Mexico City and built Catholic churches over the sites of all the temples.

17.10 The similarities between the Egyptian and Central American cultures strongly suggest some kind of linkage. It does not seem to amount to a sustained two-way exchange of ideas but probably comprised inbound survivors of probably the first Younger Dryas impact led by Thoth, remembered locally as Quetzalcoatl, who taught similar building concepts to both the Egyptians and those found in Mesoamerica. It also seems most likely that it was Quetzalcoatl or his associates who had the transport facilities to convey Africans to Central America, whose descendants later became known as the Olmecs.

17.11 Not only have we found ancient megalithic structures which stand in defiance of our conventional understanding of history but some tantalizing evidence suggesting links with the builders of megalithic structures in the Middle East.

17.12 Our traditional Western view of Central and South American history features a number of bloodthirsty tribal empires, delighting in human sacrifice and technologically backwards – no use of the wheel or horse for transport, nor brass or iron for tools and weapons. Reliance on very soft gold, silver, copper and tin resulted in metals being used mainly for decorative purposes – hence both Aztecs and Inca were defenceless against Spanish steel.

17.13 When Pizarro invaded the Inca empire in AD1533, his astonishment at the super abundance of gold in the temples banished all thoughts apart from seizure and extraction of the gold. Vast quantities of gold plate carrying engraved text, symbols and diagrams were melted down to facilitate transport back to Spain without any thought being given to the knowledge being destroyed. Only later, when the Catholic Church learned of the opportunity for conversions and sent missionaries, did anyone start to learn about the beliefs of the Inca and other indigenous peoples.

17.14 What the missionaries learned stunned them. The missionaries, Dominicans, Franciscans and Jesuits, like everyone else at that time, knew of pre Greek history solely from the Old Testament. As the missionaries mastered the local language and begun to understand the Inca belief system – it all seemed very familiar, to such an extent that the Inca were believed to be one or more of the lost tribes of Israel. The earliest record is the *Account of the Ancient Customs of the Natives of Peru* by Jesuit Blas Valera (1551 – 1597). Today, some descriptions the *Account* offers are regarded as reliable, some unique and others taken with caution – the author having had to learn various local languages and then understand complex oral traditions. The *Account* was highly regarded and quoted by historians but only edited and published by Marcos Jimenez de la Espade, a specialist in colonial Spanish history, in 1879. Today, we would not think of the Inca as one of the Lost Tribes of Israel but we do puzzle over how their tribal heritage included some of the most famous memories of the Sumerians and Egyptians – knowledge that was inaccessible to Europeans in the 16th Century.

17.15 The full extent of pre-Columbia civilizations known today has mainly been discovered in the past century. Unfortunately, we have almost nothing in terms of written records apart from monumental inscriptions. We have no equivalent of the cuneiform tablets from Mesopotamia or the Pharaonic yearbooks and priestly records from Egypt.

17.16 As with Sumer and Egypt, the generally accepted dating of the earliest civilization is increasingly challenged by evidence that these cultures seem to have sprung into existence with fully formed civil structures and extensive technical knowledge – whilst astro-archaeology is producing dates that suggest far earlier societies existed.

17.17 The civilizations predating the Spanish conquest of South America are nowadays divided into three phases – the earliest being known as the Megalithic, followed by the Ancient Empire and more recently the series of empires centred in Mesoamerica and in Peru. Careful study of the ancient constructions clearly reveals three levels of capability – with the Megalithic being the foundations, the Ancient Empire distinctive but far less impressive and the recorded culture of Inca and Aztec invariably built atop or abutting earlier styles but being relatively crude by comparison with the older levels. It is noteworthy that the first two phases are considered as possibly continental in scale, followed by fragmentation and the creation of distinctly separate and less technologically advanced local cultures.

17.18 In Central America, the best preserved cycle of legends is that of the Nahuatl people. These legends were recorded between 1540 and 1585 by Friar Bernardino de Sahagún in his work named *Historia de las cosas de la Nueva Espana*. The Nahuatl tales tell of four ages, the earliest being dated from c15600BC that lasted until the Flood, the first people having journeyed from a White Place (Azt-lan – maybe glaciated?) and associated with the number seven. Intriguingly, seven is of course an epithet of Enlil, the Lord of Earth, the 7th planet of our solar system. The people split into four tribes with the main group, known as the Mexica, travelling inland until finding an eagle perched on a cactus – the symbol they took as indicating where they should build their city. The city was named Tenochtitlan, the City of Tenoch (T'enoch). This legend has an eerie echo of the biblical tale of Cain – who was banished to wander in a distant land, where he built a city and named it after his son Enoch – who in turn had four descendants from which grew four tribes. It has been suggested that the "mark of Cain", biblically described as a permanent mark identifying Cain's descendants, might indeed be the absence of facial hair – which is unique to Amerindians. This is in marked contrast to most Mesoamerican depictions of their gods – who are invariably shown sporting beards.

17.19 Let us review the evidence that there were some survivors of the Hiawatha Impact which triggered the Younger Dryas period, as revealed by remains of a number of culturally advanced peoples at variance with the conventional historical record.

EGYPTIAN COLONIES IN CENTRAL AMERICA?

18

Were survivors of destroyed cultures acclaimed as gods?

18.1   The evidence reviewed so far strongly indicates that the conventional account that our first civilisations only emerged around 4000BC in Egypt, Sumer and the Indus Valley is no longer credible. The evidence provided by the Göbekli Tepe megaliths, 5.5m tall pillars weighing around 20 tons and covered in absolutely exquisite carvings are convincingly dated to around 9000BC and nearby small cities dating back to 11000BC, indicates an advanced society existed at that early date. This culture had extensive astronomical knowledge, had already adopted the zodiac which we continue to use and enjoying a level of agricultural production sufficient to generate surplus food to support specialised workers.

18.2   Whilst the evidence of the dating at Göbekli Tepe is irrefutable, there are also very strong arguments to support the construction of the Giza complex of pyramids and the Sphinx dating to the same time – 9023BC. Maybe this was to celebrate rebuilding after the devastating floods caused by the Kefalonia impacts c9620BC. Astro-archaeology is providing dates which place the construction of Andean megalithic observatories back many millennia earlier still.

18.3   Then we have widespread legends supported by compellingly similar graphical representations of small groups of wise men arriving in the midst of surviving communities after the Younger Dryas events and providing generous teaching and knowledge. Remarkably similar tales of the Seven Apkallu, and the same white, bearded, Falcon, Horus, Viracocha, Quetzalcoatl, appearing as a leader.

18.4   Let us consider what skills these intelligent survivors seem to have. The breadth of knowledge attributed to these newcomers almost equates to 'civilisation in a box' – including building design and construction skills, agriculture – sowing, reaping, storing produce; cooking recipes; wine-making; identification of medicinal plants and their uses; legal codes; and immense astronomical knowledge. It seems that the beneficiaries were mighty impressed and grateful.

18.5   The recipients of such bountiful gifts would naturally look up to these knowledgeable types. So, the new arrivals needed shelter. The wise newcomers would provide a design and manage those helping to build it – the result would be luxurious compared with the crude huts of the hunter gatherers – a veritable 'temple', where the 'gods' lived and issued pronouncements (commands from god and the dispensing of justice); where regular gifts from crops and hunting could be brought (offerings); no doubt some brighter locals would quickly be recruited as dedicated helpers and advisors on local practices and resources (attendant priests). This interpretation is reinforced when temple inscriptions and other records refer to temples built for gods regularly included places to house their weapons and to park their 'shem' (Sumerian term for a 'vessel'). Hence it is very easy to visualise intelligent newcomers, demonstrating their capabilities, assuming leadership and then facilitating (maybe encouraging) a process whereby they were acknowledged as superior and granted many privileges.

18.6   It is noteworthy that many of these intelligent newcomers became immortalised in the ancient records, with their names and exploits living on in monumental inscriptions and legends. Over time one can see it was inevitable that these heroes would be praised by grateful subjects, monuments built to honour them and they became remembered as 'gods'. And modern historians bought into this labelling just as easily.

18.7   One common feature of these temple complexes is the obsession with astronomy. Why was so much effort devoted to tracking the stars and planets, the voluminous records of observed and predicted eclipses and star rises recorded in cuneiform tablets from Sumer through to Babylon? Historians have long attributed the importance of having this knowledge to either mundane farming issues, such as when to plant seeds, etc., or as a control mechanism – being able to control the masses by accurately predicting highly visible events would occur in the sky. Perhaps the true reason, given our recent understanding of what may have driven the Dryas period climate volatility, was the need to accurately track the comet or meteor cloud debris which Earth seems to have overlapped orbits with. Studying the night sky will quickly reveal planets which steadily move against the background stars - so any new point of light which appears to be moving against the background might herald a new threat. We have good data on the impact events which triggered the start and the ending of the Younger Dryas period but no hard evidence of the causes of the multiple other abrupt climate changes. It must be an odds-on certainty that at least some of these sudden climate changes were triggered by other meteor impacts – therefore any culture which had such sophisticated astronomical knowledge, as we know these 'survivors' had, would naturally prioritize star gazing, building observatories and training 'observer-priests' to monitor the skies.

18.8   Let us consider where these survivors originated. The most obvious place from which one might expect survivors to have fled from would be the areas most affected by the Impacts. But, oddly, we have found no evidence at all of any megalithic culture in North America or Europe. If we had found the remains of a massive megalithic city in California or the Appalachians, then we might develop a theory of how an advanced megalithic culture was more or less wiped out and a few survivors ventured to other continents and helped spread some of their knowledge. But all the evidence from the 'black mat' shows the opposite – the Clovis culture people were definitely nomadic hunter gatherers who specialised in hunting megafauna. There is no evidence that the Clovis people constructed anything more than tents using animal skins.

18.9   There is also a complete absence of ancient megalithic remains in Europe earlier than Stonehenge. Admittedly there are a few other archaeological sites which are broadly contemporary with Stonehenge and which also create problems with conventional historical narrative but none which remotely indicate a sophisticated pre-flood culture. Examples which challenge the conventional history include: the Dhaskalio 'pyramid' on a small Greek island and Motilla del Azuer in Spain. Research indicates that Dhaskalio originally comprised 60 buildings, all clad in white marble, dating to around 2600BC – well before the Minoan civilisation and contemporary with Sumer prior to the arrival of the first Semites (the Akkadians) and contemporary with the earliest Egyptian dynasties. Motilla del Azuer, just east of Ciudad Real in southern Spain, is a unique citadel constructed around 2200BC. Expanded and occupied until around 1500BC, the design is believed to be the earliest form of the Broch found in northern and western Scotland. But, neither could be described as megalithic.

18.10 Looking at the evidence of megalithic cultures that we do have – in Egypt and Lebanon, in Central and South America and some enigmas in China and Indonesia – all are above, and in some cases, far above even current sea levels. An advanced culture must by definition specialise, and by extension must trade specialised products for a range of other specialised products. The mode of transport for heavy or bulky goods most likely to be mastered first would be that which uses water to float the goods – hence trade was likely to be water borne and ships an early development. This also means it was inevitable that many population centres would have been ports and the inhabitants living close to sea level. The far flung locations identified above are suggestive of an advanced culture that had spread across the oceans.

18.11 In exactly the same way that present day rises in sea levels are forecast to affect many leading global cities such as London, New York and Shanghai – so a supposed antediluvian megalithic culture would have been threatened by rising sea levels. We worry about current annual rises in sea levels, estimated at 2.5mm for 2023, from record ice melt and the expansion effect of rising sea temperatures. This can be compared with the challenge of living in the period of around 3000 years between c12600BC and 9600BC when the average annual rise in sea levels was 16mm - six times the rate of sea rise we are experiencing today but persisting at varying speed over as many as 100 generations.

18.12 We know where the survivors fled to – the Middle East – with evidence in Turkey, Lebanon, Sumer and Egypt; and to Central & South America – with evidence in Mexico, Peru and Bolivia. We know they did not come from North America – the evidence of the Clovis culture reveals no trace beyond hunter gatherer skills. One would assume, based on the skills quickly exhibited in their adopted homes, that these survivors would have left megalithic remains in the ruins of their overwhelmed homelands. We have some evidence suggesting a pre Younger Dryas culture in Egypt and, so far speculatively, that a maritime power may have been centred in what we call Atlantis. But, no traces have been found – neither elsewhere in Africa, nor in Australia, East or South Asia – areas least affected by the

Younger Dryas events. One major area remains, which was indirectly greatly affected, South East Asia – as rising sea levels swamped the low lying lands previously joining up the Indonesian archipelago and Australia – known as Sundaland.

18.13 Is it possible that an advanced civilisation evolved in the now largely flooded lands of Sundaland. Some do argue that the legendary Atlantis was located in this area. As a culture remembered as being accomplished sailors and traders, the Atlantean culture may have been concentrated at coastal ports. Thus their main centres of population could have been eventually overwhelmed by rising sea levels – but surely, faced with a relentless rise in sea levels, people would simply have progressively moved inland and to higher levels? The Hiawatha impact would have resulted in ash laden dark skies blotting out both sun and starlight for a long period combined with plunging temperatures. Vegetation would have withered and animals starved, persistent black rain would have been seen as a very bad omen. But for south east Asia, the fire and earthquakes told as part of the Atlantis story seem out of place.

18.14 So, the conundrum we are left with is that we have solid evidence of a post flood dispersal of technologically advanced peoples, all be it in very small numbers – but very sparse evidence of where they might have fled from. We can hope that further exploration of Tiahuanaco and Gunung Padang might provide some reliably dateable evidence from long buried organic material. An alternative, which will never gain approval or funding, would be to prise up one of the Trilithons at Baalbek or one of the megalithic anchor stones in the walls at Sacsahuaman – again to retrieve and determine accurate dating of long buried organic material from the time of construction.

18.15 From the evidence we have reviewed in this book, the most likely centre for a pre-flood advanced civilisation must be Egypt. Their technology for extracting, carving and building using huge blocks of the hardest stone is complemented by astonishing abilities in turning 15m granite columns on something resembling a lathe and polishing granite so finely as to remain highly reflective after as many as 12 millennia. One can imagine an 800m wall of tsunami sweeping clean away all human constructions along most of the length of the Nile.

18.16 One possible speculation, on my part, is that one base of the megalithic culture was around Lake Titicaca, today close to the Peruvian-Bolivian border. Certainly, there are a large number of undated megalithic sites, with some astral alignments which have been dated as possibly as far back as 15000BC. Two features of the carving are replicated in Peru (e.g. at Cutimbo on the western side of Lake Titicaca) and at Göbekli Tepe (and at other Middle Eastern sites generally far younger) – the bucket shaped 'laptop' bag that 'gods' are often depicted carrying and the style of hands being outstretched across the stomachs of human statues with fingers stretched out but not quite touching. Why did they seemingly abandon these centres? Perhaps, their observatories predicted another meteor impact, the one presumed to have ended the Younger Dryas period around 9620BC? They might have estimated an impact near their centre of operations – and decided to move as a precaution. However, whilst there is evidence of huge upheavals amongst the ruins, there is no black mat type layer (as only sparse grassland at this altitude) and no one is claiming discovery of nano-diamonds, etc., indicative of an impact. Maybe the impact was relatively close but into a deep part of the Pacific Ocean? But, whilst it could explain a decision to flee to the other side of the world – why were there so few survivors? Some have suggested that the complex constructions near the shore of Lake Titicaca resemble docks and wharfs for large numbers of ships – which makes no sense given its altitude at 3812m. But supposing a massive impact had caused tectonic plate shifts which pushed that area far above its previous level? Such a devastation would leave few survivors and have rendered any previous maritime activities impossible – therefore the few that were far away when disaster struck headed off and tried to start again, closer to sea level, around the sheltered Mediterranean.

18.17 The tales of survivors passed down to us, invariably involve very small bands – 7 being a typical number. One ancient reference which might be a remembrance of such survivors, in somewhat larger numbers, is in the Book of Enoch. Enoch is intriguing - as Islamic writers have linked Enoch with Hermes, the Greek name for Thoth – the original building designer noted in the Edfu Building texts and elsewhere. The first Book of Enoch, which is widely believed to be one of the very oldest Hebrew records, refers to a party of 'Watchers', who are also described as angels, "in all numbering 200, who descended on the summit of Mount Hermon" in the days of Jared. Most readers will be aware of the notorious references in Genesis to Watchers as being the sons of the gods who took a fancy to the daughters of men – and created a race of offspring described as Nephilim, described as 'mighty men of renown'. These references raise a host of questions:

(i) Dating - 'in the time of Jared' places these events before the Flood. Jared is described as only the 6th generation after Adam and Eve, the father of Enoch and thus a few generations earlier than Noah – placing Jared significantly before the Flood story that we have dated to c10765BC;

(ii) A party of 200 stands out compared with other groups of survivors, suggesting their transport was somewhat larger than other groups of around 7 had arrived in;

(iii) Their arrival described as "descending upon the summit of Mount Hermon" is extraordinary – the summit of Mount Hermon is at 2800m, did these Watchers arrive by spaceship?

(iv) Mount Hermon, Lebanon, is very close to Baalbek;

(v) The genetic differences between these Watchers and the human females must be very small – as not only did they produce offspring, the Nephilim, but these offspring were also fertile and the second generation became known as the Elioud.

18.18 The idea of male gods mating with human females, and of goddesses mating with human men occurs frequently in ancient records. Indeed, so frequently that I believe translators use of the term 'god' has completely misled us. Many Sumerian and Egyptian stories relate productive unions which in turn produced fertile offspring. Therefore, the 'gods' must have been just as human as we are. The more appropriate title for these more intelligent humans might be 'lord', 'king' or just 'absolute ruler'. Consider when colonialists arrived in hunter gatherer societies in North America and in sub-Saharan Africa – there was little doubt who was in charge and who had to be respected and obeyed. Typically, the invading guys took a fancy to the local girls. It is also rather telling that when the small band of Spanish led by Cortes reached Tenochtitlán in 1519, the Aztec ruler Moctezuma, considered Cortes to be a god - either an emissary of Quetzalcoatl or Quetzalcoatl himself. The arrival of men wearing unfamiliar clothes, using a previously unknown method of transport (horseback) and wielding iron swords was sufficient for them to be deemed 'gods' even by a culture comprising a relatively advanced, large urbanised population.

18.19 I also draw attention to the almost universal association of wings and or fish scales in representations of these wise sages/gods. The representation of stylised wings must surely denote that the individual could travel through the air similarly to a bird, and fish scales indicate the individual could travel across the sea, maybe even under the sea? Otherwise, why is the visual association so widespread. The stories telling of the arrival of the Apkallu to Egypt and to Peru describe ships which travelled without sails or oars.

Three technical mysteries – transportation, stone masonry, design/project management

18.20 Whilst you might justifiably retort that illustrating a 'god' with a motif showing wings means that 'god' had aerial transport is highly speculative, there are other aspects we can consider based on the solid evidence of the megalithic structures that they left behind. I briefly consider three capabilities which clearly supported these megalithic constructions:

  (i) transportation, what we might term 'heavy lift capability' over considerable elevations and over considerable distances;

  (ii) the ability to quarry and intricately shape stone blocks, some of incredible size; and,

  (iii) the ability to design complex structures of huge proportions and then manage the construction project to create magnificent edifices.

18.21 Transportation: there are various clues in the megalithic structures that we noted earlier – how could the megalithic blocks used at Machu Picchu and around Tiahuanaco have been moved enormous distances and raised to such altitudes from the source strata from which these huge blocks were hewed? Something more advanced than sheer human muscle power, ropes made from available vegetation and timber rollers must have been deployed. If relying on these alone, the workforce required and its support requirements would mean projects would have taken hundreds of years to complete – and our conventional population estimates must be seriously understated. Key elements of technology must have been used to both transport the megalithic blocks and to raise them into positions which required great dexterity. The ideas that blocks used in the Great Pyramids, 139m high, could have been pulled up to the higher levels on rollers using some kind of external scaffolding or internal passageways later filled in are both hilarious. How would the limestone casing and particularly the cap stone have been placed? One might think of bamboo scaffolding, as still used in Hong Kong, which can reach such heights – but Hong Kong scaffolding uses (i) steel bolts and wires connected to the face of the building; (ii) tough nylon ties securing all bamboo members, and (iii) is generally erected vertically rather than at an angle of 51°. Nor is Hong Kong scaffolding used to transport blocks weighing 2.5 tons! There are simply no materials which could have been used to hold together any temporary structure bearing any such weight to any height remotely close to 139m. Recent fashionable ideas of using ramps internal to the pyramid, could not have been used for the external polished white casing blocks and the capstone.

18.22 Stonehenge points to the survival of some aerial or heavy lift technology for up to 6000 years after the Flood – how could the Pembrokeshire bluestones have been located without use of an aerial survey? How could the 80 blocks weighing 4 tons each have been transported around 250 km to Stonehenge? Even the use of boats would merely halve the distance to be hauled over land – and what kind of boats existed 5000 years ago to carry a 4 ton sarcen?

18.23 Stone masonry: the megalith constructions we have considered in Egypt and in the Andes share many extraordinary features – perfectly dressed faces, angled cuts to enhance load bearing of the blocks placed overhead, precise cuts to enable exact fitting – such that on some we cannot even insert a razor blade between the blocks. Today we can use computer controlled cutting machines to achieve these characteristics – but what did the Egyptians use? The hardest metal available was bronze – and bronze saws will barely cut wood! The surfaces and features we see in the Andean megaliths include many smooth bored tubes and sharp edged rectangular insets. Having read chapter 11, please check "precision stone cutting ancient" on Google Images for detailed photographs of some of the extraordinary stone working (please ignore any references to 'ancient aliens', at least until concluding this book). As well as what seems irrefutable evidence of the use of machine tools (maybe lasers, diamond tipped power drills and boring machines?), the monumental remains also suggest some form of mass production capability.

18.24 The polygonal blocks favoured in Andean megaliths (see Google Images "polygonal megalithic blocks" for a wide range of specimens) raise a number of practical questions:

(i) if blocks of these sizes could be fitted with such exquisite precision, why not just cut them all to a standard size?

(ii) were the builders just showing off or do the complex interlocking shapes provide greater resistance against earthquakes?

(iii) were these complex shapes cut by trial and error, fitting and refitting until perfect – or by some geometric cutting device that retained memory of the angles and lengths of each face to enable the next block to be cut to fit precisely?

The grasp of geometry seems surprisingly advanced and one wonders how unaided eyesight proved the equal of modern theodolites.

18.25 Design and project management: human endeavour on the scale that the megaliths represent requires a lot of planning. These structures were not constructed by making it up as they went along – there must have detailed plans prepared prior to work commencing. Whilst there are Egyptian references to a House of Records, for example, from which plans would be withdrawn for repair works, absolutely no records or inscriptions survive from the ancient megalithic builders in the Andes. Construction management must have had plans to consult when deciding building lines and what dimensions of blocks to task workers to quarry and shape. The cap stones of the two largest Giza pyramids are at exactly the same altitude despite starting at different elevations, requiring different base sizes when adopting identical angles for the sloping sides. On this scale of project, presumably taking decades to complete, plans must have provided for both sharing across the team leadership and for succession by younger generations of leaders – requiring plans with sufficiently detailed notations for any skilled professional to fully understand.

18.26 Whilst both Egyptian hieratic numerals and Sumerian cuneiform numerals used decimal bases and relatively straightforward symbols, using large numbers would have been very laborious and prone to errors in the computations. However, the Inca had no written symbols (so far detected) but relied on a methodology using rope knots – with different types of knots in different positions on a string representing different orders of magnitude. This issue on its own would seem to disassociate the Inca from our conventional attribution awarding them authorship of the megalithic structures.

18.27 The absence of any inscriptions or even typical builders' notations is puzzling – even if humanity pre-flood was telepathic, it would still require voluminous records of design and process. Jeanette Fincke's work translating records of Ashurbanipal's learning and sources of knowledge, see 12.10 to 12.12 above, points to written records dating back prior to the Flood. We have no indication of the medium in which such texts were recorded – they may have been carefully recopied many times over the intervening millennia. But, over 9000 years the vocabulary of any language will have changed so much as to require some form of translation – hence the guidance that Ashurbanipal himself refers to adds some credibility.

18.28 Apart from the ancient Sumerian king lists and the claims of Ashurbanipal, are there any other references to pre-flood texts? Yes, according to Zecharia Sitchin, writing in *The Cosmic Code*, there are many references in both early Egyptian and Sumerian records to texts that had been written by the 'gods' in 'olden words' requiring the Olden Gods to understand them. Both Sumerian and Akkadian records refer to Kitab Ilani, translated as 'the writing of the gods', with temple inscriptions describing renovation work following 'the drawings from olden times and the writing of the Upper Heaven'. In Egyptian texts, the god Thoth, recognised as the great architect, is credited with original authorship of a number of key texts – the *Book of the Dead*, the *Book of Breathings* and the *Tales of the Magicians* – 'written by Thoth with his own fingers'. At least Thoth seems to have used hieroglyphics !! Perhaps Yahweh also used hieroglyphics to inscribe the Ten Commandments on the first pair of tablets – the ones Moses smashed in anger !! Yahweh certainly did not use Hebrew as it was not developed from the original Phoenician script until after 1000BC.

18.29 In addition, there are many references in both 1Enoch and 2Enoch (books contained in the Ethiopian bible) to the pre-flood patriarch being shown sacred books which he copied out and references to Enoch himself having written as many as 360 books over his long lifetime. Whilst 2Enoch is generally regarded as quite recent (c2200 years old), 1Enoch is equally regarded as containing some truly ancient material.

18.30 The existence of pre-flood megaliths is virtual proof of the existence of pre-flood writing – such enormous projects could not be conceived, managed and constructed purely by word of mouth. Yet, no inscriptions whatsoever have been identified at any pre-flood megalithic site. Perhaps, ten thousand years from now, another civilisation will find monstrous ruins of tangled steel from our collapsed cities and discern international communication pathways of rail lines but an absence of contemporary written records - as all our electronic storage and communication devices will have disintegrated or had their parts disassembled to retrieve and recycle precious metals.

18.31 So, to conclude on the enigma of who built the various ancient megalithic structures we have looked at and the numerous references to events prior to the earliest known periods of Egyptian and Sumerian civilization. There appears to be only three logical answers:- either a hitherto undetected advanced human civilisation with some capabilities which we have only recovered in the past century, or, some extra-terrestrial visitors, or perhaps a combination of the two. Let us examine the possibilities.

18.32 The recent assessments of ancient Egyptian stonework by professional engineers and stonemasons now strongly indicate that an advanced culture existed in Egypt prior to the Younger Dryas events. The Hiawatha impact c10765BC would have created horrific weather with torrential rain swelling the Nile to levels never before witnessed, which would have swept away many riverside communities and much of the farming resources. This would have been followed by years without sunlight - a nuclear winter leading to the loss of food sources and the breakdown of civil society. Then, just 1200 years later, I speculate that the Kefalonia impacts occurred. The precise date of these impacts should soon be defined from analysis of nano-diamonds, etc., recovered from chevrons located around the Mediterranean coasts. These impacts created a tsunami estimated at 800m high - which would have swept far up the Nile, beyond the current day border with Sudan, destroying all the habitable areas of Egypt. The resulting total devastation is just as recorded in the Edfu Temple texts.

18.33 Sumerian and Egyptian references to the arrival of the Seven Sages speak of a few survivors from afar. These survivors (of either of the catastrophes) knew where to go, the centre of civilisation as they knew it – Egypt and Sumer.

18.34 One puzzle is why such an advanced culture did not expand across more of the planet? We have speculated that pre-Younger Dryas Egyptian technology may have been responsible for Baalbek and similar megalithic foundation stones found in Jerusalem but nothing further afield. With the skills and knowledge evident in their megalithic constructions, and the trade network evident from the embalming recipes (paragraphs 11.88 to 11.96) – one might have expected to find evidence of 'colonial' outposts – also sporting megaliths. Maybe there were – evidence points to both the Harappa (Punjab) and the foundation of Goa (south west India) as being outposts of Sumer. The more likely explanation lies in trade being supported by seafaring and the network of foreign outposts being mainly ports – which were all submerged by the c50m rise in average global sea levels during the Younger Dryas period. But why is there no evidence of Egyptian megaliths anywhere else in Africa?

18.35 More recently, later cultures lacking the skills Egyptians had developed, managed to spread their culture far abroad. Consider how extensive the spread of the Greek and Roman empires – sophisticated but clearly lacking the technology of the megalithic builders. Even the British, lacking the construction skills of the megalithic builders, had developed a globe girdling empire by the 18th century. One factor may have been differential military prowess – whilst dynastic Egyptians lacked iron for weapons they somehow managed with just bronze weapons to defeat the Greek Sea Peoples armed with iron weapons on a number of occasions. However, we have direct evidence of the use of Egyptian metallurgy prior to the Younger Dryas, from the saw cuts, bore holes and rectangular finishing common on pre-dynastic stone working - which all imply the existence of advanced metallurgy.

A hitherto undetected advanced antediluvian human civilization

18.36 These early advanced people had amazing astronomical knowledge, including information we only rediscovered within the last 25 years (not just the existence of Neptune and Uranus but their respective shades of blue) – and we needed space probes to find out, not just advanced telescopes. Somehow, these people also knew the zodiac cycle of 25,920 years and the process of precession (whereby sunrise regresses back through the zodiacal houses every 2,160 years. They also knew the 1,461 year cycle of the heliacal rising of Sirius and the 18.61 year lunar cycle. To discern these facts from meticulous recordings by astronomer priests required amazingly stable civil societies lasting for thousands of years!!

18.37   The motifs used to denote 'gods' frequently incorporate wings and records tell of their sudden comings and goings using their 'shem' (vessels) to go up to heaven, etc. However, the number of 'gods' remained very small – we have a remarkable catalogue prepared by a diligent high priestess, the daughter of King Sargon of Akkad, around 2300BC. In this work, the author enumerates every temple in Sumeria, identifying the occupants, describing the principal features and with descriptions of its main features and lists of each temple's festivals and territories. Helpfully, this record quantifies the number of temples, identified as homes of the individual gods, throughout Mesopotamia in 2300BC as numbering only 42. This does not sound like the survivors of an advanced civilization here on earth – such a civilization would need to have numbered millions to enable the level of specialisation required to achieve such advanced capabilities. Indeed, one would assume that such an advanced race would easily have dominated the whole planet and, after any catastrophe, its remnants would continue to dominate the surviving parts of the planet, but that is not what we see.

18.38   If the surviving remnant were very small in number, then those advanced people would soon lose their advantages. So far, we have pieced together the basic course of events causing the devastation in 10765BC at the onset of the Younger Dryas and now, speculatively ahead of dating being verified, what is likely to have caused the sudden end of the Younger Dryas around 9620BC. We do know that sea levels continued to rise steadily throughout that period – so many coastal cities would have been overwhelmed. Small numbers of surviving people with advanced knowledge cut off from their original culture without any possibility of resupply would progressively lose knowledge that could not easily be disseminated across the local population or at least retained and handed down by the trained scribes (priests). Furthermore, they would find it very hard to establish local production capabilities to extract the ores, refine the metals and build machine tools to replace lost and worn out equipment. Strikingly, this would support the evidence found of the earliest known cultures producing the most exact constructions and the most exquisite bas reliefs, skills which then seemed to decline over successive generations.

18.39   It is very difficult to reconcile there being an advanced human civilisation on Earth in 10765BC without it having already being present outside the areas devastated by the Hiawatha impact. Yet the evidence we have suggests only a very few survivors – these that only appear in tribal legends as mere handfuls of people. Does this warn us of the effect of a nuclear winter? And why is there not more tangible and widespread evidence of their prior megalithic constructions?

Alternatively, advanced humans visited Earth from another planet

18.40   Why do I jump to the conclusion that these visitors were human? Because the numerous records of the survivors/visitors/gods successfully interbreeding with Earth born humans and producing fertile offspring – meaning their DNA must have been almost identical to ours. Is there any evidence that humans originated elsewhere? Maybe humans originated elsewhere and visited Earth, creating the final version of Homo Sapiens Sapiens by mixing in some local DNA to make a more robust localised version suitable for our ecosystem. These alien geneticists may have been responsible for the Wow2! Signal – see Part One paragraphs 19.60 to 19.73. Such visitors would possess advanced technology and be few in number, probably unable to replicate much of their technology in a remote location - such as when they were based on Earth. Maybe the visitors crashed on Earth and were unable to leave. Maybe they did their best to civilise the hunter gatherer human tribes – hence the references to small teams of wise men led by Oannes and Veracocha. What happened to the visitors, did they interbreed and get absorbed into the Earthly population? Were they rescued, if so, one might have expected further visits? Under any scenario, it is pretty obvious that any such extra-terrestrial visitors arriving on Earth thousands of years ago would have been regarded as utterly awesome and seen as 'gods'. But is there any evidence of this?

18.41   Yes, there is a mass of recorded historical references in Sumerian tablets which may be interpreted as indicating we (homo sapiens) were produced as a subservient hybrid of the visiting humans and local primates. Sumerian, Babylonian, Egyptian and Biblical records all refer to successful inter breeding between the 'gods' and humans   for such unions to be fertile implies extremely close genetic makeup. This is highly significant – it is obviously very far fetched to suggest that such genetically compatible species evolved completely independently on different planets! Therefore, one species must have created the other by relatively minor genetic modification. Even Genesis seems to point to exactly this:

PREQUEL – YOUNGER DRYAS METEOR IMPACTS, THE FLOOD & ATLANTIS

in Genesis 1:26 we have the otherwise puzzling concept of humankind being made not by God in the image of God but clearly by the gods (not El but Elohim) plural in 'their' image. Genesis, remarkably, is actually quite clear that the 'gods' (i.e. those later regarded by humans as the elite) 'made' humans after their own likeness.

18.42   As with many such suggestions which at first reading seem wildly speculative – the Sumerian records support exactly this origin!! According to the extensive writings of both Laurence Gardiner and Zecharia Sitchin, working on deciphered Sumerian cuneiform tablets, the visiting interstellar human ('gods') laboured for maybe 250,000 years to extract minerals from Earth. After millennia of complaints by those of the interstellar travellers who were forced to do hard manual labour, their leadership tried to employ local primates to do the work. When these proved unequal to the tasks they were set, it was decided to try to fashion a hybrid between their own genes and humanoids. According to the Sumerian records the early versions were indeed infertile and many attempts were made before a fertile hybrid was successfully created. One explanation is that the solution was to base the hybrid mainly on the visiting extraterrestrial's DNA but switch off parts of the brain function (maybe explaining why so much of our DNA appears to be unused 'junk') and augment the active DNA with extra brawn from local primate DNA. N.B. the genetic differences between humans and pigs is only 4% - so the differences between these 'gods' and the hybrid 'man' must have been very low indeed, differences between current humans alive today can vary by up to 1%.

18.43   The study of female mitochondria, which slowly mutates with each generation, has led to conclusions that the first female of our current human type, Homo Sapiens Sapiens, aka Eve, lived c 172,000 years ago. Excluding the megalithic structures, there is no evidence that early humans did very much – i.e. learned much or created much until shortly before the Younger Dryas event in 10765BC. The sharp rise in the human skill-set seems to have begun soon afterwards with evidence of metallurgy (at sites in Bulgaria) and the first domestication of animals and crops from around 9000BC. The Sumerian records we have unearthed, dating back as far as 5400BC (for Eridu) reveal that at that time they already enjoyed an amazingly advanced society with incredible astronomical knowledge.

18.44   The 'king lists' of both Sumeria and Egypt, of which numerous copies have been recovered, record that the original rulers of both Sumeria and Egypt were gods. The initial rulers were Enlil and Enki (known in Egypt as Ptah), both sons of Anu, regarded as the sky god, i.e. the god who lived in the sky, i.e. in 'Heaven'. The 'king lists' of both cultures record transfers of administrative power to 'demi-gods' who continued to rule for thousands of years. These demi-gods were like the biblical 'Nefilim', a cross between the gods and the hybrid humans that they had created. Stories of some of these characters survive in popular culture – Gilgamesh – famously travelled far to seek extended life claiming he was a son of a god and should be so rewarded with immortality. These half breeds desperately tried to preserve their extra quota of 'off planet' godly DNA. One widespread custom was to marry your sister by another mother – carefully adhered to by the elite in Egypt and indeed practised by Abraham marrying Sarai, his half-sister. Extraordinarily, an echo of this practice survived until a few decades ago. Even throughout the two Christian millennia, the ruling families of Europe tried to preserve their 'blue blood' by marrying nieces within their extended family – indeed at the outbreak of World War I, almost all European rulers were closely related by blood.

18.45   An Egyptian source from the Ptolemaic period corroborates the dating of the Younger Dryas and suggests it may have had a significant impact on Egypt. Mantheo, a priest living in the 3rd century BC (exact dates unknown) wrote a chronological history of Egypt's rulers, in Greek, the *Aegyptiaca*. The meaning of Mantheo's name is disputed but is thought to be 'Truth of Thoth' or 'Gift of Thoth'. In his *Aegptiaca*, Mantheo records that the 'gods' had originally come from Ur (the olden place) i.e. the city of Abraham's family. The first ruler of Egypt he names as Ptah (Enki) who Mantheo records as ruling from c29500BC to c11600BC. Ptah then handed over the rule of Egypt to one of his sons, Ra, who only ruled for 1000 years before the deluge struck c10600BC. This dating is remarkably close to the Hiawatha impact we now estimate at 10765BC. Mantheo records that Ptah then returned to Egypt, engaging in great works of reclamation and helping with the recovery.

18.46   The Sumerians were aware of Ra's Egyptian name and many Sumerian names incorporated the divine name 'Ra'. Babylon, when originally founded c3500BC, was named Dingar Ra (Gateway of Ra). Later when Ra left Egypt (becoming 'Amen Ra', 'hidden Ra, or just 'Amen') he took up residence in Babylon naming it Gateway of the Gods (Babylon) and assumed the name Marduk.

18.47   According to Sumerian tablets, around 3760BC, "Kingship was lowered from Heaven" – i.e. the gods appointed the first fully human king, Etana, to rule Sumer from the city of Kush. The first fully human pharaoh, establishing the First Dynasty in Egypt, followed many centuries later, around 3100BC. An obvious question is why both civilisations record their first fully human king only after their civilizations were fully established with numerous prospering cities already built? Who ruled each realm prior to "king number 1"? Maybe the ancient records contain some truth, maybe prior to "king number 1" these civilisations were ruled by demi-gods? Interestingly, examination of the very earliest depictions in tomb paintings (of both civilisations) commonly show servile humans unclothed but serving elaborately clothed gods. There are also references to early humans eating with their hands, off the ground, in the manner of animals of the field. The deliberately half brain dead native human mules were only slowly being educated and presumably it was the prospect of enhanced productivity that triggered their teaching!

18.48   This scenario fits the historical records (conventionally dismissed as myths) which describe the pre-dynastic rulers of Egypt as demi gods and the first rulers as gods. Describing these earlier rulers as gods maybe a translation error by archaeologists. These godly rulers were clearly known to be mortal, the earliest company of 'gods' passed away and were buried at Heracleopolis (see chapter 11). The king lists record these 'gods' as ruling for very long periods – but they were not immortal – they aged, died in combat, etc., but could live extremely long lives. These gods were few in number, just as would be expected of visiting astronauts. There are clear references to 'gods' who died – e.g. different stories relate that Dumuzi was killed by mistake and that Osiris was murdered, whilst the gods also aged – e.g. the goddess Ninharsag. Ninharsag, whom Sumerian records credit with carrying out the bioengineering which produced the first human, Adamu, was awarded the territory we currently (and mistakenly) call Sinai for her retirement. Ninharsag was by far the most popular goddess in Egypt until around 1500BC and had become affectionately known as Hathor – meaning 'the old cow'! (As explained elsewhere, the name Sinai means lands allocated to the god Sin, also known by his Sumerian name, Nannar. Originally, Sinai described the area of northern Saudi Arabia - as acknowledged by St Paul, it was only applied to the current location by Helena, the mother of Emperor Constantine.)

WERE SURVIVORS OF DESTROYED CULTURES ACCLAIMED AS GODS?

18.49   So, it seems the 'gods' of the ancient cultures were not immortal but just enjoyed very long lives – is this the basis of the biblical references to patriarchs living for hundreds of years? Those described as patriarchs in Genesis were tribal leaders, maybe at least some of these were 'demi-gods' – Noah, as told in the original saga bearing the name Ziusudra, clearly claimed to be. Therefore, it is possible that some of both his fore-bears and descendants were also demi-gods – desperately marrying their 'sisters by another mother' to try to conserve their inherited quota of godly essence!! Even the conventional historical view, based on Genesis, is that all the biblical patriarchs prior to Abraham, were not Israelite but his Sumerian forefathers.

18.50   The reference in 12.9 above, to the Schøyen fragment, which records Ziusudra (the archetype of Noah) as 'king' and as a priest to Enki is potentially quite revealing. Firstly, this far back, Sumerian history would describe Ziusudra as a demi-god (product of a union between a 'god' and a native) and for whom, presumably his father had a soft spot. Secondly, the gods, being the generally beneficent, skilled and knowledgeable humans who had survived from the antediluvian megalithic culture, called the shots. These gods determined policies and usually implemented them by communicating their requirements, via their priests, to the natives. Thirdly, the gods had sufficient astronomical skills to detect and track the likely collision course of the meteor(s) triggering the Younger Dryas – and computational skills to determine the result would be a severe rise in sea level from the consequential ice melt together with the possible triggering of a gigantic tsunami.

18.51   Obviously, kingship being 'Lowered from Heaven' in the year 3760BC was a very big event for the Sumerians. One of their princely descendants, Abraham, presumably played a role in preserving the memory of that important event – as even today, it is remembered as the starting point of the Jewish calendar – which counts years 'from when the counting of years begun'- so AD2025 equals 5785 in the Jewish calendar (3760+2025).

18.52   As detailed in later Parts of this series of books, the historical evidence shows the original Sumerian and Egyptian gods constituted a single extended family of related entities – see the Appendix at the end of this book. Each subsequent Middle Eastern culture continued to worship the same gods, and generally preserved knowledge of the same family relationships with each other, although local names were often adopted. The most extensive single proof of this quite astounding fact is the Treaty of Mitanni, signed in 1258BC between the Egyptian Pharaoh and the Hittite King – of which both complete originals have been recovered from excavations in Egypt and Turkey.

18.53   Credible references to these 'gods' seem to cease from around 500BC, perhaps because they departed around that time? I choose this date as being shortly after 539BC when, according to the famous Cyrus Cylinder Seal in the British Museum, the Persian Emperor Cyrus attributed his bloodless capture of Babylon to the fact that Marduk (previously known as the Egyptian 'god' Ra, now hidden from the Egyptians – and as such known as Amen Ra) had marched with Cyrus at the head of the Persian army. According to the records recovered, when the Babylonian army saw the god of their city, who had fallen out with their king, marching towards them, they simply threw down their weapons and the gates of Babylon were opened. Of course, in the Old Testament, the Levite priests wrote that it was Yahweh who helped Cyrus capture Babylon, and Yahweh went on to name Cyrus a Messiah (!!). However, the truth is clearly displayed in the British Museum – where the Cylinder Seal clearly credits Marduk. Moreover, it is yet another example of how the Israelites saw their god Yahweh as being in the same class as all the other 'gods' – just that Yahweh was 'theirs' and therefore the best of all the gods!!

18.54   It is also possible that the biblical record is in fact in agreement with the Cylinder Seal. Perhaps, we should infer that, Shamash (whom David's psalms identified as Yahweh around 1000BC) had departed Earth relatively soon after, maybe around 950BC. After Solomon, the Israelites seem to fall apart, succumbing first to the Assyrians and a little later to the Babylonians. Certainly, as Shamash, Yahweh made no attempt to protect his Temple or his people from defeat and deportation in 586BC. But when the Israelites saw Marduk triumphantly bring Cyrus army into Babylon unscathed, followed by Cyrus declaring that they were released and free to return to Jerusalem, they may have concluded that Marduk was in fact their Yahweh. After all, no Israelite alive would have ever seen Yahweh before.

18.55   But, is there any documented reference to the 'gods' departing. Yes, some quite extensive references. Firstly, we have the strange demise of the highly advanced Sumerian Empire c1960BC, some years after

Abraham's father, the governor of the capital city, Ur, migrated his family to the northern centre, Harran. The main records that we have documenting the end of the Sumerian civilisation are the Lamentation Texts. These describe a silent wind borne death spreading across all Sumerian cities south of Babylon, causing most people and animals to die painful deaths. There appears to have been some warning of this disaster, as many are recorded as fleeing – remnants of a Sumerian diaspora can be found in succeeding Babylonian, Hurrian (centred at Urkesh, on the Turkish/Syrian border) and other cultures. The Lamentation Texts tell of some of the 'gods' simply abandoning their people and of other 'gods' of being distraught at seeing the deaths and being forced to abandon their palace/temple. Remember, that according to the temple catalogue produced around 2300BC there were only 42 abodes of the 'gods' just a few hundred years before this calamity (See 18.37). Some have suggested the descriptions point to something akin to radiation sickness caused by a nuclear explosion.

18.56   After the demise of Sumer, only a handful of the Sumerian gods continue to be referred to in texts which imply a physical presence – for others it was their memory that was revered (as Egyptians worshipped the hidden Ra – Amen-Ra) and others prayed for the gods that had departed to return to them. Only a few key individuals continued to be referred to by Middle Eastern cultures in terms implying intimate contact – Marduk connected with Babylon; Ishkur associated with the Hittites and Hurrians (Turkey and northern Syria) where he became known as Adad and Teshub respectively; Nannar/Sin connected with Harran; Shamash/Utu who may have become known as Yahweh; and, Shamash's sister, Inanna/Ishtar who may have starred as the Queen of Sheba. By coincidence, after 2000BC we see the rise of other cultures, each attributing their origin to the arrival of a 'god' from 'heaven' to initiate a dynastic royalty. China, Japan and early South American cultures all attribute their inception to the arrival of a few gods from heaven – this may imply some 'gods' relocated into these areas and developed new civilisations.

18.57   Other texts are suggestive of some later departures. In the temple of Sin in Harran, four columns have been excavated bearing detailed inscriptions attributed to the last king of Babylon (Nabuna'id) and his mother, the High Priestess to Sin, Adda-Guppi. These tell of the departure of Nannar/Sin dated to the 610BC defeat of the Assyrian army and, after earnest praying by Adda-Guppi, Sin is recorded as returning briefly in

556BC to bless the enthronement of Nabuna'id.

18.58 A dispassionate assessment of Yahweh might conclude that he similarly departed, or was killed, prior to 586BC. The biblical story emphases that Yahweh's covenants will be everlasting, that once his temple was built - he will always dwell with his people. Solomon built and commissioned the temple in Jerusalem for Yahweh, atop the ancient megalithic platform, around 970BC. However, only 40 years later, upon Solomon's death in 931BC, the twelve tribes split - with ten peeling away to form the Northern Kingdom, Israel. Jerusalem was left controlling only Judah and Benjamin. Yahweh never seemed to return and reunite the tribes, nor prevent the breakaway ten being marched off to Ninevah by Tiglath-Pileser in 740BC. Later, King Sargon II applied the standard Assyrian policy for conquered people, marching off Yahweh's 10 tribes elsewhere and rotating into Israel people from other areas of the Assyrian Empire. These new settlers became known as Samarians, genetically now assessed to have been mainly Arameans and Amorites – descendants of the First Babylonian Empire – who intermarried with the remnants of the ten tribes. Interestingly, according to 2Kings 17:30 these newcomers mainly worshipped Nergal (first son of Enki) but also felt they had to worship the god whose land they had been transplanted into. Accordingly, both biblical and Assyrian texts record the new settlers requesting the Assyrian king to send one of Yahweh's priests to teach them his requirements – and one of the Israelite priests that had been taken captive, was duly returned. Despite being promised as his eternal abode, Yahweh allowed the temple built to his specifications by Solomon to be utterly destroyed in 586BC. Having been abandoned, the Israelites and their descendants have suffered terribly:- at the hands of successively the Romans, the Crusaders, the pogroms of the Middle Ages and the Nazis. Naturally, Yahweh's priests insist this suffering is only a result of the people's sins and that their god always graciously allows a remnant to survive. One has to be pretty desperate to believe this.

18.59 The management model devised by the advanced humans of the antediluvian megalithic culture (or, alternatively, by the space faring human visitors), proved so effective that it may have inspired the forgery of the Donation of Constantine by the Catholic Church sometime in the 8th Century. The advanced humans would naturally exploit their superior status, gained from extensive knowledge far beyond the skills of the natives they sought to rule, by positioning themselves apart, as gods.

WERE SURVIVORS OF DESTROYED CULTURES ACCLAIMED AS GODS?

Privileged natives were chosen to act as their servants (who became the priesthood), subjects were tasked to construct palaces incorporating astronomical observatories (aka temples) and provide copious food and drink – cooked to specific recipes. Details recovered from Sumerian tablets record amazing details of the provisions pledged by kings for daily delivery to individual temples. Different gods specified different selections of foodstuffs, different quantities and apparently gave detailed instructions of how different dishes should be seasoned and cooked. This detail implies real persons were dictating details of provisons and cooking they required - if it was just the priesthood demanding these supplies, they were taking quite a risk!

18.60 Ah, I can hear you thinking, does this shopping list of provisions sound like the biblical descriptions laid down for offerings by Yahweh after the Israelites escaped from Egypt? Indeed, some fundamentalist Christian writers claim that this proves the Bible is accurate - as the beastly Babylonians have merely copied ideas from the Torah. Well, not quite – the descriptions above are from Sumerian cuneiform tablets. The Sumerian civilisation disappeared quite suddenly, soon after Abraham's family migrated north to Harran around 2000BC. If one believes biblical chronology, Yahweh only started giving his dietary requirements during the later stages of the wandering around Sinai – which was many generations and at least 500 years after Abraham. These aspects are examined in much more detail in Parts 1 and 2 of this series.

18.61 The behaviour and requirements laid down by the gods seem to reflect clear traits of an elite, but an undoubtedly human, clique. Conventional history seems misled by early translation errors, seemingly based upon total disbelief that there could have been any sophisticated civilisation much before Abraham. This naturally led to historical descriptions being attributed labels such as 'gods', 'priests' and 'temples'. Whilst these labels are clearly mistaken and plainly wrong, they have become unchangeable. However, whilst there are many details which imply these 'gods' enjoyed longer lives than normal humans – they were definitely mortal, early Egyptian records tell of where the 'gods' who were killed in battle or murdered were buried and that their graves were tended and maintained.

18.62 Reading texts from the 3rd and 2nd millennia BC, one cannot but be struck by the similarity between:

(i) the detailed specifications given by various gods for the construction and adornment of their temple abodes – e.g. the specifications of the E.Ninnu temple built by King Gudea for Ninurta (a son of Enlil) at Lagash (c2150BC) and that built by Solomon for Yahweh at Jerusalem in 970BC;

(ii) the detailed dietary requirements set out as required by different gods, some of which also stipulate culinary preparations, list spices and flavourings to be utilised and the cooking procedures – with Yahweh's requirements set out for the Israelites during the Exodus; and,

(iii) the descriptions of godly transportation – in Egypt, Ra prized his Celestial Boat to travel the skies and the underworld whilst when in Babylon, as Marduk, he had a special parking place for his 'Supreme Traveller'. In the Lamentation Texts, Enlil returns to Nippur 'flying from horizon to horizon' whilst Nannar/Sin commanded his 'Boat of Heaven' and Ninurta's prized possession was the Imdugud, the 'Divine Black Bird'. The Bible records Yahweh descending upon Mount Sinai in a 'Kabod' (Exodus 24:16) which is usually translated as 'glory' but its older meaning is 'heavy' (maybe an interplanetary transport?) – surrounded by clouds of smoke; often Yahweh travels on a pillar of fire (e.g. Exodus 13:21) – maybe a personal jet-pack; whilst Elijah is recorded in 2Kings 2:11 as being met by a chariot of fire and ascending to heaven in a whirlwind. The use of aerial craft by gods and their key lieutenants seems uniform and widespread.

18.63 Up until around 1500BC, the biblical record names the Israelite god as El Elyon, the Canaanite name for Enlil. Later, from the Burning Bush interlude, Yahweh is the adopted name but various aspects point to the worship actually being of Abram's original god, Sin. By the Monarchical period, from 1000BC, internal biblical references point to Yahweh being Shamash. These three 'gods' being straight descendants of each other – father, son and grandson - implying some kind of patrilineal deity..

18.64 Our conventional history ridicules simple minded ancients for worshipping stars, effigies and other innate objects. Given the level of civilisation attained in both Sumeria and Egypt 5000 years ago, this seems unlikely. Gods were associated with members of our solar system and represented by artistic images in much the same way as images of Jesus, Mary and various apostles adorn every Catholic church today.

18.65 Whoever constructed the Giza pyramids and the Baalbek Terrace must have devoted enormous resources, yet these enigmatic constructions do not appear to serve any purpose we can think of. The early pyramids were indisputably NOT tombs but what were they for? Their very precise alignment betrays not only their date of construction but also the expert astronomical knowledge of their builders. The city of Harran with its special astronomical college, the base of the astronomer-priest cult known as the Sabians can be traced from around 8800BC (contemporary with the occupation of the Göbekli Tepe site), and the Sabians are recorded as making pilgrimages to the Giza complex from time immemorial until as late as AD1228. This could be an astonishing 10,000 year sustained relationship.

18.66 For no reason that we currently understand, many key cities in ancient times were built exactly on the 30th parallel – Giza, Eridu, Persepolis and Harappa – why? And how did the locals calculate the precise latitude? Giza, a complex of megalithic monuments and 'temples' probably dates to around 9000BC. Eridu was one of the pre flood cities of Sumeria, dominated by its 'temple'. Persepolis was selected by the Persian emperor Cyrus, where a 125,000 square metre terrace was partly carved out of a mountain side and partly formed by retaining walls, did not appear to have more than a ceremonial function. It appears to have been an isolated construction without any permanent inhabitants. One suspects that its location was decided by Marduk, after he decided to help Cyrus build an empire. The layout of the city of Harappa in the Indus Valley has marked similarities with Sumerian city plans.

18.67 Zecharia Sitchin, a writer whose research has gained a remarkabke following, provides a clear challenge to conventional histiorians. His work deciphering ancient cuneiform tablets and other historical inscriptions in both the Middle East and also in South America, led to some provocative but interesting explanations. His conclusions are firmly in the 'extra-terrestrial human visitors' camp. His views are both coherent and provide good explanations for many otherwise puzzling records. Conventional historians are contemptuous of Sitchin – which, although I also find many of his conclusions somewhat dubious, otherwise only serves to enhance his credibility.

PREQUEL – YOUNGER DRYAS METEOR IMPACTS, THE FLOOD & ATLANTIS

18.68   According to Sitchin, the ruler of the human visitors, Anu, widely identified in our ancient records as the king who lived in heaven, the sky god, etc., had two principal sons, Enki and Enlil. Initially Enki was sent to Earth and put in charge of the mission, Enki is forever symbolised in our culture as a healer and his device, the intertwined double serpent, reminiscent of the double helix of DNA, is still used worldwide as the symbol of physicians and hospitals. This alone is an extraordinary legacy. In Egypt, Enki was known as Ptah, the first divine ruler and his symbol was the Key of Life, the Ankh. Later, Anu appointed Enlil as 'Lord of Seven', (Elisheva in Hebrew, Elizabeth in English) - Earth being known as the 7th planet. Sumerian astronomy listed Pluto as the 1st planet, Neptune as 2nd, Uranus as 3rd, Saturn as 4th, Jupiter as 5th, Mars as 6th and Earth as 7th – which seems pretty strange when you think about it. How did the Sumerians know about the remoter planets of our solar system which are not visible to the naked eye and 'we' only (re)discovered with telescopes in the past 200 years? Even more puzzling is why count the numbers of planets from the 'outside' coming inwards towards the Sun – unless of course you numbered them as you travelled past them coming into our Solar System!! Curious.

18.69   With this background, following the death or retirement of the older 'gods', much of human history between c4000BC and the destruction of Sumer in 1960BC may be viewed as the titanic struggle between the sons of Enlil and the most ambitious son of Enki, Marduk (known as Ra in Egypt), for supremacy on Earth – which was seen as reflecting the precession from the Age of the Bull (Taurus being the sign of Enlil) to the Age of the Ram (Ares being the sign conveniently adopted by Marduk). This is also reflected in temple iconography throughout the period which often shows a tethered or tired Bull contrasting with a rising Ram. The divisions of the zodiac are far from precise, there is no clear dividing line – some constellations are larger than others, i.e. cover a wider segment of the sky. Both Taurus and Pieces occupy more than 30 (i.e. 360/12) degrees of arc, with Ares squeezing into significantly less than 30 degrees. This gave rise to contention over when one age ended and the next begun. It is only by convention that the zodiac is commonly divided into 12 equal segments, and by convention that we mark the transitions to around 2200BC, 40BC and AD2120 for the moves from Taurus to Ares, Ares to Pieces and Pieces to Aquarius respectively.

18.70   From translations of recovered original cuneiform tablets, we know the circular observatory built under king Gudea at Lagash for Ninurta c2160BC, established by observation that the sun still rose in the constellation of Taurus. Sumeria continued to be ruled from Lagash until around 2113BC when Ninurta appears to have departed and Enlil appointed another son, Nannar (Sin in Akkadian) whose symbol was the Moon, as god over Sumeria. Nannar moved the capital to Ur, establishing what is known today as the Ur III dynasty. The High Priest of Nippur, the cult centre of Nannar, was sent to administer Ur – his name was Terah, whose young son was called Abram. (Bells now ringing !!) Biblical Abraham's father was named Terah (Genesis 11:26-28).

18.71 The principal symbols for Enlil were the lion and the bull – which might have been seen as granting him lordship from the Age of Leo through the ages to the end of Taurus. Early Christians adopted the sign of the fish to denote their beliefs signified the dawning of a new age but the Israelite descendants of Abraham depicted their Lord as a lion, the lion of Judah. The Israelites originally worshipped Enlil, using his Canaanite name of El Elyon, as recorded throughout Genesis up to the Burning Bush incident – so the lion metaphor may originate from this. In the 1960's, the musical Hair made popular a song entitled the Dawning of the Age of Aquarius which we are now poised to enter.

18.72 This brings us full circle, our conventional view of history is based upon the foundations laid during the Reformation and the Age of Enlightenment – more specifically the period between the publication of the King James Version of the Bible, 1611, and the first translations of cuneiform writing in 1851. During this time, man's view of pre Greek history was based solely upon biblical references – and Yahweh's view of despicable 'pagan' gods whose followers worshipped inert 'idols'.

18.73 As referred to earlier, correcting false information, even for example that Columbus discovered America, is incredibly difficult – so it seems the mass of humanity is destined to remain wedded to 'fake news'. But you, having read this far, may conclude that our true history has long been supressed and can look out for future discoveries to gradually tease out our real origins.

19

Conclusions

19.1 Historians have long maintained interpretations which should be revised in the light of the evidence we now have. Firstly, when referring to the ancient civilisations of Egypt, the Fertile Crescent, Mexico and Peru, the terms applied to 'pagan gods', 'temples' and 'priests' probably need to be changed to 'ruling elite', 'palaces' and 'administrators'. Secondly, many documentary records we have which are always referred to as myths and legends need to be re-evaluated as being at least partly derived from historical truths. Serious and learned men such as Solon (see paragraph 9.1) and Mantheo (paragraph 18.45) appear to have recorded surprisingly accurate dating in references describing events which seem to mark the beginning and end of the Younger Dryas period. Given Egyptian chronology recorded only the number of years each Pharaoh ruled, the cumulative tally of the number of years was open to error from mid-year changes in monarch, from joint reigns and from regency over minors – plus the difficulty of accurately calculating the years during the chaos of the First and the Second Intermediate Periods when weak Pharaohs rotated in weeks or months. For Solon to arrive at a date which was only 20 years out after 9000 years is quite remarkable. Even Mantheo, going further back to the initial event was only 160 years out after 10400 years. If these two illustrious historians had indeed written remarkably accurately about the dating of the Younger Dryas events – perhaps we should re-evaluate the rest of their surviving writings?

19.2 The evidence points to the existence of a technologically advanced culture pre-existing all our conventional early civilisations. A culture clearly existed prior to the Flood generated by the Hiawatha Impact that had skills and knowledge which, in some disciplines, we only re-established very recently. Whilst we look to modern equipment to achieve results these ancient cultures performed, we also conclude that they lacked the metallurgy to fashion precision machine tools and the electronics for computing and lighting. However, it is entirely possible that quite different technologies may have developed in isolation.

19.3 The conclusion reached by the research documented here, is that there was either a well-developed pre flood civilisation equipped with skills and resources we find surprisingly advanced, or, Earth had a resident colony of human aliens. Naturally, we are more open to the idea of a pre-flood resident population which had been an earlier flowering of our own earthly evolution. There seems to be sufficient evidence of survivors from the pre-flood era and, comfortingly, they seem to resemble us both physically and in nutritional requirements. That they could procreate with humans and bear fertile offspring would seem to clinch the argument that they must have been Homo Sapiens Sapiens – the same as us.

19.4 But, this leaves two big problems which seem unanswerable – why were there so few survivors of the Younger Dryas impact and why did they appear to enjoy such dramatically longer lifespans.

19.5 Firstly, why were there so few survivors – possibly as few as a mere 7 Apkallu. If these survivors of a pre-flood culture brought with them what has been described as "civilisation-in-a-box" - why had they not already spread far and wide around the globe? Wherever tales of the Seven Apkallu have been handed down, their arrival has been described as sudden and unexpected – not the arrival of previously encountered peoples. As discussed earlier, so far, no evidence found has been found of a megalithic culture in North America – the area that bore the brunt of the Younger Dryas impact. If this advanced culture was based elsewhere on the planet, where we have found some megalithic remains, then significant numbers should have survived the Younger Dryas effects, recovered and even if they later died out – there should be far more widespread evidence of their civilisation.

19.6 The second problem is longevity, the one frequently sited difference between the 'gods' and other humans – their strikingly different life expectancy. Whilst admittedly mortal, the records point to lives of a few thousand years rather than what might be attributed to merely nutritional and lifestyle differences.

19.7 That these survivors from the onset of the Younger Dryas arrived with skills from a clearly developed civilisation is supported by the clutch of cities which developed soon after their arrival. The existence of a city indicates a degree of civilisation, only specialisation enables surplus food production leading to division of labour and the development of fixed habitats. We have found evidence of very ancient cities existing contemporaneous and not far distant from Göbekli Tepe – Harran, Damascus and Jericho have remains dated to 9000BC and Aleppo to as early as 11000BC. These dates reconcile with our latest estimates of the earliest cultivation of seeds and the start of agriculture – also occurring in the same region. The cultivation of the eight so called Neolithic founder crops – emmer wheat, einkorn wheat, hulled barley, peas, lentils, bitter vetch, chick peas and flax has been dated to around 9500BC. The first animals were domesticated around the same time and also in the same region – pigs from around 11000BC, followed by sheep and by 8500BC wild aurochs had been domesticated as cattle.

19.8 But their longevity points to a fundamental difference between the elite and the former hunter gatherers that they were bringing civilisation to. If we accept evidence of the exceptional life spans of the 'gods' and their advanced technology, one must then consider that these survivors were from off planet.

19.9 The numerous references to gods utilizing craft to travel across the sky are intriguing. At a superficial level one can see the linkage between those regarded as gods, being associated with stars or planets, and therefore credited with vessels to travel back and forth. But, as well as travelling in these craft, the ancient records make frequent references to the construction of temples incorporating places to store the god's craft. David longed to build a temple for Yahweh, a place for the 'Name' of the Lord. The word 'shem' used in Hebrew puzzled translators and eventually it was translated as 'name' - creating the strange formula of building a temple 'for the name of the Lord'. Recently it was realised that 'shem' is 'loan word' from Abraham's native tongue – Sumerian. In Sumerian 'shem' means vessel, with references that include travel across water, beneath water and through the air.

19.10 This conclusion leaves us with many unanswered questions. Were these survivors not just of the Younger Dryas devastation but from a space mission that went wrong? Was their space craft irreparably damaged, stranding them on Earth? Certainly, if few in number, they would lack the resources to recreate much in the way of sophisticated technology. The development of metallurgy has been traced to the same post flood period – initially focusing on gold, silver, copper and then bronze, with iron only being achieved around 3000 years ago. Certainly, there would be no hope of manufacturing lightweight composites using aluminium, titanium, etc., nor of producing silicon chips or high performance optics. On the other hand, given the numerous references to the gods utilising aerial transport, they must have enjoyed highly robust and reliable technology – because it remained functional for many millennia. Tools for precision engineering, cutting and fabricating would be unavailable – although some strange markings have been left on megalithic structures. Maybe the visitors main craft was well equipped for planetary exploration, with good stocks of spare parts and portable hand tools.

19.11 And, if they came from elsewhere, what happened to these visitors – were they ever rescued, did they depart Earth of their own accord or did they eventually die out from old age?

19.12 I have found this research compelling and whilst many questions remain unanswerable, we do have some solid reasons to reassess the conventional views put forward concerning the pagan gods of the ancient civilisations and the veracity of the text of the Old Testament. The next two Parts of this series explore these aspects in more detail.

19.13 The existence of a relatively advanced indigenous human population that developed during the millennia between the end of the last glacial maxima, c22000BC and the Hiawatha impact of 10765BC now seems irrefutable. Underwater exploration of the relatively shallow continental shelves in pursuit of mineral extraction may yield very interesting archaeological finds over coming decades. But alien, at least off planet involvement, is also very likely to have been involved at least once in human history. In Part One we shall look at startling evidence of what appears to be an alien signature buried in our own DNA.

CONCLUSIONS

Key – colours indicate name of each 'god' in principal languages:
Sumerian; *Akkadian*; Egyptian; Hebrew

* Until Moses met the Burning Bush, the god of Genesis was named El Elyon, the Canaanite name for Enlil. From Moses up to Saul, the Hebrew deity appears to have Nannar but by the Psalms of David the title had passed to Shamash. In all translations of Jewish scripture into Greek, Latin, English, etc., all names of 'god' are assumed to refer to a single entity.

Appendix

Selected family members of ruling elite – survivors of 'the Flood' or perhaps ET's?

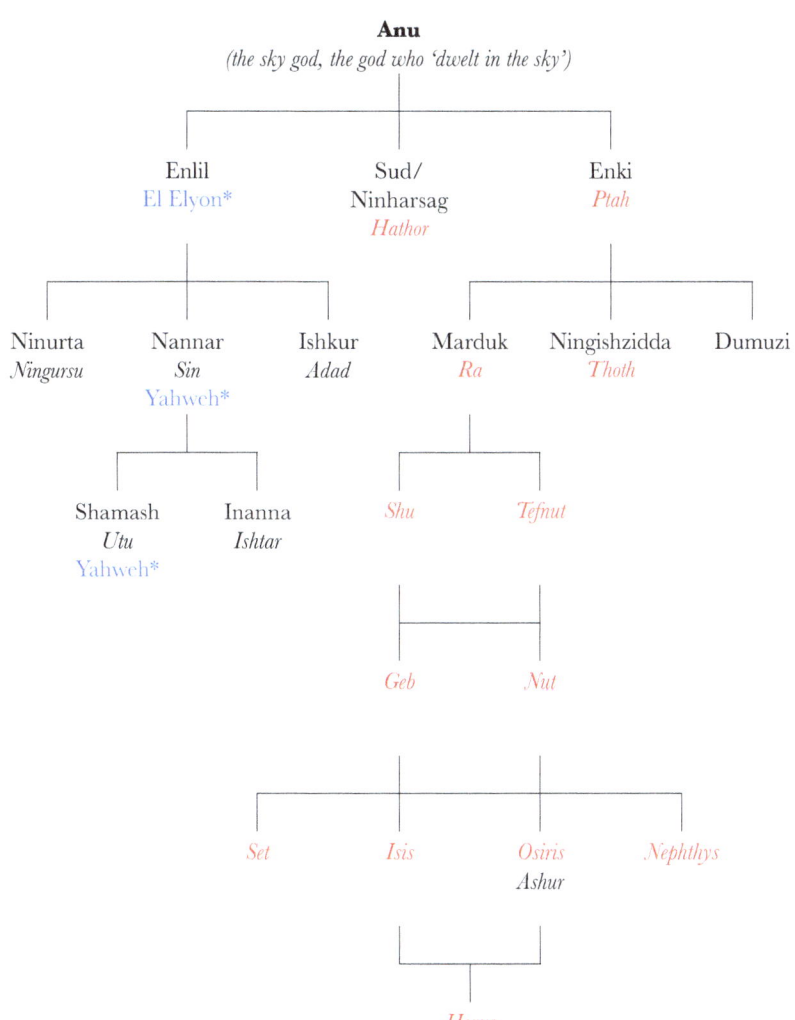

Index

Abraham	8.12, 10.7, 18.44
Abu Hureyra, Syria	8.7
Aerial craft (ancient)	18.20-18.22, 18.37, 18.62
Akapana temple complex, Tiahuanaco	13.8-13.26
Antikythera Mechanism	16 *passim*
Apkallu & 7 sages, aka Vedic Saptarishi	9.23, 9.24, 12.7, 12.10, 18.3, 18.17, 18.19, 19.5
Apis cult, Saqqara	11.25-11.32
Ashurbanipal, king of Assyria *668-627BC*	1.5, 9.18-9.20, 12.10-12.12, 18.28
Atlantis	7.44, 9 *passim*
Atlas mountains, Morocco	9.9, 9.12, 9.34
Baalbek Terrace (aka Heliopolis)	11.78-11.86, 18.14
Bedouf anomaly	5.16
Behistun Inscriptions	1.4
Bernardino de Sahagún, friar, *1499-1590*	17.18
Berossus, Babylonian astronomer-priest	12.7
Betelgeuse, Yad al Jawza	6.41-6.43
Black mat under North America	7.14-7.19, 8 *passim*
Boncuklu Tarla	10.1, 10.4, 10.5, 10.33
Budj Bim, Victoria, eruption *c35000BC*	7.46
Burkle impact	6.38, 9.30-9.32, 17.4
Cappadocia	10.25, 10.27-10.30
Carpentaria, Gulf of, Australia impacts	6.29, 9.30
Cayce, Edgar, American clairvoyant *1877-1945*	11.22
Ceres, dwarf planet	4.12
Channelled Scablands, Washington	2.2, 7.24-7.27, 9.9
Chicxulub impact	5.5, 5.18, 5.23-5.26, 6.20
Clovis culture	7.9, 7.10, 7.21-7.23, 18.8
Columbus, Christopher (Pedro Atríde?)	2.14-2.16
Cuneiform tablets recovered	1.7, 1.8

Cyrus Cylinder Seal	18.53
Damascus	10.2
Darius, king of Persia *522-486BC*	1.4
Deniliquin impact, NSW Australia	5.11
Dhaskalio, Greece	18.9
Djoser, pharaoh *c2670-2650BC*	11.47-11.49
DNA Wow2 signal	18.40-18.42
Doñana, Cadiz	9.5
Donation of Constantine	18.59
Dryas Periods *(c14000BC to c9600BC)*	6.35, 7 *passim*, 8.6, 9.7, 9.27-9.29, 11.14, 11.32, 18.7
Dryas final end date, Cariaco Basin data	11.14
Earth Impact Database (EID)	5.5, 5.6, 5.13
Ed Nadir impact, Guinea	9.10
Edfu temple and texts	9.6, 9.7, 9.17-9.26, 9.35, 11.7, 11.24, 11.62, 18.32
Egyptian technology:	11 *passim*
• Labyrinth, Hawara	11.3, 11.19-11.20
• Lathe turning	11.50, 11.51
• Lighting (artificial)	11.40
• Logistics	11.28, 11.29, 11.35-11.39, 11.81-11.83
• Project planning & documentation	11.34
• Polishing	11.28, 11.45, 11.46, 11.58-11.62
• Precision cutting	11.28, 11.41-11.44
• Precision drilling	11.52-11.57
• Schist Disc	11.70-11.76
• Stone boxes	11.25-11.32
• Vases	11.47-11.49
Emi Koussai, volcano, Chad	9.16, 9.26
Enoch, Book of	18.17, 18.29
Enki, aka Ptah	8.12, 9.22, 11.30, 18.44, 18.50, 18.68, 18.69
Etana, king of Sumer, crowned *3760BC*	6.35
Extinction Level Events (ELE)	5 *passim*, 6 *passim*

Gantenbrinck's Door star map	11.17
Giza Sphinx, pyramids & temples	2.3-7, 11.5-11.18, 18.2
Giza – Orion's Belt dating	11.12, 11.18
Giza – Regulus dating	11.11, 11.13, 11.15
Goa	12.32, 18.34
Göbekli Tepe	7.38, 7.39, 10.1, 10.4-10.24, 10.32, 18.1, 18.2, 18.16, 19.7
Gudea, king of Sumer *2144-2124BC*	12.32, 12.40-12.42, 12.44, 13.21, 18.62
Gunung Padang	14.2-14.4, 18.14
Hall of Records, under the Sphinx	11.21- 11.24, 11.66
Hangenberg Event	5.14
Harappan Indus Valley culture	11.85, 18.34
Harran	10.2, 10.7, 12.12, 18.57, 18.65, 19.7
Hawass, Dr Zahi *(born 1947)*	11.20, 11.23
He, Chinese Admiral *AD1371-1433*	2.11-2.13
Herodotus, Greek historian *c484-425BC*	9.1, 9.13, 11.21, 12.32
Hiawatha impact, Greenland, *c10765BC*	5.5, 6.37, 7 *passim*, 8 *passim*, 9.27, 10.23, 10.24, 11.5, 12.7, 18.32
Hittites	10.29, 10.30
Horus	9.18, 9.22, 9.25, 11.7, 11.24, 18.3
Hoyle, Sir Fred, British astronomer & mathematician	12.29
Iamblichus, Syrian philosopher *245-325AD*	11.21
Inerrants	2.9
Ishim impact	5.13
Jericho/Sodom & Gomorrah impact *c1650BC*	6.38, 10.2
Joshua, Book of	12.44
Jubilees, Book of	2.8
Jupiter, Temple of at Baalbek	11.79, 11.80
Karahan Tepe	10.1, 10.3
Kefalonia impacts, Mediterranean, *c9620BC*	6.38, 9.33-9.36, 10.24, 11.5, 12.7-12.9, 18.32
Kellwasser Event	5.14
Kerkwyk, Ben van, Australian researcher	11.63
Keys, David, British researcher	6.26, 6.27

Khafre, pharaoh *c2558-2532BC*	11.7
Khufu, pharaoh *c2585-2566BC*	2.3-2.7, 11.24
Krakatoa eruptions	6.27, 6.28, 9.36
Lagash, Sumeria	12.31-12.45, 18.62
Lairg Gravity Low, Scotland	5.6
Lake Taupō mega volcano	6.12
Lamentation Texts, *c1960BC*	18.55
Lateran obelisk	11.81
Local Bubble, Local Cavity	4.17-4.23
Longyou Caves, Zhejiang Province, China	10.26, 15 *passim*
Machu Picchu, Peru	13.5, 13.7, 13.29
Mantheo	18.45, 19.1
Mars	3 *passim*
Maya	17.5, 17.6
Mega volcanoes	4.34-4.36, 6.9-6.13
Menzies, Gavin, British author	2.12
Meteor impacts	4 *passim*, 5 *passim*
Milankovitch cycles, Milutim *AD1879-1958*	6.26, 6.27
Mitanni, Treaty of, *1258BC*	18.52
Mitochondria	6.2, 6.24
Mohs Hardness scale	11.58
Moons, including benefits from	3.7, 4.2-4.14, 4.37
Motilla del Azuer, Cuidad Real, Spain	18.9
Mount Mazuma eruption *5680BC*	7.46
Mount Moriah, Jerusalem	11.86
Mummification	11.88-11.96
Nannar/Sin	12.39, 12.40, 18.56, 18.57
Necho II, pharaoh *610-594BC*	12.32
Nephilim	18.17, 18.18
Nineveh	12.11
Ninharsag	18.48
Ninurta	12.40
Oannes	7.38, 7.39, 12.7, 18.3

Olmecs	17.2
Osirion, Abidos	11.33
Osiris	11.30
Pangea	5.21
Petrie, Flinders, *AD1853-1942*	2.3-4, 11.2, 11.3, 11.54, 11.55
Phoenician circumnavigation of Africa	12.32
Phoenician trading	11.85
Pillars of Hercules	9.3, 9.4
Piri Reis map	2.12
Plato, Greek philosopher	9.2-9.4
Plutarch, Roman historian, *AD46-120*	8.9, 9.1
Population bottlenecks, hominoid & human	6.4-6.8, 6.23, 6.24, 6.31
Posnansky, Arthur, Austrian chemist & archaeologist *1873-1946*	13.9-13.12
Psenophis of Heliopolis, philosopher	9.1
Quetzalcoatl, linked to Thoth	7.40, 17.2, 17.3, 17.10, 18.3, 18.18
Ra, Amen-Ra, aka Marduk	18.53, 18.56, 18.69
Rawlinson, Henry *AD1810-1895*	1.4-6
Richat Structure aka Eye of Africa	9.8-9.12, 9.26, 9.29, 9.34
Rosetta Stone	1.2
Rujum el-Hiri, Golan Heights	12.45, 12.46
Sacsahuaman	13.6
Sais, Temple of	9.2, 9.35, 11.62
Schist Disc	8.14, 11.65, 11.70-11.76
Schoch, Dr Robert, American geologist	11.10
Sea Peoples, Greek	10.30, 11.2
Serapeum, Saqqara	11.25-11.32
Shamash	11.78, 18.54
Shebtiw	9.17, 9.18, 9.21, 9.22, 9.25
Shem, Sumerian word for vessel	12.38
Shoemaker-Levy event, *AD1994*	5.20
Siberian Traps	5.16, 5.17
Snowball Earth	3.4, 4.27, 4.28, 5.13, 6.3-6.8

Solon	9.1-9.7, 9.12-9.14, 19.1
Sonchis of Sais, Egyptian philosopher	9.1
Stonehenge	12.13-12.46
Sumerian planetary knowledge	4.6-4.11, 12.3, 12.4, 18.36, 18.68
Supernova	4.16-4.26, 6.41-6.43
Tamanrasset river	9.9, 9.14, 9.34, 9.35
Thoth, Sumerian Kothar-Hasis	9.22, 12.40, 17.3, 18.3, 18.17, 18.28, 18.45
Tiahuanaco (aka Tiwanaku)	13.8-13.29, 18.14
Tiamat/Theia	4.5-4.14
Toba mega volcano, *c72000BC*	6.5, 6.13, 6.22-6.25
Toltecs	17.7, 17.8
Trou au Natron, Chad	9.16, 9.26
Tunguska event, *1912*	7.1
Thutmose IV, pharaoh *c1400-1391BC*	11.8
Ur, capital of Sumer	13.4, 18.45
Valera, Blas, Jesuit *1551 – 1597*	17.14
Vesuvius eruption, *AD79*	6.33
Viracocha	7.41, 13.2, 13.28
Volcanic Explosivity Index (VEI)	6.9-6.13, 6.22, 6.33
Vredefort impact, South Africa	5.8
Wilkes Land anomaly	5.16
Yarrabubba impact	4.28
Yellowstone NP mega volcano	4.35, 6.11, 6.25, 6.39
Ziusudra, aka Utnapishtim in Akkadian	8.11, 8.12, 12.9, 18.49, 18.50
Zodiac, ancient use of	12.3, 13.3
Zoroaster	8.9
Zoroastrian Vara (Ark)	8.9, 8.10

Bibliography

Alley, Richard B. *The Younger Dryas cold interval.* Quaternary Science Reviews, Pergamon Press, 2000

Bauval, Robert. *The Orion Mystery, unlocking the secrets of the pyramids.* Three Rivers Press, 1994.

Bretz, J Harlen. *The Channelled Scablands of the Columbia Plateau.* Journal of Geology, 1923.

Dearborn, D.S. & White, R. E. *Archaeoastronomy at Machu Picchu.* University of Arizona, 1982.

Ernenweini, E. G., and M. L. Konns. *Subsurface Imaging in Tiwanaku's Monumental Core.* Technology and Archaeology Workshop. Dumbarton Oaks Research Library and Collection, Washington, D.C., 2007

Ginzberg, Louis. *Legends of the Jews.* Wayne State University Press, 2014

Hancock, Graham. *Magicians of the Gods.* Hodder & Stoughton, 2015.

Hawkins, Gerald. *Stonehenge Decoded, Stonehenge a Neolithic Computer.* Originally published 1963 and 1965, recent edition by Barnes & Nobel, 1993.

Hunt, C. *Environment of Violence.* Polar Publishing, 1990

Hyland, Sabine. *Gods of the Andes: An early Jesuit Account of Inca Religion and Andean Christianity.* Pennsylvania State University Press, 2001

Keys, David. *Catastrophe: An Investigation into the origins of the Modern World.* Ballantine Books, 2000

Lynd, James W. *History of the Dakotas.* The manuscript was found after Lynd's death at the hands of Union soldiers in 1863 and published in 1887 by the Smithsonian Institute under his name.

Montesinos, Fernando. *Memorias Historiales.* Originally published in 1644 and known as the Quito Manuscript. Recent translation published as The Quito Manuscript: An Inca History preserved by Fernando de Montesionos. Yale University Press, 2010.

Moore, A.M.T. et al. *Evidence of Cosmic Impact at Abu Hureyra, Syria at the Younger Dryas Onset (~12.8 ka).* University of Alaska Fairbanks and the University of California, Santa Barbara, 2020

Muscheler, R. et al. *Changes in Deep-water Formation During the Younger Dryas Event Inferred from 10Be and 14C Records.* Nature 408, 567-570, 2000.

Petrie, Sir Flinders. *The Pyramids and Temples of Giza*. Field & Tuer, Ye Leadenhalle Presse, 1883.

Reymond, Eve. *The Mythical Origin of the Egyptian Temple*. Manchester University Press, 1969

Sahagún, Friar Bernardino de. *Historia de las cosas de la Nueva Espana*. Written between 1540 and 1585, referred to as the Florentine Codex because held by the Laurentian Library since 1791. Translation available as *Florentine Codex – general history of the things of New Spain*. University of Utah Press, 2012.

Sitchin, Zecharia. *When Time Began*. Bear & Company, 1993.

Sitchin, Zecharia. *The Cosmic Code*. Bear & Company, 1998.

Sjoberg, Åke W & Bergmann Eugen, et al. *Texts from Cuneiform Sources, vol.3*. Locust Valley, 1969.

Spray, John G. *Evidence for a late Triassic multiple impact event*. Nature, March 1998.

Sweatman B. & Tsikritsis, D. *Decoding Göbekli Tepe with archaeoastronomy: what does the fox say?* Mediterranean Archaeology and Archaeometry Journal, 2017

Thomas, Brian & Melott, Adrian. *Journal of Geology*, May 2019. Washburn University, Kansas

Valera, Blas. *Account of the Ancient Customs of the Natives of Peru* (1551-1597). Originally published by Marcos Jimenez de la Espade, 1879 Translated and republished as Gods of the Andes, by Sabine Hyland. The Pennsylvania State University Press, 2011.

Wilkins, Harold T. *Mysteries of Ancient South America*. 1947, republished by Adventures Unlimited Press, 2005

The Truth Will Set You Free – Series

Prequel: Younger Dryas meteor impacts, The Flood & Atlantis

As we evolved, humanity experienced periodic climate swings from ice ages to warmer periods over 100,000 and 40,000 year cycles. After the last ice age maxima, this pattern was disrupted by a series of events causing abrupt global warming and cooling – periods known as the Dryas Periods. Evidence is now emerging of the cause of some of these events – meteor impacts which decimated human societies at that time. Tribal memories passed down over millennia, originally dismissed as myths, are now being reassessed as oral history. We are now beginning to understand details of the what, when and where of events immortalised as Noah's Flood and the destruction of Atlantis. Second Edition published May 2024.

Part One: God, Enki, Ra/Marduk & Yahweh

Proof of a divine Creator is not to be found in the Bible. However, the real identity of Yahweh may be discerned from biblical texts. The most memorable figures from the Old Testament include Noah, Abraham, Moses and kings David & Solomon – one might expect these find international recognition, with references to their exceptional feats in the historical record of surrounding affected cultures. But only one of these hero's has been verified, one appears to be adopted from another culture, one surprises by his total invisibility and the kings are acknowledged only by an isolated and obscure fragment. Third Edition published September 2023.

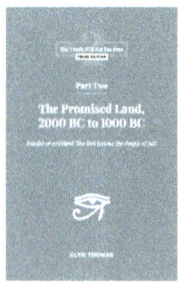

Part Two: The Promised Land, 2000 BC to 1000 BC

The Old Testament books covering the time of Abraham to David (c2000 BC to c1000 BC) tell of the Israelites led from slavery to conquer the Promised Land. However, clear evidence reveals these books were largely written during the Babylonian captivity, after 596BC, by priests with only hazy notions of geography and history. The biblical story overlooks the fact that the entire area of the Promised Land formed part of the Egyptian Empire for the greater part of the entire millennia. Third Edition published March 2024.

Part Three: Jesus, the Nazarene

Arguably, Jesus has had the most formative impact on humankind. Today, the New Testament stands as the only authoritative source of his life and teaching – but almost all of the books written about him in the first century have been destroyed. How authentic and reliable are those texts selected for the New Testament? The Old Testament is reputed to contain hundreds of prophesies concerning Jesus – are they credible? We name him Christ, meaning Messiah, a term the church has allowed to be widely misunderstood. Is Jesus part of a Trinity? Second Edition published July 2022.

Part Four: Truth Revealed – What Jesus Really Taught

This final work identifies many significant changes made to the Gospels to mould Christian beliefs in line with Church dogma. The majority of early Christian texts were ruthlessly destroyed by the Roman Church – why? What did they say? Aided by the earliest uncorrupted manuscripts and the few surviving examples of texts declared heretical, we can piece together Jesus original teaching. What is revealed dovetails well with ancient belief systems, explaining why Nazarene teaching spread like wildfire in the first century. Many of the difficult to grasp elements of conventional Christianity are exposed as being man-made. Many clues have survived, even in the New Testament, which support these findings. First Edition published August 2022.

Documents & maps are available for download from the Series website: **www.quintologypublications.com**

Texts ruled heretical by the Roman Church

Truth Series Master Index of Issues

Thomasine Creed - a radical update of the Nicaean Creed

Map of Egyptian Empire in 2nd Millenium BC

Map of impact ending the Younger Dryas Period

Symbols used on covers in this series

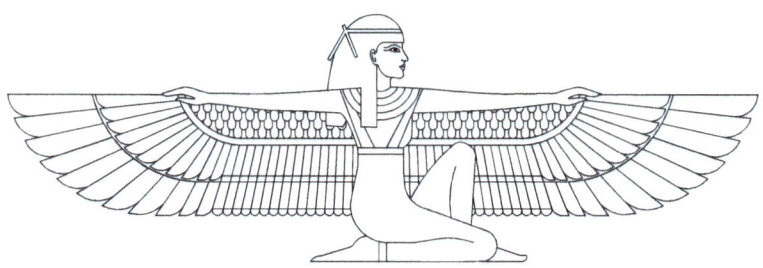

Prequel: Winged Isis

The goddess Isis was immensely popular from very ancient times. The sister and wife of Osiris, their only son was fathered after Osiris was killed and had ascended to heaven. This conception led to their son, Horus, being acclaimed as born of a perpetual virgin – and possibly an inspiration for the conception story in the gospels of Matthew and Luke. Ancient references associate Horus with the Giza pyramids and with Baalbek Terrace which are geometrically aligned to each other. The 'Winged Isis' symbolises her ability to fly, albeit with mechanical aids. Worship of Isis endured many millennia – growing to become the most popular god across the Roman Empire at the time of Jesus visit.

Part One: The Ankh

The Ankh symbolises the unity of Osiris and Isis. Osiris was murdered and rose to heaven. As a god in heaven, Osiris miraculously impregnated his wife, Isis, who gave birth to Horus. The manner of Isis conception led to her being described as a perpetual virgin, the Isis Mery. Ancient Egyptians believed that when Osiris returned to rule the Earth, he would resurrect the bodies of the dead and they would be reunited with their souls. Elements of these, already ancient, beliefs may have influenced gospel writers in the 1st Century AD.

Part Two: The Eye of Ra

Not to be confused with the eye of Horus. The Eye of Ra represents the power of the sun and the protection of Egyptian royalty. The symbol is used for this book to represent Egyptian suzerainty over the entire Promise Land for almost the entire 2nd Millennium BC.

Part Three: The Ichthys

The sign of the fish adopted by early Christians referring to the dawning of the new age of Pieces. The symbol served as a secret identification, Christians would scratch it on the ground to identify themselves to fellow believers. ΧΘΥΣ (IKhThUS) is an acronym or acrostic for the Greek phrase "Ἰησοῦς Χρῑστός Θεοῦ Υἱός Σωτήρ", which translates into English as 'Jesus Christ, Son of God, Saviour'.

Part Four: Templar symbol of two men riding one horse

Representation of the ancient belief of our binary spiritual nature. The two men represent the Spirit and the Soul riding in unity on a mortal body. Riding in unity parallels the yoked oxen, another parable denoting unity of Soul and Spirit – described by Jesus as the qualification to enter the kingdom of heaven.

www.ingramcontent.com/pod-product-compliance
Lightning Source LLC
Chambersburg PA
CBHW061745070526
44585CB00025B/2805